From Caesar to Augustus (c. 49 BC–AD 14)

This unique book provides the student of Roman history with an accessible and detailed introduction to Roman and provincial coinage in the Late Republic and Early Empire in the context of current historical themes and debates. Almost two hundred different coins are illustrated at double life size, with each described in detail, and technical Latin and numismatic terms are explained. Chapters are arranged chronologically, allowing students quickly to identify material relevant to Julius Caesar, the second triumvirate, the relationship between Antony and Cleopatra, and the principate of Augustus. Iconography, archaeological contexts, and the economy are clearly presented. A diverse array of material is brought together in a single volume to challenge and enhance our understanding of the transition from Republic to Empire.

Clare Rowan is an Associate Professor in the Department of Classics and Ancient History at the University of Warwick. She bridges the disciplines of Roman history and numismatics, with recognised research excellence, having won a European Research Council Starting Grant, while her teaching excellence has been recognised through numerous awards, including the Warwick Award for Teaching Excellence and an Australian Learning and Teaching Council Award for Programmes that Enhance Learning (shared). She is the editor of the *Coins at Warwick* blog, which encourages and disseminates studies of different coins and what they reveal about the ancient world.

D1527929

Guides to the Coinage of the Ancient World

General Editor
Andrew Meadows, *University of Oxford*

Coinage is a major source of evidence for the study of the ancient world but is often hard for those studying and teaching ancient history to grasp. Each volume in the series provides a concise introduction to the most recent scholarship and ideas for a commonly studied period or area, and suggests ways in which numismatic evidence may contribute to its social, political and economic history. The volumes are richly illustrated, with full explanatory captions, and so can also function as a numismatic sourcebook for the period or area in question.

Titles in the series

The Hellenistic World: Using Coins as Sources
by Peter Thonemann
From Caesar to Augustus (c. 49 BC–AD 14): Using Coins as Sources
by Clare Rowan

From Caesar to Augustus (c. 49 BC–AD 14)

Using Coins as Sources

CLARE ROWAN

University of Warwick

CAMBRIDGE
UNIVERSITY PRESS

CAMBRIDGE
UNIVERSITY PRESS

University Printing House, Cambridge CB2 8BS, United Kingdom

One Liberty Plaza, 20th Floor, New York, NY 10006, USA

477 Williamstown Road, Port Melbourne, VIC 3207, Australia

314–321, 3rd Floor, Plot 3, Splendor Forum, Jasola District Centre, New Delhi – 110025, India

79 Anson Road, #06–04/06, Singapore 079906

Cambridge University Press is part of the University of Cambridge.

It furthers the University's mission by disseminating knowledge in the pursuit of education, learning, and research at the highest international levels of excellence.

www.cambridge.org
Information on this title: www.cambridge.org/9781107037489
DOI: 10.1017/9781139775311

First published 2019

Printed in the United Kingdom by TJ International Ltd. Padstow Cornwall

A catalogue record for this publication is available from the British Library.

Library of Congress Cataloging-in-Publication Data
Names: Rowan, Clare, 1982– author.
Title: From Caesar to Augustus (c. 49 BC-AD 14) : using coins as sources / Clare Rowan.
Description: Cambridge, United Kingdom ; New York, New York : Cambridge University Press, 2018. | Series: Guides to the coinage of the ancient world | Includes bibliographical references and index.
Identifiers: LCCN 2018014871| ISBN 9781107037489 (hardback) | ISBN 9781107675698 (paperback)
Subjects: LCSH: Coins, Roman. | Coinage – Rome – History. | Numismatics, Roman. | Rome – History – Sources. | BISAC: HISTORY / Ancient / General.
Classification: LCC CJ833 .R69 2018 | DDC 737.4932–dc23
LC record available at https://lccn.loc.gov/2018014871

ISBN 978-1-107-03748-9 Hardback
ISBN 978-1-107-67569-8 Paperback

Contents

Tables

Figures

Preface

This book began when Andrew Meadows asked if I might write a volume for a series that aimed to provide affordable and accessible introductions to coinage for students of ancient history. I was happily assigned the period 49 BC to AD 14. The final result differs from the first volume released in the series (Peter Thonemann's *The Hellenistic World: Using Coins as Sources*), in that it focuses on particular moments in time, inviting an examination of numismatic evidence relevant to a particular individual or period of history. Since the civil wars and the Augustan age are often taught separately, the volume is more chronological than thematic. The case study approach largely reflects the way coinage is used by historians of this period, although it is hoped that the breadth of coin types covered here may provoke wider thinking about connections between the late Republic and early Empire.

The historical narrative of this period is already covered in several other excellent books; consequently this volume is not intended to provide an overview of 'what happened'. Rather this book shows how coinage can be used to enhance, challenge, and change our understanding of the period 49 BC–AD 14. The first chapter provides an entry point into the world of numismatics, exploring what money was, who made it, and how it operated in the economy, with the key literature explained. The second chapter covers the civil war and the first triumvirate, exploring the different coinage struck by the supporters of Caesar and Pompey, as well as provincial reactions. The aftermath of Caesar's assassination in 44 BC and the competition between Antony, Octavian and Sextus Pompey form a focal point for the third chapter, with the fourth focusing on Antony and Cleopatra. The principate of Augustus is examined in the fifth chapter, and the volume ends with a consideration of coinage in daily life. Often coin types are discussed in isolation as if they were viewed in some sort of ancient museum or art gallery; the reality is much messier, and I urge all readers to consider coin imagery in the light of Chapter 6.

A small volume cannot be exhaustive, and readers are encouraged to explore beyond what is covered here for further evidence and case studies. Although the traditional apprehensions ancient historians might feel towards coin evidence are diminishing, it is hoped that this volume will further encourage the use of this material in the study of antiquity. Many of the coins from this period are now freely available online in glorious colour, and direction is given to these resources, as well as a further bibliography, at the end of the volume. Here readers will also find a timeline, an index of Latin abbreviations commonly found on coins in this period and their meanings, and a glossary of technical terms. The figure captions provide the denomination, the location of the mint, the authority or moneyer responsible for the issue (where relevant), the date and a standard reference, followed by a description of the obverse (Obv.) and reverse (Rev.). Space constraints mean only an abbreviated description of each type is given. The denominations of many provincial bronze coins are uncertain, so frequently the metal and diameter of the coin is given instead. Unless specified, all coin images are reproduced at a scale of 2:1.

Thanks are due to Andrew Meadows for approaching me to write the volume in the first instance, and for providing guidance and feedback on several drafts. Alison Cooley helpfully read the Augustus chapter and provided comment. Thanks are owed to Tom Hillard and Lea Beness, who read the chapters on the late Republic, and who first taught me Republican history in Sydney as an undergraduate. The volume has also been influenced by conversations with Kathryn Welch, whose support of scholars of the Roman Republic is unflagging. Hannah Mitchell, Suzanne Frey-Kupper, Liv Yarrow, Kevin Butcher and Andrew McCabe have all provided assistance (even if they were unaware at the time), and I have been able to test out sections on the wonderful Warwick undergraduate body. The *Coinage of the Roman Revolution* panel at the Celtic Classics Conference in Dublin in 2016 both assured me I had included a representative sample of the material, and provided final points of finesse to the volume – thanks are due to Anton Powell and Nandini Pandey, who organised the panel, and to all the participants of that event. Finally, thanks are owed to the anonymous readers of the manuscript and Michael Sharp at Cambridge University Press, who waited patiently for the volume to finally appear. This book is dedicated to Ronika: as always, this is shared.

Abbreviations

The following abbreviations are used:

ACIP	Villaronga, L. and Benages, J., eds. (2011). *Ancient Coinage of the Iberian Peninsula*. Barcelona.
AE	*L'Année Épigraphique* (1888–)
AJN	*American Journal of Numismatics*
ANS	American Numismatic Society
App.	Appian, *The Civil Wars*
BMC	Poole, R.S. et al. (1873–1972). *A Catalogue of Greek Coins in the British Museum* (29 vols). London.
Caes. *BCiv.*	Julius Caesar, *The Civil War*
CIL	*Corpus Inscriptionum Latinarum* (1863–)
Dio	Cassius Dio, *Roman History*
HN *Italy*	Rutter, N. K. (2001). *Historia Numorum Italy*. London.
IG	*Inscriptiones Graecae* (Berlin, 1873–)
JRS	*Journal of Roman Studies*
Kroll	Kroll, J. (1993). *The Athenian Agora XXVI: The Greek Coins*. Princeton, NJ.
Mazard	Mazard, J. (1955). *Corpus Nummorum Numidiae Mauretaniaeque*. Paris.
NC	*The Numismatic Chronicle*
Obv.	Obverse
Rev.	Reverse
RGDA	*Res Gestae Divi Augusti*
RIC	*The Roman Imperial Coinage* (1923–) (also available digitally at http://numismatics.org/ocre/)
RPC	*Roman Provincial Coinage* (1992–) (select volumes available digitally at http://rpc.ashmus.ox.ac.uk/)
RRC	Crawford, M. H. (1974). *Roman Republican Coinage (2 vols)*. Cambridge. (Available digitally at http://numismatics.org/crro/)

RRCH   Crawford, M.H. (1969). *Roman Republican Coin Hoards*. London. (Available digitally at http://numismat ics.org/chrr/)
SEG   *Supplementum epigraphicum graecum* (1923–)
SNG   *Sylloge Nummorum Graecorum* (1931–)
Svoronos   Svoronos, J.N. (1904–8) *Ta Nomismata tou Kratous tôn Ptolemaiôn (4 vols)*. Athens.

1

Approaching Coinage in the Late Roman Republic

··

In 49 BC Julius Caesar crossed the Rubicon, sparking decades of instability that would eventually result in the rule of Augustus. Later in this same year Caesar released one of the largest coin issues the Republic had ever seen, money that communicated his position as the chief priest of Rome (*pontifex maximus*) and that carried his name: CAESAR (Fig. 2.1). The sheer volume of this coinage meant it (and its imagery) came into the hands of large numbers of people across the Mediterranean in a way not seen before; coinage had become a medium of mass communication. Moreover, coinage and the imagery it carried were tied to a single living individual. In 49 BC then, we find the beginning of a series of events that would ultimately lead to the principate, as well as the beginnings of Roman imperial coinage.

Coinage as a form of money emerged in the seventh century BC, and while Greek cities in southern Italy and Sicily adopted the medium from the sixth century BC, the first Roman coin only appears sometime after 326 BC. The Romans were remarkably slow to introduce their own coinage (RRC 1/1). Initially Roman coins matched the denominations of their Greek neighbours, but in c. 211 BC a new currency system was introduced, the denarius. We should remember that the denarius system was, extraordinarily, introduced while Rome was at war with Hannibal – how did Rome have the resources for this undertaking at this particular moment in time? Hoards suggest that Rome funded the currency reform by melting down existing precious metal currencies in the regions under her control, converting the silver into denarii (Burnett 1995). Thus the denarius was introduced as Rome was emerging as a major Mediterranean power and was accompanied by the destruction of the coinages of other cities. Roman coinage was an important representation of Roman imperialism; it is thus no surprise that the designs for the new currency were inspired by other Hellenistic powers (Rowan 2016). Rome was, according to her currency, a Hellenistic power like any other.

Although Rome continued to make use of Hellenistic-style imagery on coinages struck outside of Rome (outlined in Thonemann 2015: 169–92), coinage struck in the city itself developed in a markedly different manner. Unlike the static imagery seen on Greek money (largely unchanging from year to year), Roman coinage was increasingly decorated with a bewildering array of types. In the first century BC, officials responsible for Roman coinage chose designs that alluded to the achievements of their ancestors; direct references to living individuals were rare. Caesar's coinage, and the coins that followed, would change this. The Romans were unique in frequently changing the designs of their currency, and this meant that coinage was both a form of currency and a 'monument in miniature', a medium upon which Roman culture, mythology, and history could be inscribed. Our word 'money' comes from the Latin *moneta*, a word used to translate the Greek word *Mnemosyne*, goddess of memory (Meadows and Williams 2001). Language thus connected money to (collective) memory and history in the Roman world.

As mass produced objects that survive in large quantities, coinage gives us an insight into the views and activities of a broad array of people and cities, many of whom are not well-represented in written histories. Since the Romans treated coins as 'monuments in miniature', we can approach Roman coinage as a visual historical record. It is a record that survives almost intact, a rarity for the ancient world. What is presented here is not a definitive list of examples or interpretations; rather this volume aims to demonstrate the differing ways coinage can be used in ancient history, allowing the reader to then move forward to follow their own interests. But before we begin, Fig. 1.1 introduces some common numismatic terms. Other technical terms are explained in the glossary at the back of this volume, where you will also find a list of common Latin abbreviations found on coins from this period alongside their meanings.

1.1 What was Money in the Roman World?

Economists define money as a medium that can function as a means of account, a means of exchange, and as a store of value. The first, *means of account*, refers to the way money is used as a unit to indicate prices, or for record keeping. Today, for example, pounds and dollars are units of account (prices are given in dollars and pounds, not cents or pennies). From c. 141/0 BC the means of account for the Roman government was the sestertius, indicated by the sign IIS or HS. But in the provinces other denominations might be used (e.g. drachmae). The unit of account could also change: a tax inscription from Thessaly, for example, records a change

obverse
*the design struck from
the anvil or lower die*

reverse
*the design struck from
the held or upper die*

field
*the empty space on a
coin*

legend
*the inscription that
appears on a coin*

type
*The design that appears on a
coin*

exergue
*The area on a coin below the
ground-line of a design*

Figure 1.1. Terms used to describe a coin.

from local drachmae to denarii being used to indicate prices after an edict of Augustus (Helly 1975: 120 no. 1; Knoepfler 1988: 284 n. 72). That the varying denominational systems used across the Roman Empire resulted in different units of account in different areas is seen in the *Res Gestae Divi Augusti* (*RGDA*), which details Augustus' achievements as emperor. While the Latin text provides amounts in sestertii, the Greek versions (found in Ancyra and Apollonia in Galatia) translate these amounts into denarii. For example, the Latin text records that 300 sestertii were given to the Roman plebs, while the Greek version reports the amount as 75 denarii (*RGDA* 15; Cooley 2009: 19). Augustus' munificence was presented in denarii for Greek audiences, since this denomination was likely more familiar than the sestertius.

The sestertius was initially made of silver, but the reorganisation of the Roman monetary system from Julius Caesar onwards led to the denomination being struck in brass (Tables 1, 2). Silver sestertii were rarely produced in the Republic; the unit of account is not necessarily identical to the coins in common circulation (Burnett 1987b: 35). A price given in sestertii may have actually been paid in denarii or in another denomination. Using money to make purchases reflects its role as *a means of exchange*. Coins, particularly higher value coins, could also be hoarded or stored as savings, making them *a store of value*. Raw metal (gold or silver bullion) may also have acted in this capacity.

Table 1 Main denominations of the denarius system after c. 141/0 BC

Denomination	Metal	Value in asses
aureus	gold	400 (= 25 denarii)
denarius	silver	16
quinarius	silver	8
sestertius	silver	4
as	bronze	1
semis	bronze	½
triens	bronze	⅓
quadrans	bronze	¼
sextans	bronze	⅙
uncia	bronze	$^1/_{12}$

Table 2 Main denominations of the Roman monetary system under Augustus.

Denomination	Metal	Value in asses
aureus	gold	400 (= 25 denarii)
gold quinarius	gold	200 (= ½ an aureus)
denarius	silver	16
silver quinarius	silver	8
sestertius	orichalcum (brass)	4
dupondius	orichalcum (brass)	2
as	copper	1
semis	orichalcum (brass)	½
quadrans	copper	¼

But can money also perform other functions? Many find a strictly economic definition of money unsatisfactory since it can also play complex psychological, political, cultural and social roles in society. Just think, for example, about how people's behaviour changes upon winning the lotto, or upon finding a hoard of gold (Graeber 1996). Studies of Roman coinage have generally appreciated that money often functions in ways that go beyond a means of exchange, unit of account and store of value. Coinage in the Roman world was a 'monument in miniature', a means of communication, a medium of identity formation, as well as an object in cultic and social life. These additional functions will be explored throughout this volume.

Unlike our paper money, Roman coins were made from metal. They thus had an official face value decided by the government, and an intrinsic value (the value of the actual gold, silver, copper or brass contained in the coin). It is fiercely debated whether coins in the Roman world were generally accepted at face value (a 'nominalist' position) or whether their worth was decided by the metal value of a coin (a 'metallist' position). These debates mainly focus on the third century AD, when the silver content in Roman coinage dropped dramatically. In our period, by contrast, the purity of the coinage was high. So was the face value of a precious metal coin in this period the same as its intrinsic value?

Evidence from the late third century AD demonstrates that the market value of gold to silver was 1:12, and the exchange rates of coins under Augustus suggest (Table 1) this was also the case at the beginning of the principate: 25 denarii of c. 3.9g each (97.5g of silver in total) could be exchanged for one aureus containing c. 8g of gold (97.5 divided by 12 equals 8.125). This 1:12 ratio was likely the official government exchange rate from Julius Caesar to AD 64 (Butcher and Ponting 2014: 26, 435, 687). How many denarii an aureus was worth thus probably reflected what the government believed to be a fair exchange price between the metals. But how coinage was actually valued everyday in the marketplace is still uncertain, since we don't have enough evidence to know whether changes in the price of gold and silver regularly affected prices (e.g. if the value of gold dropped, did people conclude the aureus was worth less?) The problem of fluctuating metal prices when using coins is a recurring problem, even today – it currently costs the US government 1.7 cents to make a one-cent coin, and 8 cents for a 5-cent coin, due to the rise in metal prices. Sometimes the ideology of a currency system (e.g. the idea that the cent is the backbone of the entire US monetary system) outweighs economic rationality.

Although this book focuses on coins, other types of money existed in the Roman world. Some economic transactions, for example, must have been performed via documentation (perhaps in the form of wax tablets) rather than with physical coinage. This must have been the case for Cicero's purchase of his house on the Palatine: the price of 31.5 million sestertii would have equated to 3.5 tons of silver denarii, a sum which would have been impractical to count out or transport through the streets of Rome (Cicero, *Letters to Friends* 5.6.2; Harris 2006: 2–3). The actual transfer of the amount, then, is likely to have taken place via the exchange of official documents.

A variety of financial instruments might have served as money in the late Republic, at least for the elite (Hollander 2007: 40–52). *Permutationes* or 'bills of exchange' were a way of transferring money without having to physically move coinage, and certain references in Cicero suggest they could also function as a means of payment (e.g. Cicero, *Letters to Atticus* 5.15.2). *Syngraphae*, financial contracts for lending or borrowing money or making payments, could also function as a store of wealth. Similarly *partes* (shares in tax farming or other commercial activities) probably functioned as a store of value, and perhaps also as a means of payment. *Nomina*, or money owed to an individual, could also be used as a means of payment via the transfer of the debt from one person to another (e.g. Cicero, *Letters to Atticus* 7.18.4). These financial instruments indicate the sophistication of the Roman economy in the late Republic. But these types of money were probably only used amongst elite groups who personally knew each other; it is highly unlikely that you could write the equivalent of a cheque and hand it to a complete stranger in the Roman world. Rather these types of money could be used only within particular contexts.

Credit also existed and was extensive enough to result in several credit crises, including one in 49 BC. Cicero makes frequent reference to loans to and from friends, further highlighting the role of friendship (*amicitia*) in economic transactions. After joining Pompey's cause in 49 BC, Cicero borrowed from a variety of friends, including Atticus (Cicero, *Letters to Atticus* 11.13.4; Verboven 2002: 122). There are also indications that elite women could make and receive loans: Antony's wife Fulvia bought an estate on credit and Clodia (daughter of Appius Claudius Pulcher) lent money to her lover Marcus Caelius Rufus during their affair (Nepos, *Atticus* 9.4–5; Cicero, *Pro Caelio* 31; Verboven 2002: 123).

Bullion, or raw metal, probably also functioned as money. Gold bullion was the logical way to make large payments in this period, but since references to gold bullion and finds of gold bars are rare, the extent of bullion's role in the Roman economy remains uncertain (Harris 2006: 3; Hollander 2007: 22–4, 31). Scattered archaeological finds of bullion suggest it did play a role in the economy, if only as a store of wealth. One of the few Republican coin hoards to contain gold bars was found in Cadriano in Italy in 1811 (RRCH 357); the brief report on this find states that c. 80,000 coins were found in a pot with the bars. The last dated coin is reported to be the elephant issue of Julius Caesar, suggesting the hoard was deposited during the civil wars. A hoard from Alvarelhos in Spain contained, in addition to 5,000 denarii, 9 silver cakes (circular ingots), two inscribed with the name CAESAR (a reference to Octavian). This hoard has been interpreted as a local military treasury, suggesting that bullion could be used as a form of money, or at least transported alongside coinage in military operations (García-Bellido 2008: 285–7). The use of bullion as a means of payment is attested in ancient texts; it may be that gold and silver bullion were more commonly used as money in times of stress, or in emergencies. Caesar, for example, writes that when Varro supported Pompey he compelled Roman citizens in Spain to furnish 18 million sestertii, 20,000 pounds of silver (*argenti pondo*) and 120,000 measures of wheat (Caes. *BCiv.* 2.18). The mention of wheat reminds us that some Roman provinces (e.g. Sicily, Egypt) paid their taxes in kind rather than in cash. In these particular contexts, wheat or another product (e.g. oil) functioned as a means of payment, and hence a form of money.

1.2 Money and the Roman Economy

> . . . by bringing the royal treasures to Rome in his Alexandrian triumph he made ready money so abundant, that the rate of interest fell, and the value of real estate rose greatly . . .
>
> (Suetonius, *Augustus* 41.1)

Suetonius' observation occurs as part of a wider section in which he notes various examples of Augustus' generosity, but his statement reveals the economic forces at play in the Roman world. What the text suggests is that the influx of wealth into Rome after the capture of Egypt led to inflation and, more specifically, to a rise in real estate prices. This phenomenon might be explained by an economic theory that is frequently mentioned in studies of the Roman economy called the Quantity Theory of Money. While this theory has many variations, numismatists of the ancient world generally work with the equation proposed by the economist Irving Fisher:

$$\mathbf{M}_{(\text{oney supply})} \times \mathbf{V}_{(\text{elocity of circulation})} = \mathbf{P}_{(\text{rice level})} \times \mathbf{T}_{(\text{ransactions})}$$

According to this equation, the money supply multiplied by the speed with which it moves equals price levels multiplied by the number of transactions (Hollander 2007: 137–8). In essence, the theory suggests that there is a connection between money, the speed with which it circulates (i.e. moves from person to person), the number of transactions taking place, and prices. An increase on one side of the equation will lead to an increase on the other side, and a decrease on one side will lead to a decrease on the other. So in the case highlighted by Suetonius, it appears that the influx of money associated with the capture of Egypt (**M**) made prices (**P**, in this case the price of real estate) rise. The third-century historian Cassius Dio also comments on this phenomenon, noting that Octavian's activities upon his return to Rome in 29 BC resulted in such a vast amount of money in the city that the price of goods rose and interest rates fell (51.21.5). Similarly, a fall in the money supply can lead to a drop in prices (deflation).

The Quantity Theory of Money has proven a popular tool in studies of the ancient economy, but we need to remain cautious in its application: we do not have the same amount of information for antiquity that we have for the modern world, meaning that the values of each part of the equation are difficult, if not impossible, to accurately calculate. How, for example, can we know, even roughly, how many transactions took place in 29 BC? If there were an increase in the supply of money, but also an increase *in the amount of people using money* (Transactions), then there would be no rise in prices. These difficulties have led to the use of alternative formulae. For instance, since the number of T(ransactions) is very difficult to calculate, it is often replaced by Y, which is the total output of an economy (e.g. Hollander 2007: 138–44; Kay 2014: 87–105). The topic of prices in the ancient world is also a vexed one. We have some scattered price listings for the Republic, but we do not know whether prices fluctuated seasonally or annually, and it is unlikely that products cost the same amount throughout the Empire (e.g. the price of a pair of shoes in Rome may have been very different to the price in Germany, and we don't know if they were cheaper in summer than in winter). The inflation in Rome in 29 BC mentioned by Dio may not have been experienced elsewhere (e.g. in North Africa), and so the commonly asked question of what one could buy for a denarius is probably dependent on location, time of year and various other factors.

The best-known application of quantity theory to the Roman world is Hopkins' 'Taxes and trade in the Roman Empire' (Hopkins 1980). Hopkins, using estimations of the volume of Republican coinage, noted that the output of Roman denarii increased as much as tenfold in the period between 157 and 50 BC (other estimates range from a five to tenfold increase: see Bransbourg 2011: 120–2; Hollander 2008: 117; Kay 2014: 91–3). Noting the increase in the amount of denarii in circulation (**M**oney supply) and that there is little evidence for price rises in the period 157–50 BC (**P**rice level), Hopkins concluded that prices did not rise since the denarii were being used increasingly in expanded trade networks, and by new sectors of the population (an increase in Transactions).

The increase in the volume of money in circulation in 157–50 BC (coming from war booty, taxes, mining, and fiscal instruments other than coinage) likely created the opportunity for building programmes in Rome and elsewhere, increased military spending, and increased trade (Transactions). Trade in particular increased both in intensity and in geographical spread (Kay 2014). Here the increase in the amount of money in circulation was accompanied by an increased demand for coin, both in areas which had previously used very little coinage (e.g. rural areas), and in urban areas, where more money was spent on civic and military expenses (Hollander 2007: 138–51). This economic revolution, as it has been called, enabled a cultural revolution: the construction of monuments in Rome and the purchase of Roman material culture by provincial populations (Howgego 2013; Wallace-Hadrill 2008). The transformation of society, culture and identity that has been traced in the Roman world in the later Republic was dependent on increased wealth and money.

The complexity and scale of the Roman economy can be seen in a speech given by the Roman politician Cicero. The Hellenistic King Mithridates VI of Pontus invaded Asia in 88 BC, and famously incited a massacre of Romans and Italians in the region. In a speech delivered in support of Pompey's leadership in the Third Mithridatic War, Cicero discusses the repercussions of this event in Rome (*Pro Lege Manilia* 19; trans. Kay 2014: 245):

> For then, when very many people lost large fortunes in Asia, we know there was a collapse of credit (*fides*) at Rome, because repayments were interrupted (*solutione impedita*). It is indeed impossible for many individuals in a single state to lose their properties and their fortunes without involving still greater numbers in their ruin. Defend the Republic from this danger; and believe me when I tell you – what you see for yourselves – that this credit and system of monies, which operates at Rome in the Forum, is bound up with, and is linked with, those Asian monies (*pecuniae Asiaticae*); the loss of one inevitably undermines the other and causes its collapse.

Mithridates VI's actions evidently caused a credit crisis in Rome, which may have reduced banking operations in the Late Republic, and meant the Roman nobility in this period were more likely to borrow from each other than from institutions (Kay 2014: 235–65).

In 49 BC we hear of another credit crisis. In times of uncertainty people prefer to hoard their money rather than invest it (a modern equivalent is the proverbial hoarding of cash under a mattress). This creates a drop in the Velocity of money circulation, since money is no longer moving quickly from person to person (Kay 2014: 260–5). Any unease Romans may have felt in the lead up to the first civil war was compounded after Caesar crossed the Rubicon and seized the treasury in Rome. Cassius Dio specifically states that the uncertainty of the civil wars meant that lenders called in their debts, and those in debt found it difficult to find the coins needed for payment (41.37.2). Interest rates rose, and the price of land fell, since some had to sell their estates to meet their financial obligations (which, with falling land prices, must have been increasingly difficult). Cicero makes frequent reference to *nummorum caritas*, or the 'expensiveness of money', in this period, and the bargains to be had if one wanted to purchase land (Cicero, *Letters to Atticus* 7.18.4, 9.9.4, 10.11.2, 10.15.4). For example:

> But these days I presume all such properties have gone down in value, owing to the dearness of money (*nummorum caritatem*). (Cicero, *Letters to Atticus* 177 (9.10))

Earlier interpretations of this passage have thought it a reference to a lack of physical cash, although now scholarship is leaning towards the idea that it is a reference to high interest rates. Although the price of land fell, it appears that interest rates, rents and food became increasingly expensive, so this was not a clear-cut case of deflation (Verboven 2003). In a letter to Atticus in 49 BC, Cicero observed that no one was paying debts, and so he had advised Philotimus (his wife's freedman) to try and get money from the mint (Cicero, *Letters to Atticus* 8.7.3). This is often cited as evidence that Roman citizens could take their bullion to the mint and get it struck into coin (as in certain places in the medieval era), but how widespread this practice was is uncertain. After all, Cicero was writing as a proconsul at a time of financial crisis and so may have had opportunities not available to the average citizen (Verboven 2003).

Caesar also mentions the crisis and instituted several measures to limit its effects. Assets were valued at pre-war levels (i.e. before the drop in land prices), and it was forbidden to hold more than 15,000 drachmas in silver or gold (in the hope that people would cease hoarding money and release it again into circulation) (Caes. *BCiv.* 3.1.2; Dio 41.37.3). Later measures included the cancellation of interest incurred on loans after 49 BC, further re-evaluations of property values, the deduction of interest paid from the original loan amount, and a requirement that a proportion of a person's wealth should be invested in Italian land. These regulations indicate that the crisis must have continued for some years (Frederiksen 1966: 133–5).

It may have been this financial crisis that led to the decision to strike gold coinage regularly for the first time in Roman history, with a large gold issue struck in 46 BC (Fig. 2.10). There had been smaller gold issues in 48–47 BC, but the issue of 46 BC was on a previously unseen scale (Kay 2014: 262–4). From this point on gold coinage was frequently issued, a reflection, perhaps, of the growing expenses and demand for coin within the Roman Empire (Hollander 2007: 24). A larger empire, and an increased number of people using money, must have led to a greater demand for the coinage. The change in practice was just one of several that took place during the late Republic, ultimately forming the monetary system of the Roman Empire (Woytek 2004).

Another development was the resumption of regular bronze coinage production after a break of some 50 years. It is odd, but the Romans ceased to produce bronze coinage between 82 and 46 BC (Hollander 2007: 25). Why they did so remains unclear. The presence of large numbers of 'unofficially' produced bronze coins at this time suggests there was a demand for these smaller denominations. This is discussed more fully in Chapter 6. Lower value denominations are necessary for the functioning of the marketplace and the purchase of everyday items like bread. As anyone who has attempted to purchase a pack of gum with a $100 note may know, it is much easier to buy a small item with a small denomination (e.g. £1, $1) than with a large one (£500, $100). And anyone who does pay in a large denomination wants change. So why did the Romans cease making smaller denominations for c. 50 years? We simply don't know. Perhaps they were unaware of the need for small change outside the city of Rome, perhaps they were not concerned about providing enough denominations to facilitate daily transactions, perhaps the price of bronze changed (affecting the bronze to silver ratio), or perhaps it was simply 'benign neglect' (Bransbourg 2011: 108, 134; Hollander 2007: 38–9). The resumption of bronze coinage production in the late Republic, and its regular production under Augustus, must have been a welcome development for the Roman economy and those within it.

We thus find a complexity in the monetary and economic systems of this period. The evidence remains woefully incomplete, but in general we see an increasing supply and use of coinage in the period following c. 150 BC. Different regions and different people had different monetary experiences: the demand for and use of coin, for example, was higher in urban areas than in rural ones, and the monetary experience of a Roman wage labourer would differ from that of a farmer, which would again differ from that of a wealthy member of the elite, or someone living outside Rome. Monetary systems could also change over time. For the historian it is important to note that coinage did not exist in a vacuum; the production of coinage was connected to broader economic events, and coinage itself was just one monetary medium available. The remainder of this book largely focuses on coinage, but the Roman experience of money went far beyond what is listed in our coin reference books.

1.3 The Practicalities of Coinage Production

The official government mint in the Republic was probably located on the Arx near the temple of Juno Moneta, connected to the treasury in the temple of Saturn via a covered corridor that allowed bullion and coinage to travel safely between both locations (Tucci 2005). The Capitoline was a secure location, and the mint's association with the temple of Juno Moneta (which also housed the linen rolls recording lists of Roman magistrates and standards of measurement) provides us with a context for understanding Roman currency design. From around 130 BC, Roman coins carried annually changing imagery that referred to the ancestral achievements of the moneyers in office, a practice that can be connected to Roman memorial culture more broadly, and which Meadows and Williams have described as the 'monumentalisation' of Roman coinage (*monumenta* is connected to the Latin word *moneo*, as is *moneta*). Juno Moneta was the guarantor of weights and measures, as well as the accuracy of memory (thus the temple housed the linen rolls). So both the physical coin *and* the scene represented on it might have then been guaranteed under her auspices (Meadows and Williams 2001: 48). The Roman conceptualisation of coinage was connected to the topography of the city and to the Latin language.

Roman coinage was also struck outside Rome. During the civil wars generals struck coinage as they moved on campaign, identified in *Roman Republican Coinage* (RRC) by the term 'mint moving with', although Crawford now wishes he had used 'struck for such and such a campaign', since he suggests the purpose of the coinage produced in this period is more important than the precise location of the mint (Crawford 2012). Decentralised minting continued under Augustus, with Roman mints in Spain (at Emerita Augusta, and at two other sites, perhaps Caesaraugusta and Colonia Patricia), France (Nemausus, Lugdunum, and possibly another at Treviri), Greece (in the North Peloponnese and on Samos), Asia Minor (Ephesus, Pergamum), Syria (Antioch), Cyrenaica, Italy (perhaps Brundisium), as well as Rome.

Some cities also produced their own local coinage, most frequently bronze coins that could be used as small change. For our period these are collected in *Roman Provincial Coinage* (RPC) volume 1 (44 BC – AD 69), which includes the currency of more than 400 cities. Unlike Rome these mints were probably located in unimpressive or temporary structures; cities outside the capital did not produce coinage continuously and so did not need a permanent building (Burnett 2001). The mint of Athens in this period, for example, was in a converted building in a south-eastern corner of the agora (Camp and Kroll 2001).

We possess little information about who was responsible for the production of provincial coinages in the Roman Empire (Burnett, Amandry, and Ripolles 1992: 1–5). The proconsul, as the Roman representative in a region, might have had an influence; the appearance of a proconsul's name on some coin issues suggests such interventions sporadically took place. The emperor must have held the final authority over coinage produced in the provinces in the imperial period (though this was a gradual development rather than an instantaneous occurrence in c. 27 BC). Some provincial coins reference imperial grants allowing coin production using the Latin word *permissu*. At a more local level, the decision to issue coinage must have been made by the government of a city, a client king or his advisors, the *koinon* (a league of several city-states), or a relevant local body. Some provincial coinages name individuals: these may be the eponymous magistrates (the magistrates after whom the year was named) and/or the magistrate responsible for the production of the coinage, or the citizen who bore the cost.

An example of this last possibility might be found on Fig. 1.2 from Paestum in Italy, which names (and possibly shows on the obverse) Mineia, daughter of Marcus. Mineia acted as benefactress in the city: the building shown on the reverse is a representation of the basilica that formed part of her renovations in the local forum (Carbone 2014: nos. 43–6; Crawford 1973: 53–4). The legend S C probably refers to the Senate of Paestum. Who was the authority for this coin? Was it Mineia, who might have funded the coinage as one of her benefactions, or was it struck by the Senate to honour Mineia? Were they both responsible in some way? We can't know for certain. In Paestum a wide variety of individuals are named on the local coinage (Crawford 1973). A clearer example of an individual sponsoring the production of coinage in the city might be seen on Fig. 1.3, which names someone called Q. LAVR (Laurentius?). The reverse legend tells the user that Laurentius (?) 'out of his own money and by consent of the (local) Senate gave as a present thousands (of this coin)'.

Figure 1.2. Semis, Paestum, Augustan period (?) (HN *Italy* 1258). **Obv.** Female head, MINEIA M. F. **Rev.** Two-storey building, P(aestanorum) S(emis) S(enatus) C(onsulto).

Figure 1.3. Semis, Paestum, early first century BC (HN *Italy* 1238). **Obv.** Scales, with corn-ear on left side and weight on right side, Q LAVR PR, PAE(stanorum) in exergue. **Rev.** Coining scene with two workmen, S(ua) P(ecunia) D(ono) D(edit) S(enatus) S(ententia) MIL(ia).

Laurentius (?) thus paid for the striking of this particular coinage, perhaps to purchase grain, which is shown on the obverse.

In the Republic the decision to strike Roman coinage, and in what quantities to strike it, was made by the Senate. Three officials or moneyers were responsible for the production of coinage and were probably annually elected (Burnett 1987b: 17). They were called the *tresviri auro argento aere flando feriundo* ('the three men for casting and striking of gold, silver and bronze'), a title often represented with the abbreviation III VIR (see Fig. 1.4) or III VIR A.A.F.F. (Fig. 5.24). Republican moneyers were normally from established Roman families and were at the beginning of their political careers; moneyer was a minor office at the bottom of the *cursus honorum*, the traditional career path followed by the elite (Crawford 1974: vol. 2, 598–9). Julius Caesar increased the number of moneyers from three to four, but Augustus later lowered it again to three (Suetonius, *Augustus* 41). Much remains unknown about the operations of the Roman mint, but it is likely that the moneyers worked with the quaestors (officials connected to the treasury) to convert bullion into the amount of coinage required by the state (Burnett 1987b: 20–1). In the late Republic and early Augustan period the moneyers of Rome signed their coinage, but later their names disappear from Roman currency.

At times extra money may have been needed, and the decision was made by the Senate to produce more coinage, represented by the presence of the legend S C or EX S C on some issues, an abbreviation of the Latin phrase *ex*

Figure 1.4. Denarius, mint moving with Pompey, Q. Sicinius and C. Coponius, 49 BC (RRC 444/1a). **Obv.** Head of Apollo, star below, Q SICINIVS III VIR. **Rev.** Lion-skin hanging on upright club, bow and arrow on either side, C COPONIVS PR S C.

senatus consultum, meaning 'by decree of the Senate' (Crawford 1974: vol. 2, 608). Fig. 1.4, for example, struck by Q. Sicinius and C. Coponius in 49 BC, carries the legend S C on the reverse. This probably references the fact that the Senate, faced with the outbreak of civil war in 49 BC, decided it needed additional money (Crawford 1974: vol. 2, 608). The need to mark coinage in this way suggests that Roman coins produced outside of Rome without the approval of the Senate may have been illegal. This would mean that the issues of Caesar and other triumvirs struck in the provinces during the civil wars and discussed in the following chapters were created unlawfully (Burnett 1977: 57). But even if this were the case, we find these coins hoarded with other 'legal' denarii (suggesting 'legal' and 'illegal' circulated side by side), so these coins must have been viewed as acceptable currency in practice.

How much influence moneyers had over the design of coinage remains debated (for an overview see Noreña 2011). From the later second century BC it is evident they had control over the design of the currency they were responsible for, since the types often referred to the moneyer's ancestors. But in the late Republic and under Augustus coin designs gradually come to focus on contemporary powerful individuals. Who chose these images? Designs were most likely chosen by high-ranking (mint) officials, who possessed an understanding of official imperial ideology and who would have been able to produce imagery appropriate to a particular individual and/or event. In this way coinage can be viewed in the same way as other Roman monuments: it is unlikely the emperor himself designed every imperial relief that decorated every imperial monument throughout the Empire; rather, these monuments (and imperial coinage) were produced by officials with detailed knowledge of imperial ideology (Rowan 2013a: 212–13). Ancient authors reveal that, whatever the reality, the emperor's subjects believed that he chose his coin types, and they held him responsible for the designs (Metcalf 2006: 42; Rowan 2013c: 20). As the emperor's image slowly came to monopolise the obverse of imperial coins, this perception is not surprising.

If the letters S C on Republican coins meant senatorial approval to strike extra coinage, what did they mean during the Empire? The legend appears on Roman bronze coinage under Augustus and remained there throughout the imperial period (see Figs. 5.24, 5.69, 5.70, 5.71). Mommsen saw this as evidence of the 'dyarchy' of the principate: that the senate retained control over the production of bronze coins while the emperor took charge of gold and silver. This theory has few adherents today: the designs across all the metals are so similar they must have been the product of the same system (Carson 1956: 229–30). Burnett dispelled the suggestion that S C referred to the senatorial decrees by which Augustus was able to reform the metals of the smaller Roman denominations, using brass and copper instead of leaded bronze (see Tables 1–2 and Burnett 1977: 45–52). The precise meaning of S C remains open, though one imagines that after several decades, if not sooner, users of the coinage may simply have taken its appearance at face value as something that official Roman small change 'just had', distinguishing it from the provincial bronze coinages in circulation (Wallace-Hadrill 1986: 80–1).

The *tresviri* were the annual magistrates in charge of Roman coinage, but the mint also had a broader workforce. Our best evidence for workers at the Roman mint comes from a series of inscriptions from the reign of Trajan that name the different mint workers (CIL VI.42–4). The *familia monetalis*, as they are called in the inscriptions, consisted of inspectors and superintendents (*optio et exactor auri argenti et aeris*), as well as *officinatores* or section workers. These were a mixture of freedmen and slaves, at least by AD 115 (Burnett 1987b: 29). The mint must also have employed die engravers, who would have been skilled craftsmen, to produce the dies. Striking a coin was likely the work of three men: one held the hammer to strike the die (*malliator*), another held the flan between the two dies (*supposter*) and another held the upper (reverse) die (*signator*) (Woytek 2012b: 110). Again the situation in Rome was probably not the case for all mints. The coin in Fig. 1.3 shows only two workmen (though this may be a visual abbreviation due to the space constraints of the coin). The number and type of officials may also have differed in each mint. Provincial cities that did not regularly produce coinage probably

Figure 1.5. Denarius, Rome, M. Mettius, 44 BC (RRC 480/3). **Obv.** Wreathed head of Caesar, priestly implements (*lituus, culullus*) behind, CAESAR IMP. **Rev.** Venus standing holding Victory and sceptre, resting elbow on shield, which rests on a globe, M METTIVS. H (recut over G) in field.

made use of travelling craftsmen or mints (at least, this phenomenon has been demonstrated for the later imperial period; Kraft 1972).

In the third century AD Roman coins began to carry marks indicating which mint workshop produced them, so we know that at this time there were six workshops in total (each striking a different reverse type), but it is uncertain whether this number also existed in the period 49 BC – AD 14 (Carson 1956: 237–8). These mint or control marks (still used on coinage today) meant that the mint, year, and/or workshop for a particular coin might be identified if necessary (e.g. if there were queries surrounding the purity of the metal). For the historian, it is important to understand that sometimes parts of the coin's design were significant to the mint or production process, intended to be understood by particular officials but not by the broader public. Although some coin issues bear mint or control marks in this period, many do not. Why some coin issues were marked and others not remains a mystery, as does the meaning of many of the symbols that appear.

One issue that did use mint marks was struck by the moneyer M. Mettius in 44 BC (Fig. 1.5; Woytek 2012b: 90–6). On some coins (but not on others from the same year) different letters appear: A, B, C, D, E, G, H, I, K and L (F, it seems, was not used). Letters or numbers could be used to indicate a particular die (the best-known example from the Republic is the coinage of Crepusius in 82 BC, RRC 361/1), but this is not the case here. On Mettius' coinage the same letter appears on more than one die, and often the letter is recut (that is, the die is altered so that it would bear a different letter, with B being cut over A, C over B, and so on); on our example H is recut over

Figure 1.6. Denarius, mint moving with Mark Antony and M. Silanus, c. 33–32 BC (RRC 542/1). **Obv.** Head of Mark Antony with P. hidden in hair behind Antony's ear (circled on this example), ANTON AVG IMP III COS DES III III V R P C. **Rev.** M SILANVS AVG Q PRO COS.

G. We cannot know for certain what these letters meant. One suggestion is that the different letters perhaps referred to different sources of metal. If this is correct, the letters changed as the metal source changed. Another example of these sorts of marks can be found on Fig. 1.6, where a P. appears in the hair of Mark Antony. This is probably a die engraver's signature. Such signatures, often hidden, are also known from Greek coinage.

If you read the descriptions of Figs. 1.5 and 1.6 you will notice a description of the imagery as well as the Latin legends. The obverse (Obv.) is described first, followed by a description of the reverse (Rev.). These images, along with the other images throughout the volume, are reproduced at double life size (2:1). You can decipher the legends by consulting the list of Latin abbreviations at the end of this volume. Test it out now – on Fig. 1.6, for example, you can read the names of Mark Antony (ANTON) and Marcus Silanus (M. SILANVS). What positions did they hold?

Antony was augur (AVG), *imperator* for the third time (IMP III), consul designate for the third time (COS DES III) as well as a member of the triumvirate (III V R P C). Silanus was also an augur, a quaestor, and a proconsul. But did anyone else look this closely at Roman coins? In a famous essay called 'Numismatics and History', A.H.M. Jones, attempting to encourage numismatists into more economically orientated work, compared the designs of coins to postage stamps, and noted that if coins' legends and types were truly important 'it would seem some ancient author would have commented on them' (Jones 1956: 14). Since Jones' provocative piece, numismatists have pointed out that numerous ancient authors reference coins and coin types. Suetonius, for example, observes that Augustus struck silver coins showing his birth sign, the Capricorn, after an encounter with the astrologer Theogenes (Suetonius, *Augustus* 94.12; Fig. 5.51). Whether the story is true, or whether Suetonius (or his source) took an Augustan coin as a point of inspiration for the tale, it is clear that this particular coin (and others) *were* looked at and discussed. Recent work has also demonstrated that the Roman imperial mint likely engaged in some form of 'audience targeting', sending coins with specific messages to specific audiences (Kemmers 2006). One imagines that this type of effort, as well as the labour associated with continually changing coin types from year to year, would not have occurred if coinage was not considered a communication medium in the Roman world. Further examples of the attention paid to coin types are found throughout this volume.

1.4 Using Coin Reference Works (RRC, RIC, RPC)

Roman coin types from 49 BC – AD 14 are collected in two reference works. Republican issues prior to the battle of Actium in 31 BC can be found in Crawford's *Roman Republican Coinage* (RRC), while coinage after 31 BC can be found in the first volume of *The Roman Imperial Coinage*, now in a second edition (RIC 1^2). Both of these works are now available online (h ttp://numismatics.org/crro/, http://numismatics.org/ocre/). The coinage of provincial cities after 44 BC is catalogued in the *Roman Provincial Coinage* series (RPC 1).

RRC organises coins chronologically, with each group of coins (called a series) assigned a number (e.g. 344), followed by another number that refers to an individual coin type within the series (e.g. RRC 344/1, 344/2). RIC arranges coins by emperor and mint, with each coin type being assigned a different number (e.g. RIC 1^2 56). RPC is organised by geographical region, mint, and then chronology, with each coin type being assigned a unique number (e.g. RPC 1 456).

The dates assigned by Crawford to the coins in *Roman Republican Coinage* are based on a combination of data including metrology (weight and denominational systems), archaeological finds, overstrikes, and hoards. Crawford used the idea that coins struck around the same time will circulate together and then be hoarded or buried together. By studying a large quantity of hoards, and identifying when particular coin issues appear and then disappear (when they are present or absent in hoards), one can arrive at a relative chronology. This method lies behind much of the arrangement of RRC. It should be noted, however, that the coins themselves

Figure 1.7. Bronze coin, uncertain mint (Laodiceia-ad-Lycum?), Q. Oppius, 88 BC (?) or Caesarian period (?) (RRC 550/2e). **Obv.** Head of Venus wearing diadem, Capricorn behind. **Rev.** Victory holding wreath and palm branch, Q OPPIVS PR.

do not provide us with a precise indication of their date, and so the specific years given by Crawford remain suggestions. Crawford's chronology is largely accepted (a testament to the detailed work involved), but the dates of some issues remain debated. One such example is Fig. 1.7, which Crawford tentatively dated to 88 BC. Woytek has recently argued that it belongs instead to the Caesarian period because of its stylistic similarities to other coins of this date (Woytek 2012b: 94). Recently published find evidence strengthens the idea of a later dating; the Venus and Victory imagery on this issue then may have a Caesarian context (Barbato 2015). Further disputes about the dating of particular issues are discussed throughout the volume.

The coinage listed in *The Roman Imperial Coinage* is dated by Augustus' titles; coins carrying the title 'father of the country' (*pater patriae*), for example, are dated to after 2 BC. Within this general framework there are still some uncertainties: Augustus' titles only provide the earliest possible date for a coin (a *terminus post quem*), and some issues do not carry all of Augustus' titulature (some coins, for example, merely have the legend AVGVSTVS and so can only be dated to the period after he received this title). Consequently the dates of some coins remain open, like those struck at the mint of Rome. Only the coinage struck in Rome in 16 BC can be fixed chronologically, since the issues refer to the fact that Augustus was holding tribunician power for the seventh and eighth times (TR POT VII and VIII;

the number of times the emperor has held tribunician power is the method by which most imperial coinage is dated). But how the other issues fit around this fixed point is uncertain: in the RIC Mattingly based his dates on the idea that there was a 15-year gap between an individual holding the office of moneyer and becoming consul. This led him to place the moneyers associated with Piso, for example, in 23 BC. But the career progression of some moneyers may have taken longer than 15 years, and other arrangements have been proposed (Kemmers 2006: 41–2; Küter 2014).

Both RRC and RIC provide some indication of the volume of each issue, but we need to treat these suggestions with caution. Crawford provided an estimate of the number of dies used for each issue on the basis of 24 hoards. Crawford began with coins that had die studies (i.e. a known number of dies), and, noting how frequently these occurred in the 24 hoards, he used these results to extrapolate a die estimate for each coin issue (Crawford 1974: vol. 2, 641–93). These are merely estimates, which have proven accurate in some cases and inaccurate in others. Moreover, even if we know the number of dies, there are varying estimates on how many coins one die might produce before it breaks. The number might vary depending on the metal used (bronze, for instance, is a harder metal than gold, and would wear out a die faster), whether the metal was struck hot or cold, and the diameter of the coin. For some issues, particularly in gold, the die may not have been used until it was broken, but only until the desired amount of coins was minted. Although there are no records surviving from the ancient world about how many coins were struck per die, medieval and modern records demonstrate that it can vary radically. In the Philadelphia mint in the United States, one die could be used to make anything between one coin and two million coins; in medieval Canterbury (UK) an obverse die produced anything between 2,000 and 78,000 coins (de Callataÿ 1995: 298). For antiquity, modern scholars have postulated an average of 30,000 coins per die, but this is an *average*, not an indication of what *every* die produced.

RIC provides frequency indications for each coin issue (C=common, S=scarce, R=rare), but these are based on how many of each coin is found in major museum collections (RIC 1[2] xxi–xxii). Since museums aim to collect at least one of each type of coin, and often focus on rare or unusual types, this method does not provide a very good estimation of what was actually circulating in antiquity. The best method for estimating the relative size of a coinage is a die study (see inset 'Why study dies?' on p. 32 for a discussion), or an analysis of coin finds (Noreña 2001; Rowan 2013c: 24–8). The latter method involves collecting find and/or hoard data, and then examining how common each coin type is: if coin type A occurs frequently in hoards and coin type B only once or twice, then one can deduce that A was struck in higher numbers than B. This is a rough method, but one often applied to Roman coinage, which was struck in such large quantities that a die study is often impossible. Finds are more representative of relative frequencies than major museum holdings, but hoard data (often a person's savings, or a treasury) often contain different types of coins to single coin finds (those found alone). While hoards might be composed largely of gold or silver, single or site finds are often bronze lower denominations that have been dropped or lost.

In RRC and RIC, each slight variation in design, or obverse/reverse combination, receives its own entry. This is because reference works are created as a useful listing of each coin design and subtype. Thus the number of times a reverse or obverse type appears in a catalogue does not reflect how common it was in antiquity; it merely reflects the variations of die engravers or the workings of the mint (Krmnicek and Elkins 2014: 13–14). For example, a large issue that used a lot of dies all engraved with the same design will receive only one entry in RIC, but a small issue which had differing obverse/reverse combinations, or small differences between the dies, will receive more entries. The number of entries in the RIC does not reflect actual coin volume.

2

Competition, Legitimacy and Civil War (49–44 BC)

In 49 BC Julius Caesar crossed into Italy after negotiations surrounding the end of his command (*imperium*) in Gaul broke down. Caesar's actions sparked a civil war that would be played out across the Mediterranean and would ultimately result in the rule of Augustus. Much of our surviving history conforms to the 'official' version of events created during Augustus' principate. But an extraordinary amount of contemporary evidence also survives: the texts of Cicero and Caesar, for example, as well as the coins produced by those involved in the conflict. Like some of the texts from this period, coins offer us an insight into the viewpoints of individual Romans. But unlike texts, coins are one of the few primary sources to survive almost in their *entirety*. This means we are able to uncover the positions of both sides of the civil war, tracing the fierce competition that drove the triumvirs.

The coinage of this period increasingly focuses on individuals and contemporary events, moving away from the familial designs that had characterised earlier Roman denarii. Here coinage reflects Roman political developments of the first century BC, with a rise in prominent individuals whose terms of office often lasted more than a year and whose powers were significant. Coinage in the late Republic was a medium of self-display and communication, used alongside texts, buildings and other monuments to justify positions and consolidate power within a context of aristocratic competition. Unlike Caesar's forum or a triumphal arch, however, coinage was a monument that *moved*. It was seen both in and outside Rome, and its audience was much larger than the literate Roman elite who read Caesar or Cicero. References to coin types reveal that numismatic imagery in this period did more than just circulate amongst users; it was actively 'read', similar to any text, and then referenced to make statements about political alliances and ideology. The Roman elite took the design of their coins seriously, and so too should we as historians. Coinage from this period allows us to trace the ideology used by key individuals to legitimise their positions, as well as the reactions of provincial populations whose

Figure 2.1. Denarius, mint moving with Caesar, Julius Caesar, 49–48 BC (RRC 443/1). **Obv.** Elephant trampling snake (?), CAESAR in exergue. **Rev.** Pontifical emblems (*culullus, aspergillum*, axe, *apex*).

experiences have left little trace in literature. The debates and ideas that surfaced in this period would ultimately shape Augustus' principate, as we shall see.

2.1 From the Rubicon to Dictator for Life: Julius Caesar

Caesar's decision to cross the Rubicon in 49 BC and his subsequent acquisition of the Roman treasury were transformative moments in Roman politics and Roman coinage. Rome's wealth was now in the hands of a single man who used the bullion to strike two of the largest coin issues the Republic had ever seen (Woytek 2003: 127). One was struck in the name of Caesar, decorated with an elephant on the obverse, and priestly implements representing his religious offices on the reverse (Fig. 2.1). The issue was probably struck in a military mint that accompanied Caesar. Coins of this type are commonly found in Gaul and Spain, suggesting that minting probably took place in these regions (Woytek 2003: 127–32). The sheer quantity of money struck by Caesar changed coinage as a communication medium: the higher volume meant that more people in more areas now saw the imagery. We can see this clearly by comparing Caesar's coin issue with that struck by the moneyer Marcellinus in the previous year, 50 BC (RRC 439/1). Caesar's issue is found in numerous hoards in numerous regions (Fig. 2.3), whereas hoards containing Marcellinus' coin type are concentrated within Italy (Fig. 2.2).

Caesar's issue was thus able to communicate in a way not seen before. But what exactly was it communicating? Look closely at the coin. What was the

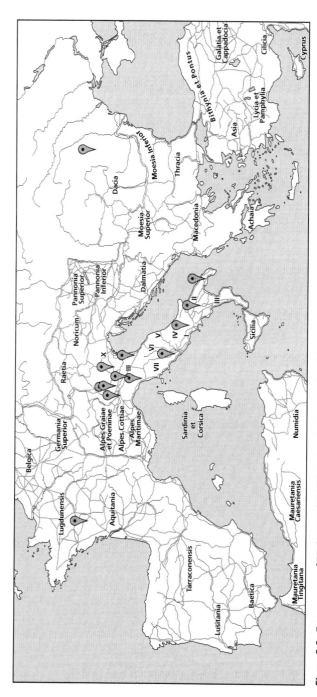

Figure 2.2. Occurrences of RRC 439/1 (50 BC) in hoards. Data retrieved from <http://numismatics.org/chrr> on <16/12/16>.

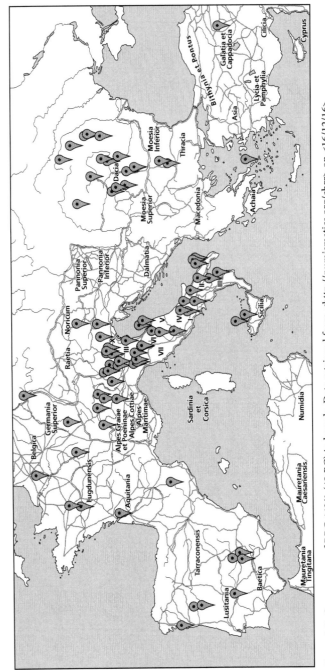

Figure 2.3. Occurrences of RRC 443/1 (49 BC) in hoards. Data retrieved from <http://numismatics.org/chrr> on <16/12/16>.

meaning of the elephant, and *what* is shown before it? Is the elephant a generic symbol of power, or a reference to Africa? It is worth noting that Caesar sent Gaius Scribonius Curio to Africa in 49 BC to fight Pompeian supporters and their ally, King Juba I of Numidia. Is the elephant a pun on Caesar's name? This is proposed by Woods 2009, since *caesai* in Punic refers to someone who had killed an elephant. Is the elephant trampling a snake, or a dragon? An elephant trampling a dragon symbolised the victory of good over evil, and was a representation of two mortal enemies. Or is the elephant standing before a Gallic war trumpet (*carnyx*), referring to Caesar's Gallic wars? As discussed below, the elephant was also a symbol of the Metelli family; was Caesar launching an attack on one of his opponents by adopting their familial symbol? Did the elephant remind people of Pompey's failed attempt to ride on an elephant chariot during his triumph? The attempt failed since the gates of Rome (*porta triumphus*) proved too small to allow the elephants through (Nousek 2008). Did the elephant remind people of Caesar's opponent Domitius Ahenobarbus, whose grandfather also famously rode in an elephant chariot? The intended meaning of the image remains a mystery. Ancient users of this coin may have been better able to understand its message, but the long list of interpretations is a reminder that different people can interpret imagery differently. As scholars, we might suggest what was *intended* by a particular image, but the audience may have interpreted it otherwise. A Roman soldier may have understood the elephant very differently to a merchant in Africa or a senator in Rome.

The reverse of Fig. 2.1 is clearer in meaning: it carries the priestly instruments that refer to Caesar's position as the chief priest of Rome (*pontifex maximus*). In the debate about the meaning of the obverse, the revolutionary nature of the reverse is often overlooked: this is the first time that these symbols had appeared together on a single coin. Romans who struck coinage while holding an office other than moneyer could refer to their magistracy; in this sense Caesar was following earlier tradition. But no other *pontifex maximus* had been responsible for the issue of coinage before. One wonders whether the extraordinary appearance of these priestly symbols reminded some Romans about the way Caesar obtained this office in the first place: the position of *pontifex maximus* normally went to men of experience (ex-consuls), but Caesar was elected in 63 BC over more experienced candidates when a law was passed that allowed the people to vote for the candidate rather than, as had been the custom, choosing from among existing priests.

Figure 2.4. Denarius, Rome, L. Hostilius Saserna, 48 BC (RRC 448/2a). **Obv.** Draped, bearded male bust with Gallic shield behind. **Rev.** Biga carrying a warrior facing backwards, holding shield and hurling spear, L HOSTILIVS SASERN.

Figure 2.5. Denarius, Rome, L. Hostilius Saserna, 48 BC (RRC 448/3). **Obv.** Female head with carnyx behind. **Rev.** Artemis holding spear and stag, L HOSTILIVS SASERNA.

While the design of Caesar's first coin issue was unusual, those that followed built upon the public image Caesar had created in his writings and orations, particularly *The Gallic War*. These coins were issued by Caesar and by moneyers that supported his cause (for example Lucius Hostilius Saserna, named on Figs. 2.4–5). One of the moneyers was Decimus Iunius Brutus Albinus, who had participated in Caesar's Gallic campaigns (he was later one of Caesar's assassins, dying in 43 BC). The imagery of military victory on Albinus' issues, like Fig. 2.7, referenced Caesar's success, but also may have recalled, in whatever small way, his own role in the Gallic campaigns. Imagery included Gallic male and female heads, Victory, military trophies, Gallic war trumpets, and a two-horse chariot (*biga*) carrying a barbarian warrior (RRC 448/1–3, Figs. 2.4–7). The publication of *The Gallic War* had meant that Caesar, although away on campaign from 58–50 BC, managed to maintain a presence in Rome and

Figure 2.6. Denarius, mint moving with Caesar, Julius Caesar, 48–47 BC (RRC 452/2). **Obv.** Female head right wearing oak wreath and diadem, LII. **Rev.** Trophy with Gallic shield and carnyx, CAE SAR on either side.

Figure 2.7. Denarius, Rome, D. Iunius Brutus Albinus, 48 BC (RRC 450/1a). **Obv.** Helmeted head of Mars. **Rev.** Two crossed carnyces, oval shield above, round shield below, ALBINVS BRVTI F.

participate in aristocratic self-display. Once the text arrived in Rome, it was read by the elite and read to the lower classes (Wiseman 1998). Caesar's activities as recorded in his own words evidently captured the Roman imagination, and so it is no surprise that Caesar's Gallic campaigns also feature on his coinage (Welch 1998: 85). Caesar had built his reputation in Rome through the reports of his Gallic activities; coins would have consolidated the message, providing a visual reminder of Caesar's achievements and his writings.

Other coin types struck by Caesar's supporters referenced contemporary events. Gaius Vibius Pansa Caetronianus struck Fig. 2.8, showing Libertas and the personification of Rome. This type likely refers to Caesar's claim that he was forced to enter Italy to defend himself against his enemies, to re-instate the plebeian tribunes who had fled to him, and to 'assert the

Figure 2.8. Denarius, Rome, C. Vibius Pansa, 48 BC (RRC 449/4). **Obv.** Laureate head of Libertas, LIBERTATIS. **Rev.** Helmeted Rome seated on a pile of arms, holding sceptre in right hand and placing foot on globe, being crowned by Victory, C PANSA C F C N.

freedom (*libertas*) of himself and the Roman people who had been oppressed by a small faction' (Caes. *BCiv.* 1.22.5; Raaflaub 2003). As these coins circulated, this issue and others would have been seen alongside the imagery recalling Caesar's achievements in Gaul. This juxtaposition of contemporary ideology and Caesar's past achievements is embodied on Fig. 2.5, which shows a female Gallic head on the obverse and the goddess Artemis on the reverse. Artemis was a chief deity in the city of Massalia, and her appearance here is probably a reference to Caesar's capture of the city in 49 BC after it had sided with Pompey (Caes. *BCiv.* 2.14; Dio 41.25.2; Crawford 1974: vol. 1, 464). Thus it was not only victory over foreign enemies that was represented on Caesar's coinage, but also victory in the civil war. The latter, however, was represented in a more abstract manner (via a deity, rather than a human captive), reflecting the Roman discomfort concerning victories over other Romans. This same awkwardness is seen again under Augustus after his defeat of Mark Antony.

From c. 47 BC Venus motifs appear (Fig. 2.9, RRC 457/1). Caesar had publicly claimed descent from the goddess during an oration at his aunt's funeral in 69 BC (Suetonius, *Julius Caesar* 6), and the goddess' appearance on coinage is probably connected to Caesar's victory at the battle of Pharsalus in 48 BC. Textual accounts mention that both Caesar and Pompey vied for Venus' support during the battle, with Pompey allegedly fearing that Caesar had a superior claim (App. 2.10.68; Plutarch, *Pompey* 68.2). Coinage struck by Pompey's supporters did not show Venus, but Pompey's theatre in Rome had included a shrine to Venus Victrix, a very public demonstration of his divine support. That Venus only appears on

Figure 2.9. Denarius, the eastern Mediterranean, Julius Caesar, 47–46 BC (RRC 458/1). **Obv.** Diademed head of Venus. **Rev.** Aeneas carrying Palladium and Anchises, CAESAR.

Caesar's coinage after his victory at Pharsalus suggests that he saw the victory as a sign that the goddess favoured him over Pompey. This may have coloured our surviving textual accounts about the battle, including the anecdote mentioned above. On Fig. 2.9 the head of Venus is combined with a reverse showing Aeneas carrying his father and the ancient cult statue of Athena Pallas (called the Palladium). Adjacent to Aeneas is Caesar's name. This juxtaposition aligned Caesar with the legendary founder of Rome and son of Venus. The goddess continued to appear on the coinage of Caesar until his assassination.

In 46 BC, having defeated Pompey and his supporters, Caesar returned to Rome and celebrated four triumphs (over Gaul, Egypt, Pontus and Africa). These celebrations saw an enormous amount of wealth paraded through the streets of Rome, including 2,822 crowns of gold (App. 2.102; Dio 43.21; Suetonius, *Julius Caesar* 38). Caesar gave a large series of gifts to his soldiers and the people of Rome during the celebrations. It is in this same year we find the first issue of aurei to be struck in quantity in the Republic (Fig. 2.10), the beginnings of the regular production of gold coinage. It is likely these aurei were struck to cover Caesar's triumphal expenses; the coins were perhaps directly given to the soldiers as part of a donative (Molinari 2003). Appian observes that Caesar used the wealth paraded in his triumph to make distributions, and so perhaps the booty brought back to Rome formed the bullion for the issue (App. 2.102).

This aureus issue is found in several hoards, and has 111 obverse and 122 reverse dies – a staggering number for a gold issue and demonstrative of Caesar's wealth at this time (Molinari 2003). By comparison, a gold issue of

Figure 2.10. Aureus, Rome, Aulus Hirtius and Julius Caesar, 46 BC (RRC 466/1). **Obv.** Veiled female head, C CAESAR COS TER. **Rev.** *Lituus*, jug and axe, A HIRTIVS PR.

47–46 BC has only one obverse and reverse die, and the earlier gold issue of Caesar from 47 BC has three obverse dies and one reverse die according to Crawford's estimations (RRC 460/1, RRC 456/1). The authorities named on Fig. 2.10 are Caesar and Aulus Hirtius, the same Hirtius who would go on to complete the text of Caesar's *Gallic War*. Hirtius was probably an urban praetor when he struck this issue, suggested by the abbreviation PR. Caesar is named as consul for the third time (COS TER). The obverse portrays a goddess (identified by Crawford as Vesta), and the reverse refers to Caesar's position as *pontifex maximus* with the portrayal of the *lituus* (the curved staff of an augur), jug and axe.

Why Study Dies?

A die study is the analysis of all known examples of a particular coin issue in order to reconstruct how many obverse and reverse dies were used in its production. The minting process means the reverse die often wears out more quickly than the obverse die (which is placed in the anvil and subject to less stress), and it is often replaced first. So an obverse die may initially be paired with a reverse die, then, after that reverse die wears out, the same obverse is paired with a new reverse die. Then the obverse die may wear out, and so this second reverse is paired with a new obverse, and so on. By reconstructing this process though a die study, we can reconstruct an internal sequence. The figure below shows a simplified version of this; often it is more complicated, particularly when multiple dies are used simultaneously.

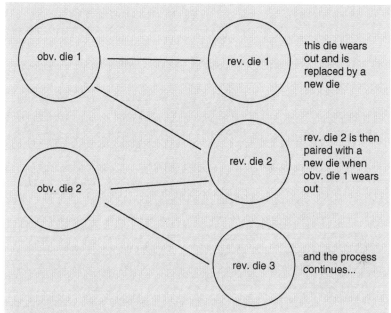

Figure 2.11. Theoretical die sequence.

Die studies assist in reconstructing coin manufacture: many dies working at once suggest an intense production, and the continued use of dies after they have broken suggests time pressure or necessity (there was no time to wait for a new die to be engraved). The number of obverse and reverse dies also allows us to reconstruct the relative size of different issues. An issue with 100 obverse dies, for example, is larger in quantity than an issue with only four. The *absolute* size of a particular coinage can also be estimated, although there are varying suggestions as to how many coins each die could produce in the pre-medieval period (ranging from 5,000 – 47,250 depending on the metal and whether the flans were cold or hot when struck). Calculations of absolute size also assume each die is used until it breaks or is worn out, which was probably not the case in all instances. Given these problems, the use of die numbers to calculate absolute quantities of coinage remains controversial.

Die analysis can also identify when the same die is used for different issues, or in multiple mints or cities. These connections (called die links) can reveal when several cities or individuals made use of a single (perhaps travelling) mint or mint-workers, or demonstrate that two issues of coinage were struck contemporaneously.

The titles that appear on the coinage struck by Caesar and his supporters reflect the positions that Caesar accumulated, which reached a peak in 44 BC (Table 3). While texts often present Caesar's honours all within one section (e.g. Dio 44.4), coinage demonstrates that there was no 'linear' development in the public use of his titles: legends like CAESAR or CAESAR IMP are interspersed with references to his dictatorships. Remarkably, Fig. 2.12 *only* provides Caesar's titles, not his name: consul for the third time, dictator for the second time, augur and *pontifex maximus*. This last position is also represented through the priestly implements shown on the reverse. Given that Caesar was the first individual in Roman history to be both *pontifex maximus* and to belong to the college of augurs, he didn't need to be named. The coin type reflects the ascendancy Caesar had gained in the Roman public sphere. Inscriptions in the provinces also reveal that there was no linear sequence for Caesar's titles, though frequent reference is made to Caesar's position as *imperator* and *pontifex maximus* (Raubitschek 1954: 73). Provinces also might have elaborated on Roman ideology, with Caesar even occasionally named as a god (*theos*).

Table 3 demonstrates that many of the coins referring to Caesar were struck outside of Rome in military mints. Even the issue of Hirtius and Caesar in Rome (RRC 466/1) was struck outside of the normal system, under Hirtius' authority as prefect rather than by a Roman moneyer (Molinari 2003: 167–8). It was only in 44 BC, the year of Caesar's assassination, that Caesar's titles appeared on 'legal' coinage struck by official Roman moneyers in the capital.

Cassius Dio records that among the honours given to Caesar was the title *parens patriae* ('father of the country') and that this title was stamped on his coinage (Dio 44.4.4). A very similar title would, of course, later be given to Augustus and successive emperors (*pater patriae*). This is one of several occasions that Dio cites numismatic evidence in his narrative; he also mentions the EID MAR coin of Brutus, discussed on p. 70. Dio was not alone in viewing coinage as a source of evidence to cite, a reflection of the Roman perception of coinage as a medium that monumentalised contemporary events and ideas. It is worth asking how, as an author writing in the third century AD, Dio came across information about these earlier coin types (the EID MAR coin, for example, was no longer in circulation). It is likely that the types were recorded in another text, or perhaps kept in an official state archive (Rowan 2013c: 28–31). Whatever the source, knowledge about coin types of the past existed within the Roman world, highlighting their secondary function as a record of events.

Table 3. The titles of Caesar on Roman coinage, 49–44 BC

Year (BC)	Titles of Caesar	Translation	Mint	Reference	Denomination
49–48	CAESAR	*Caesar*	moving with Caesar	RRC 443/1	denarius
48–47	CAESAR	*Caesar*	moving with Caesar	RRC 452/1–5	452/1: aureus; 452/2–5: denarii
47	CAESAR DICT ITER	*Caesar, dictator for the second time*	east	RRC 456/1	aureus
	CAESAR IMP COS ITER	*Caesar, imperator, consul for the second time*	Sicily	RRC 457/1	denarius
47–46	CAESAR	*Caesar*	Africa	RRC 458/1	denarius
46	C CAESAR COS TER	*Gaius Caesar, consul for the third time*	Rome	RRC 466/1	aureus
	COS TERT DICT ITER AVGVR PONT MAX	*Consul for the third time, dictator for the second time, augur, pontifex maximus*	uncertain	RRC 467/1	denarius
46–45	CAESAR	*Caesar*	Spain	RRC 468/1	denarius
45	C CAES DIC TER	*Gaius Caesar, dictator for a third time*	Rome	RRC 475/1–2	both aurei
	CAESAR DIC TER	*Caesar, dictator for a third time*	uncertain	RRC 476/1	bronze coin (uncertain value)
44	CAESAR DICT QVART	*Caesar, dictator for a fourth time*	Rome	RRC 480/ 1–28	1–22: denarii
	CAESAR IMP or IMPER	*Caesar, imperator*			23–5: quinarii
	CAESAR IM P M	*Caesar, imperator, pontifex maximus*			26–8: sestertii

Table 3. (cont.)

Year (BC)	Titles of Caesar	Translation	Mint	Reference	Denomination
	CAESAR DICT PERPETVO	*Caesar, dictator for life*			
	CAESAR DICT IN PERPETVO				
	CAESAR PARENS PATRIAE	*Caesar, father of the country*			
	CAESAR DIC QVAR COS QVINC	*Caesar, dictator for the fourth time, consul for the fifth time*	Rome	RRC 481/1	aureus
	CAESAR IMP	*Caesar, imperator*	uncertain	RRC 482/1	denarius

Figure 2.12. Denarius, uncertain mint, Julius Caesar, 46 BC (RRC 467/1b). **Obv.**
Head of Ceres, COS TERT DICT ITER. **Rev.** Pontifical emblems (*culullus,*
aspergillum, jug and *lituus*), AVGVR PONT MAX.

Figure 2.13. Denarius, Rome, C. Cossutius Maridianus, 44 BC (RRC 480/19). **Obv.**
Wreathed and veiled head of Julius Caesar, *apex* behind, *lituus* before, CAESAR
PARENS PATRIAE. **Rev.** C COSSVTIVS and MARIDIANVS arranged in a cross;
in the angles, AAA FF.

Fig. 2.13 is one of the coins that carries the title *parens patriae*, accompanied by a portrait of Caesar and other symbols referring to his positions. Caesar's title of *imperator* and the honour of wearing triumphal dress at the games (Dio 43.43.1) and while sacrificing (App. 2.106) are referenced via his laurel wreath, worn beneath a toga that has been pulled over his head (the traditional attire worn when sacrificing to most deities). The veiled head, the augur's staff before Caesar's portrait, as well as the flamen's cap behind, refer to his positions as *pontifex maximus* and augur. One side of a small coin is loaded with meanings.

Controversy exists over whether the *parens patriae* issues of Caesar were struck during his lifetime or after his death, a problem connected to the uncertain chronology of the issues of 44 BC as a whole (Alföldi 1958; Buttrey 1956; Crawford 1974: vol. 1, 492–5; Kraay 1954). A large number of coin types were struck in this year, and it is difficult to be certain which coins were issued before, and which after, Caesar's assassination on the Ides of March. Archaeological evidence can rarely provide such a close date range, and so the reconstruction has largely been determined by connecting particular coin types to known historical circumstances. This is not an ideal methodology, since a coin could commemorate an event after it had been held, or advertise that it was forthcoming. Moreover, it can be difficult to tie a specific image to a specific event. For example, the obverse portrait of Caesar as *parens patriae* was also used for an issue showing a *desultor* on the reverse, a rider who jumped from horse to horse during games (Fig. 3.3). The *desultor* may refer to any or all of the games (*ludi*) held in 44 BC, so we can't provide it a specific date (Woytek 2003: 425). Recent scholarship has asserted that it is likely that all coins showing Caesar's portrait were struck in his lifetime (Woytek 2003: 427; for a discussion see "The mysterious case of Caesar and the *desultor*" on p. 59). The coins themselves cannot really be dated so closely, but the weight of the evidence does suggest this is the case (who would strike Caesar's portrait after he had just been assassinated?). The title of *parens patriae*, then, appeared on coinage just before Caesar's death.

Sulla's Dream or an Ode to Caesar?

Figure 2.14.
Denarius, Rome,
L. Aemilius Buca,
44 BC (RRC 480/1).

One of the few coins not to carry a direct reference to Caesar in 44 BC is this issue of Lucius Aemilius Buca. The obverse shows Venus and gives the name of the moneyer. The reverse has proven more difficult to interpret. Plutarch records that a Cappadocian goddess visited the Roman general Sulla in a dream before his battle with Marius (Plutarch, *Sulla* 9.4), and the scene here has frequently been interpreted as 'Sulla's dream' (Buca was a relative of Sulla; Crawford 1974: vol. 1, 493). This in turn has sparked various theories as to how Buca was able to strike this rather 'independent' image in a year otherwise dominated by Caesarian iconography. But this interpretation is unlikely; the scene is more reminiscent of the goddess Selene descending to her lover Endymion on Mt Latmos, accompanied by her charioteer, winged Aura (Fears 1975; Morawiecki 1983: 24). This imagery is a popular motif on funerary sarcophagi, and consequently Fears interpreted this piece as a funeral tribute to Caesar after his death. This interpretation moves the coin from the beginning of 44 BC to after the Ides of March. More recently, Woytek has pointed out that many of Buca's coins from this year display references to Luna, the Roman version of the Greek Selene (e.g. the appearance of the crescent behind Caesar's head on RRC 480/4, and the portrait of Luna on Buca's sestertii, RRC 480/26). He concludes the issue was probably struck before Caesar's death as a 'private' type of significance to the moneyer, reclassifying it as an 'independent' image (Woytek 2003: 430–2). In fact, since Luna is often shown with a diadem, might it be that it is Luna, and not Venus, shown on the obverse?

The appearance of Caesar's portrait on Roman denarii in 44 BC is often seen as a revolutionary moment in Roman history (Fig. 2.15). But coins had depicted living Romans before (notably the portrait of Titus Quinctius Flamininus in the east in the second century BC, and Sulla's portrayal as *triumphator* in 82 BC; see RRC 548, 367/1–5 and Pollini 2012: 72–3). Caesar's appearance on denarii is the culmination of these earlier developments. In fact, the city of Nicaea in Bithynia was the first to strike coins with

Figure 2.15. Denarius, Rome, M. Mettius, 44 BC (RRC 480/3). **Obv.** Wreathed head of Caesar, priestly implements (*lituus* and *culullus*) behind, CAESAR IMP. **Rev.** Venus holding Victory and sceptre, resting elbow on shield that rests on globe, M METTIVS. I in field.

Figure 2.16. Brass 24mm, Nicaea (Bithynia), C. Vibius Pansa, proconsul, 47/6 BC (RPC 1 2026). **Obv.** Bare head of Caesar, ΝΙΚΑΙΕΩΝ. **Rev.** ΕΠΙ ΓΑΙΟΥ ΟΥΒΙΟΥ ΠΑΝΣΑ, Nike advancing right holding palm and wreath, monograms to left and right.

Caesar's portrait on them in 47/6 BC (Fig. 2.16), several years before Caesar's portrait appeared on coinage at Rome. The proconsul of Bithynia and Pontus at the time was the same Gaius Vibius Pansa who struck the Libertas coin at the outbreak of the civil war (Fig. 2.8; Weinstock 1971: 297). The provinces thus provided an important precedent. Why Nicaea adopted the portrait of Caesar when they did and whether Vibius Pansa had any influence remains unknown, but it is important to remember that Greek cities had become accustomed to ruler portraiture under the Hellenistic monarchs. Indeed, Nysa-Scythopolis in Syria struck coins that probably show the laureate portrait of the Roman governor of Syria, Gabinius, in the 50s BC (RPC 1 4825–6; Erkelenz 2002: 73). One must then question the extent to which contemporary Romans deemed Caesar's portrait on coinage 'revolutionary'. The practice continued after Caesar's assassination, even on coins made by the assassins themselves (Eck 1984: 130). If Caesar's portrait were as radical as is believed today, it would be unlikely that Brutus would have followed Caesar's example.

2.2 The Battle for Legitimacy: Pompeians after the Death of Pompey

Following Caesar's entry into Italy, Pompey the Great and his supporters left to establish a base in Greece. In contrast to Caesar's coinage, which

Figure 2.17. Denarius, Apollonia Mordiaeum (Pisidia), L. Lentulus and C. Marcellus, 49 BC (RRC 445/1b). **Obv.** Triskeles with the winged head of Medusa in centre and corn-ears between legs. **Rev.** Jupiter standing, holding thunderbolt in right hand and eagle in left, LENT MAR (in ligature) COS.

Figure 2.18. Denarius, Rome, Faustus Cornelius Sulla, 56 BC (RRC 426/4b). **Obv.** Head of Hercules, S C. **Rev.** Globe surrounded by four wreaths; below left, *aplustre*, below right, corn-ear.

focused on Caesar, the coins struck by the Pompeian side carried more traditional designs – deities and types referring to ancestral achievements. The consuls of 49 BC, for example, released an issue with an image of Jupiter on one side and a triskeles on the other (the triskeles was a symbol of Sicily, and then of the Marcelli ever since the capture of Syracuse in 212 BC by Marcus Claudius Marcellus) (Fig. 2.17).

This conservatism stands in contrast to the coinage of the 50s BC, which bore direct reference to Pompey. One of these earlier issues carried three trophies referring to Pompey's three triumphs over Africa, Asia and Europe, an image that reportedly was placed on Pompey's signet ring (RRC 426/3; Dio 42.18.3). Fig. 2.18 commemorates these triumphs via three wreaths. The fourth, larger wreath at the top of this coin is probably a representation of the *corona aurea*, the golden crown that was seen as a sign of kingship in Rome and worn by *triumphators*; Pompey was given the honour of being allowed to wear this crown at the games (Velleius Paterculus 2.40.4; Crawford 1974: vol. 1, 488 n. 1). The globe in the centre of the design may refer to the trophy of the inhabited world Cassius Dio records was paraded in Pompey's triumph (Dio 37.21.2), while the *aplustre* (ship's stern) and corn-ear at the bottom refer to Pompey's achievements in securing the grain supply to Rome. These coins and others referencing Pompey's achievements have been found in hoards from the 50s BC onwards. The coins and their messages were already in circulation as the civil war broke out (see, for example, the hoards of Brandosa (BRA) and Mignano (MIG) in Italy, which both have a *terminus post quem* of 49 BC, available online at http://numismatics.org/chrr/). In this context Pompey had an advantage over his rival.

After the defeat at Pharsalus and Pompey's death in Egypt in 48 BC, opposition to Caesar continued in Africa under the command of Metellus Scipio, who had previously commanded forces in Syria. Along with other Pompeian commanders, Scipio was subjected to criticism by the Caesarian side – in *The Civil War* Caesar attacked their legitimacy, noting that Scipio (and others) did not wait for the ratification of the appointments by the assembly and left Rome without taking the appropriate auspices, amongst other irregularities (Caes. *BCiv*. 1.6.6–7). Caesar wrote 'all rights, divine and human, were thrown into confusion'. Whether Caesar's accusations are true or not, we find a clear response to them on Scipio's coinage, which display an inordinate emphasis on Scipio's offices, and their legitimacy (Linderski 1996; Steel 2013: 197–8).

Fig. 2.19 provides an excellent example of the crowded symbolism of Scipio's coinage. The obverse carries a reference to Jupiter, underlining Scipio's divine support. The *sella curulis*, the chair that symbolised Scipio's magistracy, appears on the reverse. Directly above the chair is a set of balanced scales (referring to fairness and justice, just as in the modern world), suggesting that his office was both justly acquired and/or justly conducted. Within the scales is a cornucopia (a sign of abundance), and to the right of the chair is grain, further emphasising the material benefits Scipio's position has brought to the Roman world. The many references and symbols may have led to many different interpretations by the viewer. Some, for instance, might have seen the scales as a rebuttal of the Caesarian claims of Scipio's cruelty.

The Caesarians also called Scipio's military experience into question, and it is not surprising that we find an emphasis on military achievements on

Figure 2.19. Denarius, African mint, Q. Metellus Scipio and P. Crassus, 47–46 BC (RRC 460/2). **Obv.** Bust of Jupiter right, eagle's head and sceptre below, METEL PIVS SCIP IMP. **Rev.** Curule chair with scales balanced on cornucopia above, corn-ear on left, dragon's head (?) on right, CRASS IVN LEG PRO PR.

Figure 2.20. Denarius, African mint, Q. Metellus Scipio and P. Crassus, 47–46 BC (RRC 460/3). **Obv.** Female head with turreted crown, corn-ear on left, caduceus on right, *rostrum* below, uncertain rectangular object above, CRASS IVN LEG PRO PR, laurel wreath as border. **Rev.** Trophy, *lituus* on left, jug on right, METEL PIVS SCIP IMP.

Fig. 2.20. The military trophy on the reverse, probably a reference to Scipio's victories in Syria, was perhaps meant as a 'reply' to Caesar's coinage that highlighted his success in Gaul (Fig. 2.6). The coin type may also have been a public response to the Caesarian allegation that Scipio gave *himself* the title of *imperator* after having *lost* in Syria (Caes. *BCiv.* 3.31.1). Victorious generals might be proclaimed *imperator* by their troops (indeed generals needed this acclamation to apply for a triumph from the Senate) but could not assume the title for themselves. Scipio's coin carries the title here, further emphasised by the selection of the laurel wreath, a symbol of a *triumphator*, as a border on the obverse – perhaps again a reply to the claims of his opposition.

Figure 2.21. Denarius, North Italian mint, Q. Caecilius Metellus Pius, 81 BC (RRC 374/2). **Obv.** Diademed head of Pietas right; stork before. **Rev.** Jug and *lituus*, IMPER within wreath.

Again this coin is loaded with multiple symbols, including the corn-ear, a *rostrum* (referencing naval victory or superiority), a laurel wreath (military triumph), and a caduceus (associated with the god Hermes and a symbol of prosperity). On either side of the military trophy is a jug and *lituus*. In the context of Caesarian claims about the irregularities of Scipio's command, the *lituus*, a symbol of the augurate at Rome, may have communicated that the gods *had* been consulted (Linderski 1996: 181). But a *lituus* and jug had also appeared on the coinage of one of Scipio's ancestors in 81 BC (Fig. 2.21). The appearance of these items on coins of 47/6 BC, then, may have referenced Scipio's ancestry, underlining his name Pius. In fact, any or all of these meanings might have been read into the image depending on the viewer. The jug and *lituus* were polyvalent, allowing multiple messages and meanings to be communicated to different viewers: the legitimacy of Scipio's position (despite Caesar's attempt to tarnish it), the role of the gods in supporting Rome and her magistrates, and the reputable lineage from which Scipio descended.

This combination of familial history and contemporary politics can also be seen on Fig. 2.22, which has a reverse decorated with an elephant accompanied by the legend SCIPIO IMP. Although one might be tempted to see this as a 'reply' to Caesar's elephant coin (Fig. 2.1), there is little to support this hypothesis. The elephant had been a symbol of the Metelli since the victory of L. Caecilius Metellus over Hasdrubal at Panormus during the First Punic War in 250 BC, and elephants had previously appeared on the coinage of several moneyers from the family (Linderski 1996: 173). Indeed, Q. Caecilius Metellus Pius, the same moneyer who struck Fig. 2.21 in 81 BC, also released an issue displaying an elephant with the initials of his name in

Figure 2.22. Denarius, African mint, Q. Metellus Scipio, 47–46 BC (RRC 459/1). **Obv.** Laureate head of Jupiter, Q METEL PIVS. **Rev.** Elephant, SCIPIO IMP.

Figure 2.23. Denarius, North Italian mint, Q. Caecilius Metellus Pius, 81 BC (RRC 374/1). **Obv.** Diademed head of Pietas with stork before. **Rev.** Elephant, Q C M P I in exergue.

the exergue: Q.C.M.P.I. (the 'I' referring to his title as *imperator*; Fig. 2.23). As with the *lituus* and jug, Scipio may have been using an ancestral type in keeping with Republican tradition. Nonetheless, the elephant was a topical motif, particularly since Caesar's own elephant issue was very large, and so others may have interpreted the image within the competing claims of the civil war (particularly if they didn't have an intimate knowledge of Roman elite family symbols). Since the issue was struck in Africa, the image might also have been interpreted as a reference to the elephants of King Juba I, who supported Scipio against Caesar (Dio 43.3.5–4.1). Juba himself released coins with an elephant on the reverse (Fig. 2.24), and so any users of Scipio's currency in Africa may have seen the elephant as a local symbol rather than (or in addition to) a reference to the Roman general.

Metellus Scipio had a strong client base in Africa, assuring him local support. Literary sources mention prophecies that a Scipio could not be defeated in the region (Suetonius, *Julius Caesar* 59; Plutarch, *Life of Julius*

Figure 2.24. Bronze 29mm, Numidia, Juba I (60–46 BC). **Obv.** Head of Jupiter Ammon with curled horns. **Rev.** Elephant walking, neo-punic legend above.

Figure 2.25. Denarius, African mint, Q. Metellus Scipio and Eppius, 47–46 BC (RRC 461/1). **Obv.** Head of Africa wearing elephant's skin, corn-ear on right, plough below, Q METELL SCIPIO IMP. **Rev.** Hercules resting on club which is on a rock, EPPIVS LEG F C.

Caesar 52.2; Dio 42.57.5). Pro-Caesarian literature attempted to blacken Scipio by suggesting that the commander and his supporters were deferring to Juba, going so far as to suggest that Scipio had promised the province of Africa to the king (e.g. Caesar, *African War* 57; Dio 43.4.6). It is clear that we cannot take this tradition at face value, but Scipio's coinage does reveal that he actively sought and/or commemorated local support. Several of his coins show local imagery. Fig. 2.25, for example, displays the head of Africa on the obverse, a design inspired by local Mauretanian coinage (Salzmann 1974: 177). But while the image was local, it was used in a Roman context: a corn-ear is placed before the head, reflecting the Roman idea of Africa as a breadbasket (not a vision found on contemporary monuments of local

Figure 2.26. Denarius, African mint, Q. Metellus Scipio and P. Crassus, 47–46 BC (RRC 460/4). **Obv.** Sekhmet holding *ankh*, labelled as G(enius) T(errae) A(fricae), Q METEL PIVS SCIPIO IMP. **Rev.** Victory holding winged caduceus and *patera*, P CRASSVS IVN LEG PRO PR.

kings). Numismatic imagery within imperial or colonial contexts often reflects the 'conqueror's vision' of a particular region rather than local identity (Rowan 2014a). Scipio's coin is an example of this practice in the Roman world.

The reverse of Fig. 2.25 shows Hercules, a Roman deity who also had a local African cult – the Mauretanian kings traced their ancestry to Sophax, the son of Hercules (Salzmann 1974: 176). As with his other coins, Scipio's numismatic imagery could appeal to multiple people on multiple levels. The local deity Sekhmet also appears on Scipio's issues (Fig. 2.26). These local images no doubt referred to the alliance of Scipio with Juba and Scipio's support in Africa. If the coins were intended to be used locally, the designs may also have been chosen with a local audience in mind, making the denarii (a coin denomination not found in any quantity in Africa before this period) more likely to be accepted (Coltelloni-Trannoy 1999: 76). Not many coins of this type have been found in Africa, however, although they are found in hoards in Italy and elsewhere. This may be because the type was not struck in large quantities in comparison with other denarii of this era, or because there are less published coin finds from Africa in comparison to other regions.

Pompey's sons, meanwhile, were active in Spain. When rebellion broke out against the Caesarian governor in 48 BC, cities in Spain appealed to the Pompeian faction in Africa, who sent Gnaeus Pompey (son of Pompey the Great) to the region in 47 BC. His brother Sextus Pompey soon followed; Pompey had been popular in Spain and his sons inherited this support

Figure 2.27. Denarius, Spanish mint, Gnaeus Pompeius and M. Publicius, 46–45 BC (RRC 469/1a). **Obv.** Helmeted head of Roma, M POBLICI LEG PRO PR. **Rev.** Female figure with shield slung on back, holding two spears in left hand and giving palm branch to soldier standing on the prow of a ship with right hand, CN MAGNVS IMP.

(Lowe 2002: 65). Unlike Scipio, neither brother had an official position; their presence in the area could only be justified by the fact that they were the sons of Pompey the Great. Dynasty won out over Roman law (Steel 2013: 203). The brothers had to rely on the memory of their father for legitimacy and so it is no surprise that he features on their coinage. Pompey's sons cast themselves as pious avengers of their deceased father, a self-representation that enabled Gnaeus and Sextus to capitalise on Pompey's popularity in Iberia and later in Sicily (discussed in Section 3.3).

Coinage commemorated the close relationship between the Pompeians and Spain. Fig. 2.27 shows Roma on the obverse, with a reverse naming Gnaeus Pompeius as *imperator* and showing a female figure giving a palm branch to a soldier arriving by ship. The female figure is most likely the personification of Hispania (Spain); the image thus communicates the welcome of the younger Pompey and his forces in the region (Welch 2012: 102). Other issues show Spanish cities lending support to a (Pompeian) soldier, with a portrait of Pompey the Great on the obverse (Fig. 2.28; Buttrey 1960a). As well as creating legitimacy, these representations of Pompey the Great also fell within the Republican tradition of coin types commemorating ancestral achievements.

The self-presentation of the brothers as the pious avengers of their father is most clearly seen on the coinage of Sextus, who struck issues showing Pompey the Great on the obverse and Pietas holding a palm branch on the reverse (Figs. 2.29–31). On Fig. 2.30 the portrait faces left instead of right, leading to the suggestion that it is the younger Gnaeus Pompey who is

Figure 2.28. Denarius, Spanish mint, Gnaeus Pompeius and M. Minatius Sabinus, 46–45 BC (RRC 470/1b). **Obv.** Head of Pompey the Great, CN MAGN IMP. **Rev.** Spanish city raising right hand to greet soldier, who receives shield from another kneeling Spanish city, M MINAT SABI PR Q.

Figure 2.29. Denarius, Spanish mint, Sextus Pompey, 45–44 BC (RRC 477/1a). **Obv.** Head of Pompey the Great, SEX MAGNVS IMP B. **Rev.** Pietas holding palm branch and sceptre, PIETAS.

Figure 2.30. Denarius, Spanish mint, Sextus Pompey, 45–44 BC (RRC 477/2). **Obv.** Head of Pompey the Great, SEX MAGNVS IMP SAL. **Rev.** Pietas holding palm branch and sceptre, PIETAS.

Figure 2.31. Denarius, Spanish mint, Sextus Pompey, 45–44 BC (RRC 477/3a). **Obv.** Head of Pompey the Great, SEX MAGN PIVS IMP SAL. **Rev.** Pietas holding palm branch and sceptre, PIETAS.

shown, or even Sextus himself. But such a representation would be remarkable – Caesar's portrait had probably not yet appeared on coinage. Moreover, the 'lick' of hair over the forehead on Fig. 2.30 is characteristic of the portraiture of Pompey, and so it is probably he who is shown here (Buttrey 1960b: 84; *contra* Welch 2012: 108). This is further reinforced by the fact that the portrait is clean-shaven – Pompey's sons are traditionally shown with beards of mourning. Nonetheless, the combination of Pompey's portrait with a legend naming Sextus (IMP SEX MAGNVS or IMP SEX MAGNVS SAL) means that there is room for interpretative confusion – users of the coins may have seen Pompey the Great *or* his son in the image, and perhaps this ambiguity was intentional. Given that Sextus relied on his father to legitimise his position, it is not surprising that he would wish to be as closely aligned with Pompey as possible.

Sextus also adopted the title 'Pius'. We can actually see the moment this occurs on Fig. 2.31. The obverse die, having already been used to strike some coins, was altered to include this additional title. PIVS is squeezed into the only available space, directly above Pompey's head (Buttrey 1960b: 90). That coinage production would stop so that Sextus' new titulature could be added further reveals the importance placed on coinage as a medium of self-representation and communication.

2.3 Caesar's Elephant in the Provinces

Just as Roman coinage reveals the ideologies of the Roman elite involved in the first civil war, so too the iconography chosen by the provincial elite for

Figure 2.32. Bronze 16–17mm, Treviri (Titelberg?), Aulus Hirtius, c. 45 BC (RPC 1 501). **Obv.** Elephant trampling snake (?), A HIRTIVS. **Rev.** Pontifical emblems (*culullus, aspergillum,* axe, *apex*).

their local (provincial) coinage provides important information. Coinage, along with provincial inscriptions and other monuments, provides us with glimpses of the experience of Roman rule. Provincial coins often carry themes of local interest: local festivals, cults, mythologies and historical events. They also include local representations of Roman rule. At times cities adopted the imagery of Roman coinage for their own local issues, indicating not only that people were paying attention to the designs of coinage, but also that coinage formed a medium in an on-going dialogue between Rome and the provinces. The following discussion focuses on one example, although there are many others: the adoption of Caesar's unusual elephant design.

The imagery associated with Caesar's elephant coin (Fig. 2.1) reappears on coinage struck by Aulus Hirtius. Hirtius had accompanied Caesar to Spain in 49 BC (when the elephant issue was struck) and remained a supporter of Caesar until his assassination, striking Fig. 2.10. In 45 BC Hirtius was governor of Gaul and was responsible for a local bronze coinage that directly referenced Caesar's earlier issue: an elephant trampling a 'snake' was placed on the obverse, with Caesar's pontifical emblems on the reverse (Fig. 2.32; on the date see Woytek 2003: 124). The only difference in the design is that the legend CAESAR has been replaced with A HIRTIVS. The type must have been chosen to underline Hirtius' support of Caesar – but what, I wonder, would the local Gallic population have made of the imagery? 505 examples of these coins have been found at Titelberg in Luxembourg, making this site (a major settlement of the Treviri tribe) the most likely location for the mint (Metzler 1995; Reding 1972: 60). As the coinage was used locally, the imagery on it may have gradually come to be associated with the city rather than with Caesar.

Figure 2.33. Bronze 22mm, Osicerda, 49–40 BC (ACIP 1292–3). **Obv.** Victory holding wreath, OSI. **Rev.** Elephant trampling snake (?), USEKERTE in Iberian script below.

Figure 2.34. Silver quinarius, Rome, A. Licinius Nerva, 47 BC (RRC 454/3). **Obv.** Helmeted head of Minerva, NERVA. **Rev.** Victory with wreath and palm branch, A LICINIV.

The Treviri may have come to see the images as 'theirs'. This may explain why the imagery was used again as a type by another Roman proconsul of Gaul in 30–29 BC: the imagery was now local (RPC 1 502).

The city of Usekerte-Osicerda in Spain also imitated Caesar's denarius type, showing an elephant trampling a 'snake' on the reverse of one of their bi-lingual coin issues with the name of the city in Iberian script below (Fig. 2.33). The obverse of the coin gives the city's name in Latin accompanied by an image of Victory holding a wreath and palm. The Victory is also taken directly from Roman coinage: see Fig. 2.34 (Justo 1996–7: 322). The adoption of Roman iconography here may have been intended as a statement of support for Caesar. The historical context is probably the battle of Ilerda, fought between Caesar and the Pompeians Lucius Afranius and Marcus Petreius close to the city (Justo 1996–7). If this is the context, the victory of Caesar is communicated via the obverse Victory type, while the elephant trampling the 'snake' image makes direct reference to Caesar himself. The city was well within the circulation region of Caesar's elephant

Figure 2.35. Bronze 21–22mm, Mauretania, 33–25 BC (RPC 1 879). **Obv.** Head of Zeus Ammon, IMP CAESAR. **Rev.** Elephant trampling snake (?), DIVI F in exergue.

denarii and would have been aware of Caesar's numismatic iconography. The civic elite, having 'read' Caesar's coinage (as well as the types of other Roman coins), transformed the imagery into their own 'monument in miniature' commemorating Caesar's victories.

Caesar's numismatic iconography was also adopted in Africa, perhaps because of the elephant's association with the region. A single image could simultaneously refer to Africa, Caesar, Roman power and, later on, Octavian. It was undoubtedly the double association of the elephant with Africa and with Rome that made the image attractive as a type for Roman Mauretania in the period 33–25 BC. Fig. 2.35 has the head of the local god Zeus Ammon on the obverse (identifiable through his curled ram's horns) accompanied by the legend IMP CAESAR, while the reverse shows an elephant trampling a 'snake', with DIVI F ('son of a god') in the exergue. The imagery is both 'local' and 'Roman', with the legend IMP CAESAR and the elephant now referring to Octavian as son of the deified Caesar.

The elephant and 'snake' reappear in the city of Hadrumetum in North Africa in 6–5 BC. The obverse of Fig. 2.36 shows a portrait of the governor, Africanus Fabius Maximus, with the legend naming him as proconsul and *septemvir epulonum* (VII EPVLO, the *septemviri epulonum* were a religious college in Rome). The reverse shows the elephant and 'snake' and names the quaestor C. Livineius Gallus. The mention of the quaestor, unique on African coinage, was perhaps meant to recall Livineius Regulus (the father of Gallus), who had been a commander in Hadrumetum during Caesar's

Figure 2.36. Bronze 22–23mm, Hadrumetum, Fabius Africanus (proconsul) and C. Livineius Gallus, 6–5 BC (RPC 1 781). **Obv.** Bare head of Africanus right, AFR FA MAX COS PROCOS VII EPVLO. **Rev.** Elephant trampling snake (?), C LIVIN GALLVS Q PRO PR.

campaigns (Caesar, *African War* 89.3; Coltelloni-Trannoy 1999: 74). A Caesarian context is certainly suggested by the choice of imagery. Caesar's denarii have not been found in any quantity in North Africa, perhaps because of the poor publication of finds from the region (Burnett 1987a: 176). However, the imagery could have travelled to the area in another way, perhaps via the movement of individuals well versed in Roman ideology. The image of the elephant and 'snake' here, struck after Caesar's death, may have evoked Caesar in the minds of the users, but also the deeds of Livineius Regulus, Augustus and the Roman presence in the region more generally.

The client king Ptolemaeus also struck the elephant and 'snake' type when he ruled Mauretania as sole king from AD 23–40 (Mazard 1955: 403–4; Salzmann 1974). Since the king struck other issues that referenced Augustan iconography (alongside more local types), we might understand the image here as a reference to the Roman support Ptolemaeus enjoyed. Educated in Rome, the client king was well versed in Roman iconographic language. Caesar's elephant again gained new associations without necessarily losing the older ones.

Thus as Caesar's elephant and 'snake' type travelled, the image gained new associations and meanings. Coins are different to other monuments since they move between different people and are 'seen' in ever-changing contexts. With each new context a coin image may gain and/or retain

Figure 2.37. Bronze 17–18mm, Thrace, Rhaescuporis I and Cotys II, c. 48–42 BC (RPC 1 1703). **Obv.** Diademed bust, ΒΑΣΙΛΕΥΣ ΚΟΤΥΣ. **Rev.** Trophy, ΒΑΣΙΛΕΩΣ ΡΑΙΣΚΟΥΠΟΡΙΔΟΣ.

meanings; as an 'image in motion' its viewing context is unstable (Mwangi 2002: 35). Caesar's soldiers may have had a particular association with the elephant and 'snake' image, which may have changed as the coins travelled from soldiers to merchants, to local populations and eventually, for some issues, beyond the boundaries of the Roman Empire (hoards containing the coin have been found in Romania, for example). Similarly, reuse of the image meant that additional meaning was 'added' onto the original reference: associations with Augustus, Roman power, Caesarian supporters, or local identity emerged. But in spite of the multiple associations a coin image may have had (which modern scholarship is hard-pressed to fully reconstruct), the repeated use of the Caesarian coin type clearly demonstrates that an iconographic dialogue took place on coins of this period, with coin imagery 'read' and re-used. Although the unusual imagery of Caesar's denarius may have made it attractive to imitate, it was undoubtedly the sheer quantities in which the issue was struck that enabled it to act as a communicative medium across the Empire, and which led to it being adopted in numerous provinces and contexts.

Although the coinage of Caesar has formed the focus here, the dialogue was not limited to his types alone. The late Republic saw widespread interaction between the coinage of Romans, the provinces, and Rome's client kings. Coins of the Thracian king Rhaescuporis I, for example, reproduce the types of his Roman ally Brutus (Figs. 2.37–8; Youroukova 1976: 50–2). Rhaescuporis supported Brutus at Philippi and in his campaigns against the Thracian tribes. The resultant victories are likely the

Figure 2.38. Aureus, mint moving with Brutus and Cassius, Brutus and M. Servilius, 43–42 BC (RRC 505/4). **Obv.** Laureate head of Apollo, M SERVILIVS LEG. **Rev.** Trophy, Q. CAEPIO BRVTVS IMP.

Figure 2.39. Denarius, African mint, Juba II, 25 BC–AD 24 (Mazard 129). **Obv.** Diademed head of Juba II, REX IVBA. **Rev.** Head of Africa wearing elephant skin, corn-ear before.

occasion for the striking of coinage by both Rhaescuporis and Brutus. The Mauretanian King Juba II was also inspired by the issues of Metellus Pius Scipio on his coinage: the bust of Africa on Fig. 2.39 has a corn-ear before her, demonstrating that the prototype for the image was ultimately Roman (see Fig. 2.25) (Salzmann 1974: 177).

3

Competition and Conflict after Caesar (44–36 BC)

Caesar's assassination in 44 BC heralded a sustained period of conflict: the assassins seem to have had no firm plans for what to do after Caesar's death. Caesar's position as dictator for life had provided a precedent for one-man rule in the Republic, one that could not be easily forgotten. What should Rome, post-Caesar, look like? There were many different ideas on this score, and as events unfolded alliances were made and broken, claims and counterclaims developed and refuted. This uncertainty was exacerbated by the fact that two men claimed to be Caesar's heir: Antony and Octavian.

What can coinage add to our understanding of this period? Many of the main political players (Octavian, Antony, Brutus, Cassius, Sextus Pompey) struck coinage that reveals their ideologies and alliances at different periods. Although the written record may have later been reshaped, coins that were already in circulation were harder to alter, and these provide an insight into the views of Octavian's opposition. As with the coinage discussed in the previous chapter, it is clear that the elite viewed and responded to the coinage released by others; along with texts and other monuments, coinage formed a medium of communication for those who sought power. Coinage was a 'monument in miniature' taken seriously by all involved in Roman politics. And in spite of the many alliances formed in this period, the coin types reveal intense competition, suggesting that, ultimately, any agreement or compromise between political leaders was doomed to fail (Newman 1990: 62).

3.1 Caesar's Inheritance: Antony versus Octavian

Two men in Rome claimed to be Caesar's heir. Mark Antony, Caesar's co-consul for 44 BC and nominated governor of Italy, was a logical political successor. But Caesar's will designated another heir: Octavian, who, in accordance with Caesar's wishes, began calling himself Caesar. Who Julius Caesar's heir was mattered: the 'true' heir could count on Caesar's strong support amongst the Roman plebeians and the army, as well as the

Figure 3.1. Denarius, Rome, P. Sepullius Macer, 44 BC (RRC 480/21). **Obv.** Tetrastyle temple with globe in pediment, CLEMENTIAE CAESARIS. **Rev.** *Desultor* holding reins and whip; palm branch and wreath behind, P SEPVLLIVS MACER.

allegiance of pro-Caesarians amongst the Roman elite. The need of both Antony and Octavian to demonstrate their superior claim shaped many of their decisions immediately following 44 BC (Richardson 2012: 10–46). The importance of being Caesar's heir is also seen on coinage.

Antony's connection to Caesar was communicated via portraiture and an emphasis on religious offices. Antony was part of the college of the *luperci Iulii* (priests responsible for a festival honouring Caesar) and was a nominated priest of the cult to Caesar and his Clemency (Dio 44.6.4). Caesar's pardon of the Romans who had opposed him during the civil war was seen as an embodiment of his outstanding clemency (*clementia*) and a temple in honour of this *clementia* was decreed towards the end of his life. Caesar himself emphasises his *clementia* in his writings, so whether this honour was spontaneous or something more orchestrated is up for debate (App. 2.106; Dio 44.6.4; Plutarch, *Life of Julius Caesar* 57.3; Weinstock 1971: 241–3). The temple appeared on coins soon after Caesar's death (Fig. 3.1). Antony, as priest of this cult, would no doubt have supported the structure's representation. Caesar's assassination must have resulted in great uncertainty, including with regards to what to put on the coinage. The moneyer of Fig. 3.1, Sepullius Macer, seems to have overcome this uncertainty (could he show Caesar's portrait?) by representing the temple (Woytek 2003: 427).

The implied reference to Antony as priest of the cult (and hence his connection to Caesar) is made apparent by another issue struck by Macer, Fig. 3.2. This type has the *same* reverse as the temple coin (a horse rider who jumped from horse to horse during public spectacles), but the obverse shows Antony veiled (emphasising his role as priest), accompanied by

Figure 3.2. Denarius, Rome, P. Sepullius Macer, 44 BC (RRC 480/22). **Obv.** Bearded and veiled head of Mark Antony; *lituus* before, jug behind. **Rev.** *Desultor* holding reins and whip; palm branch and wreath behind, P SEPVLLIVS MACER.

Figure 3.3. Denarius, Rome, P. Sepullius Macer, 44 BC (RRC 480/20). **Obv.** Wreathed and veiled head of Julius Caesar, *lituus* before, *apex* behind, CAESAR PARENS PATRIAE. **Rev.** *Desultor* holding reins and whip, palm branch and wreath behind, P SEPVLLIVS MACER.

priestly implements, and bearded as a sign of mourning for Caesar. Although this portrait emphasised Antony's role as a priest, the image might also have reminded people of Caesar's own portraiture before his death: the dictator was also veiled and shown with objects associated with his priesthoods (compare Antony's portrait, for example, with Fig. 2.13). These iconographic similarities demonstrate how Antony presented himself as Caesar's heir (Newman 1990: 53).

The Mysterious Case of Caesar and the *Desultor*

In RRC a third coin issue is listed showing a *desultor* (Fig. 3.3). The obverse is a wreathed and veiled head of Julius Caesar accompanied by an augural staff and a priestly cap with the legend declaring 'Caesar, father of the country'. This is the same obverse as Fig. 2.13. This particular issue has formed the crux of many modern discussions surrounding the use of Caesar's portrait before and after his death, but what is not often mentioned is that the issue is only known from *a single specimen* (a *unicum*), housed in the Cabinet des Médailles in Paris. A coin that is only known from one example, when other coins from the same year and moneyer survive in quantity, must arouse suspicion. This coin may in fact be a minting error: one of the dies from the previous series was accidentally combined with the *desultor* reverse, creating a combination of obverse and reverse iconography that was never originally intended (Woytek 2003: 427). Since the resulting coin is likely a mistake, we should remove it from our discussions of Caesarian portraiture.

Antony's self-presentation as Caesar's successor continued with the production of a double portrait type in 43 BC, showing Antony on the obverse (named as *imperator*) and the laureate head of Caesar (named as dictator) on the reverse (Fig. 3.4). The *lituus* and jug, which were shown on either side of Antony's portrait on Fig. 3.2, are now spread over the obverse *and* reverse, underlining the connection of Antony to the deceased dictator. When combined with the double portrait design and the identical placement of the legends (to the right of each portrait), the overall effect is one that closely aligns Antony with Caesar.

Perhaps as a response to Antony's coinage, Octavian also struck a double portrait type in 43 BC. Fig. 3.5 shows the older and younger Caesar with their respective religious offices listed. Both sides of the coin carry the legend C CAESAR with Octavian named as consul and augur, and the deceased

Figure 3.4. Denarius, mint in Gallia Transalpina and Cisalpina, Mark Antony, 43 BC (RRC 488/1). **Obv.** Bearded head of Mark Antony, *lituus* behind, M ANTON IMP. **Rev.** Laureate head of Caesar right, jug behind, CAESAR DIC.

Figure 3.5. Aureus, mint in Gallia Cisalpina and Italy, Octavian, 43 BC (RRC 490/ 2). **Obv.** Bearded head of Octavian right, C CAESAR COS PONT AVG. **Rev.** Laureate head of Caesar, C CAESAR DICT PERP PONT MAX.

Figure 3.6. Denarius, mint in Gallia Cisalpina and Italy, Octavian, 43 BC (RRC 490/ 1). **Obv.** Bearded head of Octavian right, C CAESAR IMP. **Rev.** Equestrian statue left, with raised right hand, S C in exergue.

Julius Caesar as dictator for life and *pontifex maximus*. Octavian, however, took the competition with Antony one step further: he also released coinage showing the equestrian statue that had been voted to him by the Senate in January 43 BC (communicated on the coin through the legend S C), underlining the fact that *he* had the official support of the Republic, while Antony had, by this stage, become a public enemy or *hostis* (Fig. 3.6).

In January 42 BC Caesar officially became a god or *divus*, meaning that Octavian became the son of a god (Koortbojian 2013: 8). Between 41 and 39 BC Octavian began using the title DIVI IVLI F ('son of the deified Julius') on his coinage (Alföldi and Giard 1984). Sextus Pompey, son of Pompey the Great, also claimed divinity for his father around this time (see page 73). Octavian and Sextus must have been responding to one another's claims; Sextus, in fact, may have been the first to issue coins that suggested a divine lineage (Newman 1990: 61). The appearance of DIVI F on coins of Octavian

Figure 3.7.
Aureus, Rome,
Q. Voconius
Vitulus, 40 BC (?)
(RRC 526/1).
Obv. Bearded
head of Octavian
right, DIVI IVLI
F. **Rev.** Calf left,
Q VOCONIVS,
VITVLVS in
exergue.

Figure 3.8. Denarius, Rome, Q. Voconius Vitulus, 40 BC (?) (RRC 526/2). **Obv.**
Laureate head of Caesar right, *lituus* behind, DIVI IVLI. **Rev.** Calf left,
Q VOCONIVS, VITVLVS in exergue.

was accompanied by a further development of the double portrait type.
A series was released that included an aureus issue carrying a portrait of
Octavian (Fig. 3.7) and a denarius issue showing the portrait of Julius
Caesar (Fig. 3.8). The same reverse type (a calf) was used for both, while
the obverse legend differed only by the addition of an F (DIVI IVLI F on the
aureus and DIVI IVLI on the denarius). The overall effect is similar to the
issues of Macer discussed above (Figs. 3.1–2), but here the connection is
even more pronounced. The calf was a reference to the moneyer responsible
for the series, Q. Voconius Vitulus (*vitulus* in Latin means a bull calf). This
combination of types, with one side referring to Octavian and the other to
the Roman moneyer, is also seen in the early years of the principate,
discussed in Chapter 5.

Octavian's claim to be Caesar's legitimate heir is also highlighted on
bronze issues showing Octavian on one side and Caesar on the other

Figure 3.9. Leaded bronze 29–30mm, Italian mint, Octavian, c. 38 BC (?) (RRC 535/1 = RPC 1 620). **Obv.** Bearded head of Octavian right, CAESAR DIVI F. **Rev.** Wreathed head of Caesar, DIVOS IVLIVS.

Figure 3.10. Bronze 29–30mm, Italian mint, Octavian, c. 38 BC (?) (RRC 535/2 = RPC 1 621). **Obv.** Bearded head of Octavian right, star in front, DIVI F. **Rev.** DIVOS IVLIVS in a laurel wreath.

(Fig. 3.9), and the representation of a bearded Octavian with the star associated with Caesar's deification before him (Fig. 3.10). On a later issue (Fig. 3.11) Caesar and Octavian are shown together on the same side of the coin.

In 38 BC, as these coins were released, Antony was in the east. He was unable to match Octavian's claim to be son of a god, so his response was to

Figure 3.11. Denarius, mint moving with Octavian, Octavian and Agrippa, 38 BC (RRC 534/2). **Obv.** Laureate head of Caesar and bearded head of Octavian facing each other, on left, DIVOS IVLIVS, on right DIVI F. **Rev.** M AGRIPPA COS DESIG.

Figure 3.12. Aureus, mint moving with Mark Antony, Mark Antony, 38 BC (RRC 533/3b). **Obv.** Head of Mark Antony right, M ANTONIVS M Γ M N AVGVR IMP TIIRT. **Rev.** Head of Octavia right, COS DIISIG ITIIR IIT TIIRT III VIR R P C.

stress his own ancestry in the traditional Roman manner. Antony released coins with the legend M F M N (= MARCI FILIVS MARCI NEPOS, 'son of Marcus, grandson of Marcus'), a lineage that was perhaps intended to communicate a more traditional Republican ideal in contrast to the divine lineage of his competitor (Fig. 3.12). Octavia appears on the reverse, but she is not mentioned in the legend. This means that Antony's titles can occupy *both* sides of the coin, creating an impressive list: augur, *imperator* for the third time, designated consul for the second and third times, and triumvir. Octavia's appearance suggests her importance; texts record her central role in the negotiations between her husband and brother in the exchange of military resources at this time (e.g. App. 5.95; Richardson 2012: 56). The alliance between Antony and Octavian is referenced on coinage even as other components of the coin design reveal continuing competition

Figure 3.13. Denarius, Rome, L. Servius Rufus, 43–41 BC (RRC 515/2). **Obv.**
Bearded male head (probably Brutus), L SERVIVS RVFVS. **Rev.** Dioscuri standing
facing.

Figure 3.14. Denarius, Rome, C. Numonius Vaala, 43–41 BC (RRC 514/2). **Obv.**
Male head (Cassius?), C NVMONIVS VAALA. **Rev.** Soldier rushing left, attacking
rampart defended by two further soldiers, VAALA in exergue.

between the two. Looking closely at Fig. 3.12 you'll see that the legend is
a bit garbled. This is probably because the series was struck in the eastern
Mediterranean, and the die engraver was probably more comfortable with
Greek than Latin: the F has been rendered as a gamma (Γ) and letter E as II.

3.2 Apollo and Libertas on the Coinage of Brutus and Cassius

Nicolaus of Damascus, a friend of King Herod the Great and tutor to
the children of Antony and Cleopatra, observes that three men were
the most influential in the plot to assassinate Caesar: Decimus Brutus,
Gaius Cassius and Marcus Brutus (Nicolaus of Damascus, *Life
of Augustus* 19; Toher 2003). Cassius and Brutus styled themselves as
the 'Liberators', and it has been suggested that the portraits of both
Cassius (Fig. 3.14) and Brutus (Fig. 3.13) appear on Roman coinage in

43 BC, the year following Caesar's death. Woytek has argued that the college of moneyers Crawford placed in 41 BC may actually belong to 43 BC (Buttrey 1956: 37; Woytek 2003: 438–50). Crawford has since disagreed (Crawford 2012).

So were Figs. 3.13–14 struck in 43 BC or 41 BC? As mentioned in the introduction, the dates assigned to coins in RRC are estimates, and the hoard evidence for these two issues is small, meaning they are difficult to date with certainty. Neither portrait is named, so the viewer cannot be *sure* that they are seeing Brutus or Cassius. It does seem unlikely that Brutus would appear on the coinage of 41 BC, after he had been defeated at Philippi. But since the portraits are unnamed, Crawford suggests that the moneyers may have struck these issues in 41 BC with plausible deniability, communicating the 'right' message to sympathisers, while to others the moneyer Rufus might say 'Oh no, that's not Brutus, that's my uncle Fred'. The debate remains open: either the coins were struck in 43 BC, or they were struck later, after Brutus' defeat. Of course, the two portraits may not be Brutus and Cassius at all! We have no other known portraits of Cassius, but compare Fig. 3.13 with the portrait of Brutus on Figs. 3.19–20. Do you think the same person is shown?

Brutus and Cassius both eventually fled Rome for the eastern Mediterranean. While Antony and Octavian competed to win the allegiance of Caesar's supporters, Cassius and Brutus presented themselves as the champions of Libertas with the support of Apollo (Hollstein 1994). Both Brutus and Cassius could claim a particular connection to Apollo. Cassius was a *quindecemvir*, a member of the priestly college in Rome responsible for Apollo's cult, while Brutus was associated with the god through the actions of his legendary ancestor L. Iunius Brutus (see inset 'Family business? Brutus and his ancestry', p. 67). Brutus had also been placed in charge of games for Apollo in Rome (the *ludi Apollinares*); he paid for the games but they were held in his absence after he fled the capital (Hollstein 1994: 128–32). Coins of Brutus and Cassius carry images of Apollo and his attributes: the tripod, laurel branch or lyre (Figs. 3.15–16; RRC 498–506). As the deity connected with the expulsion of the Tarquin kings from Rome at the very beginnings of the Republic, Apollo was associated with freedom from tyranny or *libera res publica*, a connection articulated on coinage through the representation of Libertas.

Figure 3.15. Aureus, mint moving with Cassius, Cassius and M. Aquinus, 43–42 BC (RRC 498/1). **Obv.** Diademed head of Libertas right, M AQVINVS LEG, LIBERTAS. **Rev.** Tripod with cauldron, decorated with two laurel branches, C CASSI PR COS.

Figure 3.16. Denarius, mint moving with Brutus, Brutus, 43–42 BC (RRC 501/1). **Obv.** Head of Libertas right, LEIBERTAS. **Rev.** Plectrum, lyre and laurel branch tied with fillet, CAEPIO BRVTVS PRO COS.

Family Business? Brutus and His Ancestry

Brutus came from a family famously associated with *libertas* and the expulsion of monarchs. Nicolaus of Damascus observes that the reputation of Brutus' family was influential in the uprising against Caesar (Nicolaus of Damascus, *Life of Augustus* 19). According to legend, L. Iunius Brutus drove out the last of the Tarquin kings after interpreting an oracle of Apollo from Delphi. Brutus then became the first consul in 509 BC (Cicero, *Letters to Brutus* 53). As a moneyer in 55/54 BC Brutus celebrated this ancestry: Fig. 3.18 shows Libertas on the obverse, and L. Iunius Brutus walking with two lictors and an *accensus* (one of the poorer members of the Roman legions) on the reverse (Ceruti 1993–4). Brutus also struck a coin type with the portrait of L. Iunius Brutus on the obverse, and another ancestor, C. Servilius Ahala, on the reverse

Figure 3.17. Denarius, Rome, Brutus, 55/54 BC (RRC 433/2). **Obv.** Head of L. Iunius Brutus, BRVTVS. **Rev.** Head of C. Servilius Ahala, AHALA.

Figure 3.18. Denarius, Rome, Brutus, 55/54 BC (RRC 433/1). **Obv.** Head of Libertas, LIBERTAS. **Rev.** L. Iunius Brutus (cos. 509 BC) waking between two lictors and preceded by an *accensus*, BRVTVS in exergue.

(Fig. 3.17). Ahala had killed Spurius Maelius in 439 BC after Spurius had begun to style himself as a king. Brutus was descended from this other tyrannicide via his mother Servilia, and the reference here may reflect the growing visibility of Roman women in this period. But Brutus also had a more direct connection: he had been formally adopted into the Servilii by his uncle in 59 BC after his father was killed by Pompey the Great.

That Brutus connected his role as an assassin of Caesar with the actions of his ancestors is demonstrated on Fig. 3.19, an aureus struck with his legate Pedanius Costa. On the obverse is a portrait of L. Iunius Brutus, the first consul of Rome (PRIM COS), while the reverse carries the portrait of Brutus himself. The oak wreath on both sides of the coin is the *corona civica*, the wreath awarded for saving a Roman citizen's life. Neither Brutus nor his ancestor was formally awarded the honour, but the message the wreath communicates is that both are the saviours of Roman citizens. The oak wreath was later adopted by Sextus Pompey on his coinage (see Fig. 3.29;

Figure 3.19. Aureus, mint moving with Brutus, Brutus and Pedanius Costa, 43–42 BC (RRC 506/1). **Obv.** Bearded head of L. Iunius Brutus, L BRVTVS PRIM COS. Oak wreath as border. **Rev.** Bearded head of M. Brutus, M BRVTVS IMP COSTA LEG. Oak wreath as border.

Figure 3.20. Denarius, mint moving with Brutus, Brutus and L. Plaetorius Cestianus, 43–42 BC (RRC 508/3). **Obv.** Bearded head of Brutus right, BRVT IMP L PLAET CEST. **Rev.** Pileus between two daggers, EID MAR below.

DeRose Evans 1992: 147). Just as Antony and Octavian connected themselves to Caesar, and Sextus Pompey underscored his relationship to his deceased father, so too Brutus represented his actions within the context of his ancestry. That so many involved in the civil war should reference their heritage reveals the dominance of familial achievement in the elite Roman mindset. There was also a clear iconographic dialogue between the differing groups that arose after Caesar: just as Sextus Pompey responded to Brutus' aureus, so too Brutus himself was probably influenced by the double portrait types of Octavian and Antony in formulating the design of Fig. 3.19.

Brutus' portrait also appears on Fig. 3.20, the famous issue that directly refers to the assassination of Caesar. The reverse displays a *pileus* (the liberty cap worn by slaves when they were granted freedom) between two

Figure 3.21. Aureus, mint moving with Brutus and Cassius, Cassius and
M. Servilius, 43–42 BC (RRC 505/1). **Obv.** Laureate head of Apollo right, C CASSI
IMP. **Rev.** *Aplustre* with branches ending in roses, M SERVILIVS LEG.

daggers accompanied by the date of Caesar's death (EID MAR, the Ides
of March). The issue was struck with Plaetorius Cestianus, who is named
alongside Brutus in the obverse legend. This particular coin is mentioned by
Cassius Dio, who writes that Brutus 'stamped upon the coins which were
being minted his own likeness and a cap and two daggers, indicating by this
and by the inscription that he and Cassius had liberated the fatherland' (Dio
47.25.3). Cassius' portrait never appears on coins struck in the east, suggesting that although there were points of similarity between the two, Brutus and
Cassius could also diverge in their self-representations. Why Brutus should
have placed his portrait on coinage and Cassius not needs further study.
Perhaps Brutus' ancestry, as well as his education and literary reputation,
meant that he was better suited as a figurehead for the Liberators' cause, and
he may have been chosen over Cassius for this purpose in the lead up to
Philippi (Mattingly 1948: 451; Richardson 2012: 44).

Both Cassius and Brutus also referenced their military achievements
on coinage. Once it became apparent that armed conflict was inevitable,
Brutus and Cassius decided to fund their campaign by attacking regions
that supported the triumvirs. Cassius attacked and sacked Rhodes, then
demanded tribute from Asia before moving onto Cappadocia, while
Brutus moved against Lycia. These campaigns gave them bullion for
coinage, and their coinage in turn commemorated the campaigns.
Brutus' coins celebrating his Thracian campaigns have already been mentioned (Fig. 2.38); Appian observes that he used the treasures from Thrace
to strike coinage (App. 4.75). Cassius' victory over Rhodes (App. 4.65–74)
was celebrated with two main types. Fig. 3.21 shows an *aplustre* (the

Figure 3.22. Denarius, mint moving with Brutus and Cassius, Cassius and M. Servilius, 43–42 BC (RRC 505/3). **Obv.** Laureate head of Apollo right, C CASSEI IMP. **Rev.** Crab holding *aplustre* in its claws, rose and untied diadem below, M SERVILIVS LEG.

ornamental stern of a ship and a symbol of naval victory), with its branches ending in roses. The ancient Greek word for rose was *rhodon*, and the similarities between the words *rhodon* and *Rhodos* meant that the flower became an emblem of the island. So Fig. 3.21 communicates a naval victory over the area.

Fig. 3.22 shows a crab holding an *aplustre* with a rose and an untied diadem. The crab was the emblem of Cos, close to Myndus, where the naval battle against Rhodes took place (Woytek 2003: 507). The diadem was traditionally associated with kings, so its representation here as untied connects the defeat of Rhodes with Cassius' on-going battle against tyranny (Hollstein 1994: 122–6). This is further suggested by the inclusion of Apollo on the obverse (often mistakenly identified as Libertas; Popovitch 2013: 92; Woytek 2003: 506). Cassius' use of local imagery to communicate his victories is an excellent example of how 'Roman' ideology was continuously influenced by the provinces, particularly in the late Republic when Roman politics came to be played on a larger geographical stage.

Texts are confused about who used 'Apollo' as a watchword at the battle of Philippi in 42 BC (Plutarch writes it was used by Brutus, Valerius Maximus that it was Octavian and Antony) suggesting that the god was significant to both sides of the conflict (Plutarch, *Brutus* 24.7; Valerius Maximus 1.5.7). Plutarch records that Antony had plans to repair the temple of Apollo at Delphi after Philippi (Plutarch, *Antony* 24; Roller 2007: 90). Apollo, then, was a god that was not only important to the Liberators. Antony and Octavian also claimed his support, and when Octavian became Augustus, Apollo would feature heavily in his ideology (Miller 2009: 23–30; Moles 1983: 250–1).

3.3 Piety, Neptune and the Sea: Sextus Pompey

Also important in understanding the development of ideology under Augustus is Sextus Pompey's self-presentation as a pious son. Sextus remained an active political player in this period, posing a very real threat to the triumvirs. In 43 BC he was appointed as commander of the fleet and sea coasts (*praefectus classis et orae maritimae*), perhaps a response to the naval power of Cassius in the east (App. 3.4; Dio 46.40.3; Velleius Paterculus 2.73.2; Welch 2012: 166). After being declared a public enemy by the triumvirs Sextus moved to Sicily and was based on the island from c. 42–36 BC. Although he had been proscribed (declared an enemy of the state), Sextus continued to advertise his position as commander of the fleet on his coinage, as well as the fact that this position had been given to him by the Senate (EX S C, see Figs. 3.25–6). Sextus' coinage also continued to display him as the pious avenger of his father Pompey the Great, forming a link with the earlier issues he and his brother had struck in Spain (see pages 48–50). But Sextus also emerges as a great innovator. He aligns, and even assimilates, his deceased father to the god Neptune, a deity fitting for his role as a naval commander. Just like Octavian, Sextus claimed to be the son of a god.

One of the first issues struck for Sextus in Sicily was by his supporter Q. Nasidius (Fig. 3.23; App. 5.139; Dio 15.13.5). Although RRC assigns these coins to Massalia (44–43 BC), there is now a general consensus they were struck elsewhere (perhaps in Sicily) at some point after 43 BC (Crawford 2012; Woytek 2003: 505). The obverse carries a portrait of

Figure 3.23. Denarius, Sicily, Q. Nasidius, c. 42–38 BC (RRC 483/2). **Obv.** Head of Pompey the Great right, trident before and dolphin below, NEPTVNI. **Rev.** Ship sailing right, star above, Q NASIDIVS below.

Figure 3.24. As, Sicily, Sextus Pompey, 42–38 BC (RRC 479/1). **Obv.** Laureate head of Janus with the features of Pompey the Great, MGN above. **Rev.** Prow, PIVS IMP.

Pompey the Great aligned with Neptune. A dolphin and trident are placed on either side, and the legend confirms that we are meant to read the image as a representation of Pompey-Neptune: NEPTVNI. Dio records that after the naval victory over Salvidienus Rufus in 42 BC, Sextus presented himself as the son of Neptune 'since his father had once ruled the whole sea' (App. 5.100; Dio 48.19.2, 48.48.5). The reverse displays a galley with a star above it, perhaps simultaneously referring to Sextus' naval skill and Nasidius' own role as a naval commander, since the galley sits above his name. The other coin type released by Nasidius is extremely rare, but shows Pompey as Neptune on the obverse and a naval battle scene on the reverse (RRC 483/1).

The divinisation of the deceased Pompey is also seen on bronze coinage released around the same time (Fig. 3.24; Lowe 2002: 78; Pollini 1990: 340). Traditional Republican asses bore the double-head of Janus on the obverse and a prow on the reverse (meaning that the Roman version of 'heads or tails' was called 'heads or ship': Macrobius, *Saturnalia* 1.7.21). Sextus' issue showed the god Janus with the facial features of Pompey. Initially dated to the period after 45 BC and assigned to mints in Spain and Sicily (Crawford 1974: vol. 1, 94; Welch 2012: 109), the coins are now believed to have been struck only in Sicily between 42 and 38 BC. This is due to the large number of specimens found on the island and the die axes of the series, which differ from the Roman bronzes struck in Spain (Frey-Kupper 2013: 275; Woytek

2003: 501; Sextus likely became *imperator* for the second time in 38 BC, and this title is absent from the asses, suggesting they were struck before this point). This was a large issue of bronze coinage, with 193 obverse dies (Martini 1995). If there was any ambiguity surrounding Pompey's association with Janus here, it is dispelled by the legend MGN at the top of the obverse, a clear reference to Pompey's title of *Magnus*, just as the legend on Fig. 3.23 clearly identifies the portrait of Pompey with Neptune. These asses are heavier than normal, conforming to a weight standard that existed before 91 BC (Lowe 2002: 78). We don't know why Sextus would strike coins with such a heavy weight, but his coins, along with the bronzes of the triumvirs, released small change into the economy after a significant pause in production.

On asses Sextus is referred to only as Pius (PIVS) and *imperator* (IMP), and we find this emphasis on titles instead of his name on silver coinage as well. These coins (RRC 511) are difficult to date, although it is agreed they belong to Sextus' period in Sicily, c. 42–36 BC (Woytek 1995 argues for a date of after 38 BC, Welch 2012: 184 a date before 39 BC). These denarii again emphasise Sextus' naval supremacy, with one bearing the image of Neptune and a naval trophy (RRC 511/2a), and Fig. 3.25 displaying a lighthouse on the obverse with Scylla poised to strike on the reverse. Scylla was a legendary monster believed to reside alongside the strait of Messina between Sicily and Italy, and her appearance here probably refers to a naval victory of Sextus in the region. Possible contenders are the victory over Quintus Salvidienus Rufus, the close friend of Octavian, in 42 BC (the

Figure 3.25. Denarius, Sicily, Sextus Pompey, 42–36 BC (RRC 511/4a). **Obv.** Lighthouse (*pharos*) surmounted by a statue of Zeus Pelorus (or Neptune?); before is a ship with *aquila* in the prow and a sceptre tied with a fillet at the stern, MAG PIVS IMP ITER. **Rev.** Scylla wielding rudder in both hands, PRAEF CLAS ET ORAE MARIT EX S C.

Figure 3.26. Denarius, Sicily, Sextus Pompey, 42–36 BC (RRC 511/3). **Obv.** Head of Pompey the Great with jug behind and *lituus* before, MAG PIVS IMP ITER. **Rev.** Neptune holding *aplustre* with cloak over left arm, right foot on prow; the Catanaean brothers on either side, carrying their parents, PRAEF CLAS ET ORAE MARIT EX S C.

battle took place 'around Scyllaeum'), or the destruction of Octavian's fleet by storm in 38 BC (App. 4.85; Powell 2002: 122; Welch 2012: 185). If the latter interpretation is correct, then the coins precisely mirror Appian's account of the event: Sextus' fleet remained safe in the harbour (shown on the obverse and communicated by the ship before a lighthouse), while Octavian's forces were battered (shown on the reverse with a vicious-looking Scylla). Whatever the intention of the design, viewers might have recalled either battle, or both, when looking at the coin.

A merging of Sextus' emphasis on *pietas* with this maritime ideology can be found on Fig. 3.26, which carries the head of Pompey the Great on the obverse and Neptune between the Catanaean brothers on the reverse. The Catanaean brothers were embodiments of familial piety in Sicily. According to myth, during the eruption of Mount Etna the two brothers Amphinomos and Anapios carried their parents out of Catana, while others fled carrying only gold and silver. The two brothers were slowed by the weight of their parents, but, miraculously, the flowing lava parted around them, although it consumed the less pious citizens who had chosen to carry only wealth (Powell 2002: 123–4). Sextus adeptly manipulated this local myth for his audience – most of his silver coinage is found in Sicily (Crawford 2012). The two brothers, shown on the reverse, bring to mind Sextus and his deceased brother Gnaeus, since Neptune (a reference to Pompey the Great) is placed between them. Sextus is thus cast as the pious son of Neptune-Pompey. The facial features of Neptune on the reverse might recall those of Pompey the Great, although this is clearer on some specimens than others (La Rocca 1987–8; Powell 2002: 123; Welch 2012: 188). This coin issue established a connection between the family of Sextus, the Sicilian myth, and the god Neptune.

Aeneas, Amphinomos or Anapios?

Figure 3.27. Aureus, Rome, L. Livineius Regulus, 42 BC (RRC 494/3a). **Obv.** Head of Octavian, C CAESAR III VIR R P C. **Rev.** One figure carrying another, L REGVLVS IIII VIR A P F.

Fig. 3.27, struck in 42 BC for Octavian, has traditionally been interpreted as Aeneas carrying Anchises, a reference to Octavian's Julian heritage. Given that Caesar had used Aeneas on his coinage the conclusion is a sensible one, but we may have been too hasty in seeing what we expect rather than what is actually portrayed (a lesson too that at times coin publications may be mistaken in their descriptions). Zarrow 2003 suggested instead that the reverse shows one of the Catanaean brothers, meaning that **both** Sextus and Octavian aligned themselves with the myth (just as they both cast themselves as sons of a god). Before Virgil the Catanaean myth was a far better allusion to *pietas* than Aeneas. Unlike the coinage of Caesar (Fig. 2.9), the figure here is not carrying the Palladium, only a parent. And the iconography is similar to an earlier Roman denarius that shows one of the Catanaean brothers on the reverse and Pietas on the obverse (Fig. 3.28).

It was Virgil's *Aeneid* that contributed to the idea of 'pious Aeneas' (Galinsky 1969). The *Aeneid* was only finished in 19 BC, more than twenty years after the release of Fig. 3.27. Without an identifying legend, we cannot be absolutely sure of the correct identification (and perhaps it attracted multiple interpretations), but if the aureus portrays one of the Catanaean brothers, we have further evidence of the iconographic dialogue that took place between Octavian and Sextus in this period.

Figure 3.28. Denarius, Rome, M. Herennius, 108/7 BC (RRC 308/1a). **Obv.** Diademed head of Pietas, PIETAS. **Rev.** One of the Catanaean brothers carrying his father on his shoulders, M HERENNI.

Figure 3.29. Aureus, Sicily, Sextus Pompey, 42–36 BC (RRC 511/1). **Obv.** Head of Sextus Pompey, bearded, MAG PIVS IMP ITER, within oak wreath. **Rev.** Heads of Pompey the Great (clean-shaven) and Gnaeus Pompey Junior (bearded) facing each other, *lituus* on left, tripod on right, PRAEF CLAS ET ORAE MARIT EX S C.

The filial piety of Sextus was also communicated via an aureus issue, with Sextus shown on the obverse within a *corona civica*, or oak wreath, and his deceased father and brother on the reverse (Fig. 3.29). Like the contemporary portraits of Octavian and Antony, Sextus is bearded, demonstrating that he is in mourning. The *corona civica* probably refers to Sextus' salvation of Romans from the proscriptions: those proscribed by the triumvirs had a price on their heads, and Sextus offered double the amount to anyone who brought them to him instead, saving their lives (Powell suggests these aurei may even have formed the payment. See App. 4.36; Dio 47.12.2; Powell 2002: 119). Although Crawford estimated 15 obverse and 15 reverse dies for this type, a die study demonstrated that there are only 2 obverse dies

Figure 3.30. Aureus, mint moving with Ahenobarbus, Cn. Domitius Ahenobarbus, 41 BC (RRC 519/1). **Obv.** Male head right, AHENOBAR. **Rev.** Tetrastyle temple, NE PT on either side, around, CN DOMITIVS L F IMP.

and 3 reverse, meaning the issue is smaller than initially believed (and that Crawford's method may be problematic for smaller issues, DeRose Evans 1987: 109). As discussed in the introduction, the die estimates in RRC are based on 24 hoards; here, as elsewhere, the numbers are not definitive. The small number of dies does suggest a presentation piece (i.e. a coin intended to be presented to a select group, rather than to form a large payment) like that suggested by Powell.

Brutus also appeared bearded within a *corona civica* on aurei (Fig. 3.19), and the parallels hint at a broader Republican strategy in opposition to the triumvirs (Welch 2012: 191–5). At the very least, Sextus' issues demonstrate a knowledge of, and conscious reference to, the coinage of Brutus and other Republicans. Some broader thematic strategy amongst those opposing the triumvirs is further suggested by the messages of naval achievement that we have traced on the coins of Sextus and Cassius, also found on the coinage of the Republican commander Gnaeus Domitius Ahenobarbus. His aureus issue shows an ancestral portrait and a temple of Neptune (Fig. 3.30). Pliny records that a Cn. Domitius built a shrine to Neptune in the Flaminian Circus in Rome, but it is unclear which Domitius this is. Consequently, we cannot know whether this is the temple shown here; as discussed on pages 139–44, the portrayal of temples on coins did not necessarily reflect existing structures (Pliny, *Natural History* 36.4.26). The beard on the portrait of Ahenobarbus' denarius issue (Fig. 3.31) suggests this may be a representation of Ahenobarbus himself (shown in mourning like Octavian, Antony, and Sextus), although this is not certain (it may be

Figure 3.31. Denarius, mint moving with Ahenobarbus, Cn. Domitius Ahenobarbus, 41 BC (RRC 519/2). **Obv.** Bearded male head (Ahenobarbus?), AHENOBAR. **Rev.** Trophy on prow, with two spears and a shield, CN DOMITIVS IMP.

another ancestor). The reverse of the denarius advertises a naval victory, likely that at Brundisium in 42 BC when Ahenobarbus defeated the triumviral supporter Gnaeus Domitius Calvinus (Bieber 1973: 881; Welch 2012: 519). These coins were probably struck after Philippi and before Ahenobarbus reconciled with Antony in 40 BC (see Fig. 4.14 for a denarius struck after the reconciliation).

3.4 The Second Triumvirate and Roman Women

Our exploration suggests that there was no neat 'Republicans' versus 'Triumvirs' divide. Numismatic and textual evidence suggests, in fact, that the triumvirate was 'a surface harmony' that covered intense rivalry: even as the triumvirs advertised their alliance they sought to undermine each other (Newman 1990: 62). Uneasy alliances were accompanied by marriages and divorces, and it is in this period of Roman history that portraits of Roman women appear on coinage. The civil wars saw an unprecedented public role played by women: when the triumvirs attempted to tax wealthy women, for example, Hortensia spoke out against it in the Roman forum (App. 4.32–33), while Fulvia (Antony's first wife) and Octavia (Octavian's sister and Antony's second wife) played active roles in negotiations between the triumvirs and in securing support. This was the backdrop to Augustus' later decision to grant women increased rights (Cooley 2013).

The formation of the second triumvirate was commemorated on multiple coin emissions, reflective of the growing use of the coinage to mark contemporary (as opposed to historical) events. Close analysis of these

Figure 3.32. Aureus, mint in Cisalpine Gaul. Mark Antony, 43 BC (RRC 492/1). **Obv.** Bearded head of Mark Antony right, *lituus* behind, M ANTONIVS III VIR R P C. **Rev.** Bearded head of Octavian right, C CAESAR III VIR R P C.

coins demonstrate that in addition to messages of unity and alliance, coinage was used to make subtle claims about the superiority of one triumvir over another. One example is Fig. 3.32, an aureus of Mark Antony from 43 BC. At first glance, Octavian and Antony appear equal, with each shown on one side of the coin, and each named as *triumvirs for confirming the Republic with consular power (III vir r(ei) p(ublicae) c(onstituendae) (consulari potestate))*. But when we look closer, Antony has a *lituus* behind his head, while Octavian's portrait is not accompanied by any symbols. This gives the impression that Antony holds a superior position (Newman 1990: 60). This slighting of Octavian is demonstrated by another aureus that shows Antony on one side and Lepidus on the other. Here *both* triumvirs are portrayed with priestly symbols, Antony with the *lituus* of an augur and Lepidus with an *aspergillum* and *simpulum* (instruments used to sprinkle sacred water and make libations) (RRC 492/2). We see the same competition on the double portrait types struck for Octavian: on these Octavian is given the additional title of *pontifex maximus*, abbreviated as PONT (C CAESAR IMP III VIR R P C PONT AVG), an honour absent from Antony's side of the coin (M ANTONIVS IMP III VIR R P C AVG) (RRC 493/1). Even as they were united against the liberators, Antony and Octavian were in competition with each other, suggesting that any alliance was ultimately doomed to fail.

In 42 BC a large amount of precious metal coinage was struck at Rome and many of the coins commemorated the triumviral alliance (RRC 494/1–46). We may plausibly link this large issue of coinage (some 46 individual types) with bullion flowing in from the proscriptions (Woytek 2003: 466).

A type from this year showing Venus and Apollo (RRC 494/34) is the most common Republican aureus – it must have been struck in very large quantities, suggesting the amount of wealth the proscriptions brought into the treasury was significant (although evidently not large enough, given the move to tax the wealthiest Roman women). By contrast, gold coins carrying portraits of the triumvirs were struck in much smaller numbers, which meant they would be seen by fewer people. These coins may have been intended to commemorate the alliance, or to be given to a particular group; at any rate their broader communicative potential was small. Buttrey performed a die study of the series, and was only able to find 112 examples of the 15 triumviral aureus types. In total Buttrey identified 18 obverse and 22 reverse dies, with only one coin found in a hoard (compare this against the size of Caesar's gold issue on p. 31). The bulk of the coinage from 42 BC, then, focused on 'personal' types of the moneyers, alluding to familial history or other motifs (Buttrey 1956: 33).

The marriage of Antony to Octavia in 40 BC was commemorated with the release of an aureus issue the following year (RRC 527/1; Wood 2001: 41–6). The obverse carried a portrait of Mark Antony accompanied by the legend M ANTON IMP III VIR R P C, and the reverse a portrait of Octavia with no accompanying legend. The appearance of a living Roman woman on a coin should be seen as part of the increasing use of portraiture on coinage and the increasing public role and legal freedoms granted to women in this period (Cooley 2013; Wood 2001: 13). It should be noted, however, that this was a small issue: only *one* specimen of the coin is known, found in a hoard in Castagneto in Italy in 1883 and now in Berlin (Crawford 1974: vol. 1, 531; see ww2.smb.museum/ikmk/object.php?id=18202297 for an image). This suggests that the aureus was meant to be commemorative rather than to act as a communicative medium on a large scale. Thus the first unambiguous representation of a woman on a Roman coin probably had an intended (and presumably receptive) audience in mind. A later aureus also showing Octavia has already been discussed (Fig. 3.12).

The appearance of Octavia on the aureus of 40 BC was the culmination of more ambiguous experimentation. Antony's earlier wife Fulvia, who played an active role in politics (even raising eight legions for Antony in the lead up to the Perusine War), may have appeared on coinage before her death in 40 BC (App. 4.5.32, 5.10.93–5; Dio 48.4–15, 48.54; Cooley 2013: 28). The city of Eumenea in Asia changed its name to Fulvia (probably in 41 BC), and coins were released that appear to show Fulvia as Nike (Fig. 3.33; RPC 1 3139–40). If this is Fulvia, the lack of a legend and the

Figure 3.33. Leaded bronze 18mm, Fulvia/Eumenea, Zmertorix Philonidou, c. 41–40 BC (RPC 1 3139). **Obv.** Draped bust of Fulvia as Nike with wings. **Rev.** Athena with spear and shield, ΦΟΥΛΟΥΙΑΝΩΝ ΖΜΕΡΤΟΡΙΓΟΣ ΦΙΛΩΝΙΔΟΥ.

Figure 3.34. Quinarius, Lugdunum, 42 BC (RPC 1 513 = RRC 489/6). **Obv.** Bust of Fulvia as Victory, III VIR R P C. **Rev.** Lion, ANTONI above, IMP in exergue, A XLI on either side.

addition of the wings makes the image ambiguous, though given the name of the town this is the most likely interpretation.

Fulvia also appears in the guise of Victory on silver quinarii of Lugdunum (Lyon, France), a colony founded by Antony's supporter Munatius Plancus in 43 BC (Fig. 3.34). This is an odd series of coins: some quinarii were struck in the name of Lugdunum, and others in the name of Antony, although all coins carry the same imagery (RRC 489/5–6 = RPC 1 512–13). This creates a bit of a quandary: if the civic elite of Lugdunum were responsible for the types, then they, like the citizens of Fulvia, were choosing to honour Antony's wife on their local coinage. But that the coins carried the name of Antony suggests that he was the authority for the issue and that it was an official Roman type: viewers would have held Antony responsible for the coin's design. With two different legends suggesting two different authorities, the coins have been catalogued both in RRC and in RPC, in essence labelled as both a 'provincial' *and* a 'Roman' series. We encounter similar problems under Augustus, and it is a reminder that the division between 'provincial' and 'Roman' can be somewhat artificial and, at times, unhelpful.

Figure 3.35. Cistophorus, Ephesus (?), c. 39 BC (RPC 1 2201). **Obv.** Head of Antony wearing ivy wreath right, *lituus* below, M ANTONIVS IMP COS DESIG ITER TERT, all within wreath of ivy leaves and flowers. **Rev.** III VIR R P C, draped bust of Octavia above *cista* flanked by snakes.

The denomination and the lion reverse type of Fig. 3.34 is more in keeping with local Gallic silver currency than with the Roman monetary system. The lion had appeared on earlier Greek coins struck by the city before the late Republic. But the appearance of the same unusual iconography (Fulvia as Nike) in geographically distant parts of the empire at around the same time suggests that these images are Fulvia, and are coming from a Roman source. The alignment of Antony's wife with a goddess may be a response to the divine connections claimed by Octavian and Sextus Pompey. (Incidentally, the XL and XLI on the quinarii are a reference to Antony's age at the time of minting, an unusual addition, but something that Caesar had also done – note the LII on Fig. 2.6). Similar to male Roman portraits, the portraits of Roman women appeared on provincial coinage before official Roman issues.

Octavia also appears on cistophori struck in Asia, probably at Ephesus (Figs. 3.35–6, Burnett, Amandry and Ripolles 1992: 377). The cistophorus denomination had been introduced to the region by the Hellenistic kings of Pergamum: the obverse of these coins carried a *cista mystica* or sacred basket from which snakes emerged (this design gave the coins their name), while the reverse bore two snakes coiling around a bow case. Unusually, the coinage bore no reference to the Attalid kings of Pergamon; the

Figure 3.36. Cistophorus, Ephesus (?), c. 39 BC (RPC 1 2202). **Obv.** Jugate heads of Antony and Octavia, M ANTONIVS IMP COS DESIG ITER ET TERT. **Rev.** III VIR R P C. Dionysus standing on *cista* between snakes.

legends on the coins named cities in the kingdom, not rulers. This was part of the Attalid strategy of presenting their kingdom as a federation or alliance of cities, a type of *koinon* (Thonemann 2013: 30–3). Like other precious metal currencies in the east, the Romans kept the denomination in use after their conquest of the region in the second century BC with little alteration to the design. It was only under Antony that this changed: some elements of the original cistophori design were kept (probably to ensure the denomination remained recognisable), but the coins now carried portraits of Antony and Octavia, with the legend naming Antony and his positions in Latin. For the people of a region whose coinage traditionally carried no portrait or reference to a ruler, this must have been a noticeable change.

Fig. 3.35 displays Antony wearing an ivy wreath on the obverse with the bust of Octavia on the reverse, while Fig. 3.36 displays jugate busts of Octavia and Antony on the obverse with Dionysus on the reverse. As on the aurei, Octavia is not named in the legend, creating space for a lengthy description of Antony's positions. Antony had been hailed as 'the New Dionysus' in Ephesus (and in Athens, see p. 102), and this explains the appearance of Dionysus and the ivy wreath worn by Antony.

Antony in the East after Actium

Figure 3.37. Cistophorus, reign of Hadrian, Alabanda (Metcalf 35). **Obv.** Bust of Hadrian, HADRIANVS AVGVSTVS P P. **Rev.** Apollo holding raven and branch, COS III.

Although the textual accounts of the late Republic were reshaped after Antony's defeat (Roller 2007), Antony's coinage continued to circulate well into the imperial period. His cistophori circulated until at least the reign of Hadrian, when many were overstruck as part of a renewal of silver currency in the region (Metcalf 1980: 115–20). Fig. 3.37 is an example of this. Antony's now worn coin has been struck again with new designs, although in this instance the process was imperfect: the snake and basket design of Antony's original coin can still be seen on the obverse, while the legend of the original coin is still visible on the reverse (one can see the TERT M ANT of the original coin). When studying the iconography of Roman coins, we should consider that meanings and associations might change over time. Even after the marriage of Antony and Octavia ended, and Antony was defeated, these coins (and their images) continued to circulate. The imagery would no longer have had contemporary meaning, but rather these coins would have functioned as long-lasting 'mini monuments' that gave Antony a visual presence in the principate.

Table 4 The 'fleet coinage' of Mark Antony

Denomination	Obverse image	Reverse image
Sestertius	Bare head of Antony on the left facing a bust of Octavia on the right	A *quadriga* of hippocamps surmounted by two figures (Antony and Octavia?), HS, Δ and a square object
Tressis	Busts of Antony and Octavian on the left, facing a bust of Octavia on the right	Three ships sailing, Γ and triskeles below
Dupondius	Bare head of Antony on the left facing the bust of Octavia on the right	Two ships sailing, two caps of the Dioscuri above, B below
As	Jugate heads of Antony and Octavia	One ship sailing, A and the head of Medusa (?) below
Semis	Bare head of Antony	Prow, S above
Quadrans	Janiform head, probably of Antony and Octavian	Stem of prow, three dots in field

3.5 The 'Fleet Coinage' of Mark Antony

Octavia is also depicted on the bronze coins struck in the eastern provinces after Antony received the region at the Treaty of Brundisium in 40 BC (Table 4; RPC 1 1453–70). These coins were struck by Antony's fleet prefects – Lucius Calpurnius Bibulus, Lucius Sempronius Atratinus and Marcus Oppius Cato – which is why they are called the 'fleet coinage' in modern scholarship. The 'fleet coinage' coincides with the spread of the Roman denarius to the eastern Mediterranean, and the two phenomena must be connected: the bronzes, which introduced Roman-style denominations to the area, provided small change to be used alongside Roman silver coinage.

In order to make identifying the different denominations easier for people not accustomed to Roman money, Greek letters indicating marks of value were placed on the coins (a delta indicating four, a gamma three, beta two, alpha one), and the images were also designed to serve as an interpretative aid. For example, the sestertius (4 asses) bore a quadriga (a chariot with four horses) on the reverse, the tressis (3 asses) three ships and a triskeles, the dupondius (2 asses) two ships and the two caps of the Dioscuri, the as one ship, the semis (half an as) the prow of a ship, and the quadrans (quarter of an as) merely the stem of a ship's prow. The system was intended to communicate the values of these coins to new users (Amandry 1990: 84). The system was

Figure 3.38. Sestertius, Peloponnesian mint, 34mm, L. Sempronius Atratinus, 38 BC (RPC 1 1453). **Obv.** Bare head of Antony on left facing bust of Octavia on right, M ANT IMP TER COS DES ITER ET TER III VIR R P C. **Rev.** *Quadriga* of hippocamps surmounted by two people embracing (Antony and Octavia?), HS to left, Δ and square object below, L ATRATINVS AVGVR COS DESIG.

innovative: the sestertius, which had previously only been struck in silver, was now struck in bronze, and the tressis and dupondius denominations had not been struck since the third century BC (Amandry 1986). Although the fleet coinage system was abandoned after Antony's defeat, it (and the other innovations of the late Republic) must have served as inspiration for Augustus' later reforms of the monetary system (see Table 2; Amandry and Barrandon 2008).

The obverses of these coins carried the busts of Octavia, Octavian and Antony in various configurations. The obverse of the quadrans carried a portrait of Janus with features that resemble Antony and Octavian (though this is clearer on some examples than others), perhaps a direct reply to the Pompey-Janus issue of Sextus (Fig. 3.24). The legends named the three fleet prefects and Antony as triumvir. The sestertius displayed two figures on a *quadriga* of hippocamps, commonly believed to represent Antony and Octavia as Poseidon and Amphitrite (Fig. 3.38; Bahrfeldt 1905: 35). Once again, we find a Neptune motif employed on the coinage of this period. Like Apollo, Octavian would later claim Neptune's support, and Octavian's Actium victory monument was dedicated to Neptune and Mars (Lange 2009: 118).

When considering the audience or impact of a particular numismatic image, it is important to look at its circulation area. The fleet coins and the

Figure 3.39. Bronze 17mm, Ephesus, after 43 BC (RPC 1 2569). **Obv.** Jugate bare heads of the triumvirs right. **Rev.** Cult statue of Artemis of Ephesus, EΦE.

Figure 3.40. Bronze 13mm, Ephesus, after 43 BC (RPC 1 2574). **Obv.** Draped bust of Octavia right. **Rev.** Bee, APXIE ΓPAM ΓΛΑΥΚΩΝ EΦE.

cistophori were largely, if not exclusively, used in the east of the empire; those living in this region would have encountered the numismatic portrait of Octavia more frequently than those living in the west. Each region would have had a different experience of the triumvirate and its ideologies, just as they would later have a different experience of the principate. The Janus-Pompey coins of Sextus, for example, were an important circulating currency in Sicily, while the Divos Iulius coins of Octavian (Figs. 3.9–10) have a high frequency of finds in Italy.

Coinage produced locally in provincial mints added another layer of difference. Ephesus, for example, struck bronze civic coins showing the triumvirs and Octavia. While the silver cistophori produced in Ephesus were for regional use and did not carry a legend referring to the city, these bronze coins were struck for local use and were labelled as coins of the city (Butcher 2005). Uniquely, the magistrates of Ephesus showed the three triumvirs jugate, combined with a reverse portraying the famous local cult statue of Artemis (Fig. 3.39, RPC 1 2569–73). A coin was also struck with Octavia on the obverse, with a bee (a symbol of Ephesus) on the reverse, accompanied by a legend naming Ephesus and Glaucon as *archiereus* and *grammateus* (Fig. 3.40). These coins and their imagery would have circulated within the city of Ephesus and its hinterland. Their iconography displays a connection between Roman power and local culture that would become common on provincial coinage during the Roman Empire.

4

The View from the East: Cleopatra and Mark Antony (38–31 BC)

Antony's relationship with Cleopatra and his treatment of Octavia were a crucial part of Octavian's justification for war in the lead up to Actium. Plutarch's *Life of Antony* reveals the sort of arguments that must have been put forward: Antony is taken 'captive' by Cleopatra (25.1) and surrenders his power to command (*imperium*) to a woman (60.1), with his actions finally forcing Octavian to declare war on the Egyptian queen. By campaigning against Cleopatra rather than Antony, Octavian could avoid the appearance of another civil war. But numismatic evidence reveals the other side of the conflict: how Antony and his supporters represented themselves. Numismatic evidence remains uninfluenced by Augustan ideology and reveals the support both Antony and Cleopatra received in the east.

4.1 Cleopatra and the Monetary System of Ptolemaic Egypt

Cleopatra VII came to power in a region that possessed an unusual economic arrangement for antiquity. The Ptolemaic kingdom had a closed currency system, meaning that *only* Ptolemaic coinage could be used within its borders; foreign coin was not accepted (Lorber 2012). This stipulation had political advantages (inhabitants within the kingdom only saw Ptolemaic coinage and its associated iconography), as well as tangible economic benefits. By striking Ptolemaic silver tetradrachms at a reduced weight (c. 14.27 g instead of the accepted Attic standard of c. 17.2 g), and then (it seems) compelling merchants who visited Egypt to convert their Attic weight currency into Ptolemaic silver, the government reaped a profit, either by charging for the exchange, or by simply giving out lighter coins in exchange for heavier ones (Howgego 1995: 52–4; von Reden 2007). Foreign gold coin also had to be exchanged for local currency.

We find very few foreign precious metal coins in Egypt, suggesting that this policy was largely successful. By tightly controlling their monetary system the Ptolemies were also able to introduce other innovations.

Significantly, the Ptolemaic dynasty increased the role of bronze coinage, which came to be used for a variety of purposes, including the payment of taxes (von Reden 2007). Since bronze coins were probably a fiduciary currency (that is, the value of the coin depended on trust that the government would accept it at a particular value, rather than the value being based on the metal content of the coin), this policy also had economic benefits for the Ptolemaic dynasty. By demanding taxes be paid in bronze coin (rather than in grain or in kind), the Ptolemies also increased the monetisation of the populace as most of the population would have to encounter coinage at some point in their everyday life, if only to obtain the appropriate coin to pay their tax.

As queen, Cleopatra released silver tetradrachms of significantly reduced silver content, following the model of her father Ptolemy XII (Lorber 2012: 227–8). This was achieved through debasement, the mixing of silver with other metals (e.g. lead) to produce coins that weighed the appropriate amount, but contained less silver. This was another mechanism by which the Ptolemaic dynasty was able to profit economically from coinage (in this instance, by producing more coins from the same amount of silver). A significant quantity of bronze coinage was also minted during Cleopatra's rule carrying her name in Greek, increasing supply after a period of shortage. These coins carried the ruler's portrait on the obverse, and an eagle on a thunderbolt on the reverse, imagery commonly found on Ptolemaic coins (Fig. 4.1). In contrast to

Figure 4.1. Bronze 80 drachma piece, Alexandria, Cleopatra VII, 51–30 BC (Svoronos 1871). **Obv.** Diademed and draped bust of Cleopatra VII. **Rev.** Eagle standing on thunderbolt, ΒΑCΙΛΙCCHC ΚΛΕΟΠΑΤΡΑC.

Figure 4.2. Bronze 29–30mm, Paphos (Cyprus), Cleopatra VII, 47–31 BC (RPC 1 3901). **Obv.** Bust of Cleopatra as Aphrodite with a crown (*stephane*), with Ptolemy XV Caesarion as Eros in her arms and sceptre at shoulder. **Rev.** Two cornucopiae joined at the bottom and bound with fillet, monogram in field, ΚΛΕΟΠΑΤΡΑΣ ΒΑΣΙΛΙΣΣΗΣ.

the Roman world, the iconography of Ptolemaic coinage was largely unchanging.

Coinage was also struck at the mint of Paphos on the island of Cyprus. Having briefly been a Roman province, Cyprus was returned to the Ptolemies by Julius Caesar in 48 BC. Under Cleopatra's rule, bronze coins showing the head of Zeus Ammon and an eagle (or two) on a thunderbolt were struck (RPC 1 3902–3), as well as an issue showing Cleopatra as the goddess Aphrodite with her son Ptolemy XV Caesarion as Eros (the mythological son of Aphrodite) in her arms (Fig. 4.2). The reverse of this issue is a common Ptolemaic type: two cornucopiae (horns of plenty symbolising abundance) bound by a ribbon or fillet. The unusual obverse may have been chosen to mark Caesarion's birth in 47 BC, although the coin itself does not carry any indication of date and may have been struck as much as 10 years later (Baldus 1973: 33). Cyprus had a well-known cult of Aphrodite, and Cleopatra's representation here may have been intended to connect her to local culture, although there was also an established cult of 'Cleopatra-Aphrodite' in the Ptolemaic kingdom (Cheshire 2007). But intentionally or not, this coin type also alludes to Caesarion's father, Julius Caesar, and his connection to Venus. Appian notes that when Caesar built the temple of Venus Genetrix in Rome 'he placed a beautiful image of Cleopatra by the side of the goddess', which

Appian observes was still there in his day (App. 2.102; Dio 51.22.3). Thus the Aphrodite/Venus connection of Cleopatra existed both in Rome and within her own kingdom.

The closed monetary system continued after the Roman conquest of Egypt by Augustus (Bland 1996: 114). The continuation of the Ptolemaic system may be explained by the fact that Romans often kept local administrative structures in place after conquests, but it may also have been due to the special status Egypt had as a province. This status is reflected in the mint at Alexandria. In contrast to other provincial coinage, which was produced by local elites, the mint at Alexandria was probably under the control of someone from the imperial administration (likely the *ideologus* or *diocetes*; Milne 1971: xviii). The Alexandrian mint was probably managed in the interests of the emperor, and might even be viewed as a branch of the mint at Rome (Bland 1996: 114). Consequently, the imagery used at the mint of Alexandria in the imperial period is often very similar to that used at the Roman mint (see Figs. 5.30–4 for an example).

4.2 The Coinage of Antony and Cleopatra

Antony was assigned the east as part of the agreement at Brundisium in 40 BC, and this region became his main base of operations until his death. Coins struck at this time featured Octavia (discussed in the previous chapter, p. 81), as well as Antony himself: an aureus issue showed him as a maritime victor (RRC 533/1, only one set of dies known), and Fig. 4.3 shows him as an augur. Antony's third imperial acclamation in 37 BC was marked with trophy

Figure 4.3. Denarius, mint moving with Antony, Mark Antony, 38 BC (RRC 533/2). **Obv.** Antony togate and veiled holding *lituus*, M ANTONIVS M F M N AVGVR IMP TERT. **Rev.** Radiate head of Sol, III VIR R P C COS DESIG ITER ET TERT.

Figure 4.4. Denarius, mint moving with Antony, Mark Antony, 36 BC (RRC 539/1). **Obv.** Head of Mark Antony, ANTONIVS AVGVR COS DES ITER ET TERT. **Rev.** Armenian tiara with bow and arrow behind, IMP TERTIO III VIR R P C.

Figure 4.5. Aureus, mint moving with Antony, Mark Antony, 34 BC (RRC 541/2). **Obv.** Head of Mark Antony, ANTON AVG IMP III COS DES III III V R P C. **Rev.** Head of Marcus Antonius Antyllus, M ANTONIVS M F F.

types (RRC 536), and his victories in Armenia during his ultimately unsuccessful Parthian campaign were also celebrated (Fig. 4.4). Unable to claim victory over the Parthians, Antony may have resorted to emphasising the victory he *had* achieved. Crawford believed that on Fig. 4.4 Antony is shown looking upwards. This is characteristic of the portraiture of Alexander the Great, and perhaps Antony is aligning himself to the famous Macedonian general here (Crawford 1974: vol. 2, 743, 747 n.5).

In 34 BC, two double portrait types were struck showing Antony and his eldest son, Marcus Antonius Antyllus. On one issue (RRC 541/1) Antony's titles occupy both the obverse and reverse of the coin, meaning an impressive list could accumulate: M ANTONI M F M N AVG IMP TERT COS ITER DESIG TERT III VIR R P C (*Marcus Antonius, son of Marcus, grandson of Marcus, augur, imperator for the third time, consul for the second time, consul designate for the third time, triumvir for confirming the Republic with consular power*). On the other issue, Fig. 4.5, Antyllus is

Figure 4.6. Denarius, mint moving with Antony, Mark Antony and Cleopatra, 32 BC (RRC 543/1). **Obv.** Diademed and draped bust of Cleopatra, prow below, CLEOPATRAE REGINAE REGVM FILIORVM REGVM. **Rev.** Head of Antony, Armenian tiara behind, ANTONI ARMENIA DEVICTA.

named as the son of Antony. Antyllus was Antony's heir and betrothed to Octavian's daughter Julia. But his appearance on Roman coinage is unusual, and suggests the beginnings of a dynastic policy by Antony. Indeed, on the other issue Antony advertises his own parentage (M F M N). The overall effect is very similar to what we find in the later Empire: the parentage of the current ruler is included in inscriptions, with the appointed successor also named. By contrast, Octavian's coinage would not begin to address problems of succession until well into the principate.

Coinage showing Antony and Cleopatra began to be struck in 36 BC, although Antony would not divorce Octavia until 32 BC. It was in this year that Fig. 4.6 was struck, with Cleopatra on one side of the coin and Antony on the other. A similar design, but with a different legend, was struck for use within Syria on the local tetradrachm standard (Fig. 4.7; RPC 1 4094–6). The style of the tetradrachms is very similar to the denarii, suggesting they were products of the same mint (Butcher 2004: 58). Die analysis has demonstrated that it is Cleopatra's portrait that is on the obverse of both series; but to users there were, in a sense, two obverses or coining authorities. The use of the double portrait might refer to the fact that the coinage was paid for by Cleopatra but used by Antony (Butcher 2004: 57). Although there has been much debate about the significance of these portraits, we should remember that double portrait types had been regularly used since Caesar's death. Users may thus have seen little unusual in the choice of design. What *was* unusual, however, was the appearance of a Hellenistic Queen, who is named as *Cleopatra, Queen of Kings and of the Children of Kings.*

Figure 4.7. Tetradrachm, Antioch (?), Cleopatra VII and Mark Antony, c. 36 BC (RPC 1 4094). **Obv.** Diademed and draped bust of Cleopatra, ΒΑΣΙΛΙΣΣΑ ΚΛΕΟΠΑΤΡΑ ΘΕΑ ΝΕΩΤΕΡΑ. **Rev.** Head of Antony, ΑΝΤΩΝΙΟΣ ΑΥΤΟΚΡΑΤΩΡ ΤΡΙΤΟΝ ΤΡΙΩΝ ΑΝΔΡΩΝ.

Find spots indicate that the tetradrachms circulated both in Roman Syria and the section of Syria that fell under Cleopatra's rule after the donations of Alexandria. The two portraits likely made it easier for these coins to circulate in two empires: Antony's portrait acted as a guarantor of the coin in the Roman-controlled part of Syria, while Cleopatra's portrait acted as guarantor in areas officially ruled by Cleopatra's son Ptolemy Philadelphus (Baldus 1987: 147). The iconography of these coins also provides some clues as to how the relationship between the two was publicly represented. The imagery does not communicate a 'joint reign' (which would be visualised with jugate busts), but rather a 'jointness of reign' (Buttrey 1954: 108). Each is a ruler in his or her own right.

On Fig. 4.7 Cleopatra is named as *thea neotera*. Buttrey interpreted the legend to mean 'Queen Cleopatra Thea the Younger' (Buttrey 1954: 104). He suggested that Cleopatra VII adopted the title after the donations of Alexandria to connect herself with the Seleucid queen Cleopatra Thea Eueteria, who ruled Syria from 125–121/0 BC. Others interpret the title as a reference to Cleopatra as a 'new goddess' pointing out that *thea neotera* is also used outside of Syria. Other regions could hardly have had a 'new' Cleopatra Thea when they did not have an initial one (Butcher 2004: 55). Given Cleopatra's alignment with Aphrodite, her divinity as pharaoh in Egypt, and Antony's own alignment with the god Dionysus, the declaration

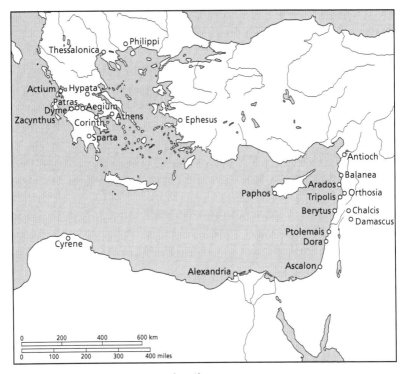

Figure 4.8. Map of places mentioned in Chapter 4.

of the queen as a 'new goddess' is unsurprising. On the tetradrachm Antony is styled as *imperator* for the third time and triumvir, while the denarius refers to his conquest of Armenia. For both Antony and Cleopatra the tetradrachm issue carried a different legend (in a different language) to the denarius issue, probably because the different denominations were intended for different regions and audiences.

4.3 Antony's Supporters: Atratinus and Sosius

Although we often focus on the triumvirs, the subordinates of Octavian and Antony also had key roles in this period and were often at the forefront of Roman-provincial interaction. A good example is Lucius Sempronius Atratinus, Antony's legate in Greece from c. 39–36 BC (Broughton 1951–2: vol. 2, 389). Atratinus was one of the prefects responsible for the fleet coinage of Antony discussed in the previous chapter (pages 86–7).

Figure 4.9.
Bronze 19mm,
Sparta, 43–31
BC (RPC 1
1101). **Obv.**
Bare head of
Atratinus,
ATPATINOC.
Rev. Eagle
standing right,
ΛΑ ΦΙ ΔΙ.

As a representative of Antony and the Roman government, Atratinus also received honours in the east. The city of Patras honoured him as a patron and benefactor ([πάτ]ρωνος [καί εὐεργέτου]; SEG XXX, 1980, no. 433; Amandry 2008: 430). Hypata in Thessaly erected an honorary inscription for him (*IG* IX,2 39), and Sparta struck a coin issue in Atratinus' name with his portrait on the obverse (Fig. 4.9, Grunauer-von Hoerschelmann 1978: 39). The coins were probably meant as an honour for the prefect, similar to the erection of an inscription or statue. Atratinus' name also appears on coinage of Entella and Lilybaeum in Sicily (RPC 1 653, 655, 2226), issues that were probably struck when he was sent by Antony to support Octavian against Sextus Pompey in 36 BC. Atratinus demonstrates that Antony's power in the east (and Roman rule more generally) could be experienced via interactions with subordinates, rather than (or in addition to) direct contact with Antony himself. Local populations viewed such subordinates as useful intermediaries between themselves and Antony, which explains the honours frequently granted to these individuals (Balzat and Millis 2013).

Gaius Sosius provides a complementary case study. Perhaps best known in the modern day for his connection with the temple of Apollo Sosianus in Rome, Sosius commanded a section of Antony's fleet and fought for him at Actium. In 38 BC he was governor of Syria and Cilicia, but before and after this post he was stationed at Antony's naval base on the island of Zacynthus (Achaea). There he was responsible for several issues of local coinage (Shipley 1930). The first issue, released in 39 BC and presented here as Fig. 4.10, may refer to the alliance of Antony and Cleopatra. If so, Sosius referenced the

Figure 4.10. Bronze 19–21mm, Zacynthus, C. Sosius, 39 BC (RPC 1 1290). **Obv.** Head of Antony, IMP. **Rev.** Eagle on thunderbolt with caduceus on the right, ZA, C SOSIVS Q.

Figure 4.11. Bronze 17mm, Zacynthus, C. Sosius, c. 34 BC (RPC 1 1292). **Obv.** Head of Apollo, ZA. **Rev.** Tripod, C SOSIVS COS DESIG.

alliance several years before Cleopatra's portrait appeared on Antony's own coins. The obverse carries Antony's portrait and names him as *imperator*, while the reverse bears the eagle on a thunderbolt type normally seen on Ptolemaic coinage, accompanied by Sosius' own name and a reference to his position as quaestor. The eagle was a polyvalent image, and it might have evoked Jupiter or Roman power in the mind of the user, although on other Greek issues it does seem to have referred to Cleopatra (see p. 104). It thus might refer to Cleopatra here. Later coins of Sosius focus on his own position and achievements: an issue of 36 BC bears a military trophy and names him as *imperator* (RPC 1 1291; Shipley 1930: 78). This was a reference to his victory in Judea in 37 BC, which resulted in King Herod being placed on the throne. Although the reverse of this issue references Sosius' military victory, the obverse carries a portrait of Antony, perhaps reflecting the fact that Sosius' achievements were achieved under Antony's patronage.

Sosius' next issue of coinage on Zacynthus was in 34 BC (Fig. 4.11), with a design showing Apollo and a tripod. Sosius is named as consul designate.

Figure 4.12. Silver stater, 10.87 g, Zacynthus c. 5–4th centuries BC. **Obv.** Head of Apollo. **Rev.** Tripod, I A Δ 1.

The *fasti* (official public lists) record that Sosius held a triumph for his victories in Judea in 34 BC (AE 1930, 60), and he remained in Rome afterwards to support Antony's cause. Some think that it was as *triumphator* that Sosius undertook the rebuilding of the temple of Apollo in the Campus Martius (Shipley 1930: 84). The decision by a supporter of Antony to rebuild a temple to Apollo in Rome shortly after Octavian had vowed his temple to Apollo on the Palatine in 36 BC would have been politically provocative. However, others argue that the temple was built after Actium, after Sosius had switched sides and sought to prove himself to Octavian (Hölscher 2009: 318–19). The controversy surrounding the temple is ongoing, but it does provide some possible associations for Sosius' coinage. Fig. 4.11 may have been a reference to his building activity in Rome (Shipley 1930: 85). If the temple is to be dated later, the imagery of Apollo may have later come to be associated with Augustus (indeed, even if Sosius vowed the temple in 34 BC, the meanings of this numismatic imagery likely changed over time). To add to the complexity, the type is also similar to the local coinage of the island issued before the Roman conquest (Fig. 4.12). Zacynthus possessed an important cult centre of Apollo, which must have influenced its choice of coin design. Fig. 4.11 is the only issue of Sosius to refer to local iconography, and so the imagery might have been read as a reference to Sosius, to Augustus, or to the island and its cult, or all or none of these, depending on the viewer and the year they encountered the coin.

Sosius' fourth coin issue dates to 32 BC, after he had assumed the consulship and then been forced to flee Rome because of his support for Antony (Dio 50.1.2–6). In spite of this Sosius refers to himself as consul on

Figure 4.13. Leaded bronze 22mm, Corinth, P. Aebutius and C. Pinnius, 39–36 BC (RPC 1 1124). **Obv.** CORINT, bare head of Antony. **Rev.** P AEBVTIO C PINNIO II VIR, prow.

the coin (Antony and Sosius no doubt continued to argue he held the position), while the iconography of Neptune (obverse) and dolphin and trident (reverse) refer to his position as a naval commander of Antony's fleet (RPC 1 1293).

4.4 Support in the Provinces

A contrast to the negative traditions surrounding Antony and Cleopatra that were fostered by Octavian and his supporters is found in the demonstrations of support for Antony on provincial coinage. Corinth, for example, was an important base for Antony prior to Actium and epigraphy reveals that prominent civic positions in the town were held by Antony's supporters at this time (Rizakis 2001: 42). One of the civic magistrates (called a *duovir*) from this period was M. Insteius Tectus (RPC 1 1118–21), who was perhaps a relative of the M. Insteius who commanded Antony's fleet at Actium, or possibly even the same individual (Plutarch, *Mark Antony* 67.7; Amandry 1988: 36; Rizakis 2001: 42). The presence of Antony and his followers in the colony was undoubtedly the context behind a provincial coin issue that took its imagery directly from one of Antony's denarii (Amandry 1988: 36–7). Fig. 4.13 imitates Fig. 4.14, but when copying the original design the die engraver did not allow for the fact that he was engraving a negative image to be struck onto a flan; consequently the result is a mirror image of the original.

Antony continued Caesar's practice of founding colonies in the east. Caesar had been the first to establish colonies outside of the Italian

Figure 4.14. Denarius, mint moving with Antony, Mark Antony and Cn. Domitius Ahenobarbus, 40 BC (RRC 521/2). **Obv.** Bare head of Antony right, *lituus* behind, ANT IMP III VIR R P C. **Rev.** Prow with star above, CN DOMIT AHENOBARBVS IMP.

Figure 4.15. Bronze 21mm, Philippi, Q. Paquius Rufus, 42–30 BC (RPC 1 1647). **Obv.** Head of Antony, A(ntoni) I(ussu) C(olonia) V(ictrix) P(hilippensis). **Rev.** Togate figure seated left on *sella curulis* holding writing board (?) with urn at feet. Q PAQVIVS RVF LEG C D.

Peninsula, meaning that these settlements could function as political, military and economic control points. In Achaea Caesar had founded Corinth, Buthrotum, Photike and Dyme. In 42 BC, perhaps soon after the battle against Brutus and Cassius, Antony founded a colony at Philippi (Papageorgiadou-Bani 2004: 31). Two coin types were struck by Antony's legate, Q. Paquius Rufus, in connection with the foundation. The obverses carry a portrait of Antony and a legend naming the colony, stating it was founded on Antony's orders. One reverse displays a ploughing scene, a foundation ritual that mimicked the creation of the *pomerium* (sacred boundary) in Rome (RPC 1 1646). The other type, Fig. 4.15, has a scene from the land allotment ceremony. A togate man (perhaps Antony) is seated on a curule chair holding the lists used to allot land, with the urn containing the lots before him. The legend names Rufus (the C D probably refers to the fact the colony had been founded, perhaps standing for *coloniae deducendae* or *coloniam deduxit*). Under Caesar an 'ideology of colonisation' began to develop; Roman colonies were seen as 'mini-Romes' (this was not necessarily the reality, but it was an ideology that accompanied Roman colonisation from this period). This no doubt contributed to the iconography chosen: the ploughing scene, for example, stresses the similarities between Philippi's foundation and that of Rome. Once released into circulation, these images would then foster the idea that the inhabitants were living in a 'mini-Rome' (Rowan 2014a: 152). Octavian later re-founded Philippi and named it after himself; similarly it appears that Antony re-founded the Caesarian colony of Dyme, changing its name from Colonia Iulia Dumaeorum to Colonia Iulia Antonia Dumaeorum (RPC 1 1285; Amandry 1981: 55).

Coinage attests to the benefactions Antony bestowed on cities in the east, which must have been a motivating factor behind local honours for the triumvir. One of the more remarkable cases is the city of Thessalonica in Macedonia, which, along with Sparta, remained loyal to the triumvirs by refusing to join Brutus and Cassius. As a consequence, both cities were reportedly promised to the assassins' soldiers as plunder (App. 4.16.118; Plutarch, *Brutus* 46.1; Voutiras 2011: 459). Thessalonica in particular appears to have been loyal to Antony, and the city was rewarded by becoming a self-governing or 'free city' (*civitas libera*) after 42 BC. This honour was celebrated with an issue that showed Eleutheria (freedom) on the obverse, with Nike on the reverse commemorating the victory at Philippi (Fig. 4.16). Two further issues of the same period refer to games called the *agonothesia* (RPC 1 1552), perhaps held to celebrate the victory at Philippi, and to the *homonoia* or friendship of the city with Rome (Fig. 4.17). The city also adopted a new, Antonian era calendar: that is, years began to be counted from 42 BC (Voutiras 2011: 460).

As well as honours for Antony's subordinates, cities also voted honours for the triumvir himself. Texts report that Antony presented himself as the New Dionysus, and that he was addressed as such in Athens when he wintered there in 39–37 BC. He also reportedly married Athena, requiring the Athenians to pay a dowry (Dio 48.39.2; Plutarch, *Mark Antony* 24.3; Hoff 1989: 273). Coins released by Athens after the marriage are debased and of a lower weight than earlier issues, suggesting that the dowry was significant and that the Athenians were financially poorer for Antony's stay (Kroll 1972: 99–100). The Athenians celebrated an *Antonian Panathenaia* in honour of Antony as the New Dionysus in 39/8 BC (*IG* II^2 1043, lines

Figure 4.16. Leaded bronze 27mm, Thessalonica, 37 BC (RPC 1 1551). **Obv.** Bust of Eleutheria, ΘΕΣΣΑΛΟΝΙΚΕΩΝ ΕΛΕΥΘΕΡΙΑΣ. **Rev.** Nike advancing with wreath and palm, M ANT AYT Γ KAI AYT.

Figure 4.17. Leaded bronze 20mm, Thessalonica, 37 BC (RPC 1 1553). **Obv.** Bust of Homonoia, OMONOIA. **Rev.** Horse galloping, ΘΕΣΣΑΛΟΝ ΡΩΜ.

22–3), and at around the same time struck coinage showing Dionysus (Fig. 4.18). The type is so unusual for Athenian coinage that it must refer to Antony (Kroll 1972: 98–9). One issue combined the Dionysus obverse with a reverse showing the bust of Athena, perhaps referring to Antony's marriage to the goddess (Kroll 1993: 142). But Octavia was also identified with Athena in the city, and so the coin may refer to Antony and his Roman wife (Raubitschek 1946).

The Ephesian cistophoric coinage referencing the association between Antony and Dionysus has been discussed on pages 83–4, and further

Figure 4.18. Bronze 21mm, Athens, 39–37 BC (Kroll 140). **Obv.** Head of Dionysus. **Rev.** Athena holding spear, AΘE.

Figure 4.19. Bronze 20mm, Aegium, Theoxios and Kletaios, shortly before 31 BC (Kroll 3). **Obv.** Head of Dionysus wearing ivy wreath, ΑΙΓΙΕΩΝ. **Rev.** Eagle standing left, ΘΕΟΞΙΟΣ ΚΛΗΤΑΙΟΣ.

evidence is found in Aegium (Achaea). Amongst the bronzes produced by the city is an issue showing Dionysus on the obverse and an eagle on the reverse (Fig. 4.19). This coin perhaps refers to the relationship of Cleopatra (the eagle) and Antony (Dionysus) (Kroll 1996: 51). Athens also struck coinage with an eagle, the only time the animal appeared on the city's currency, suggesting it is a reference to Antony's alliance with Cleopatra (Kroll 1993: 145; Haug 2008: 412). The Ptolemaic eagle also appears on coinage of Argos and Megalopolis in Cappadocia (Kroll 1996: 51).

Fig. 4.20, struck by the magistrate Agias the son of Lyson, may be connected with the stay of Cleopatra and Antony in the city of Patras in 32/31 BC (Kroll 1996: 52). The obverse names Cleopatra and bears her portrait, while the reverse is decorated with the headdress of Isis. Haug 2008 makes the intriguing suggestion that Agias, and perhaps other Greeks in the region,

Figure 4.20. Bronze 21mm, Patras, Agias the son of Lyson, 32–31 BC (?) (RPC 1 1245). **Obv.** Diademed bust of Cleopatra, ΒΑΣΙΛΙΣΣΑ ΚΛΕΟΠΑΤΡΑ. **Rev.** Headdress of Isis, ΑΓΙΑΣ ΛΥΣΩΝΟΣ ΠΑΤΡΕΩΝ.

turned towards Cleopatra as a Hellenistic-style alternative to Roman domination; of interest here is that it is Cleopatra who is referred to on the city's coins – Antony is completely absent. A coin struck honouring Cleopatra at a time when she was a declared enemy of Rome must have been an intentional statement and, in contrast to the surviving literary tradition, suggests that not all Greek subjects were entirely content with Roman rule.

The independent city of Ascalon in Syria struck silver tetradrachms featuring Cleopatra's portrait, in all likelihood because of the city's relationship with the queen (Gitler and Master 2010). The Syrian cities of Balanea and Aradus struck coinage bearing Antony's portrait. In the case of Balanea this was probably in response to concessions granted by Antony; the city also adopted a new Antonian era (RPC 1 4456–9, 4466–8; Baldus 1987: 126). What these provincial coins demonstrate is the power of Antony to grant concessions to cities as he set out to reorganise the Roman east. This power was recognised by the civic elite of these regions, who honoured Antony and his officers in the hope of benefactions, or in recognition of them. Although our literary historical account is shaped by the ideology of Octavian, coinage, as a contemporary and unaltered document, demonstrates that many in the east recognised and commemorated the relationship between Antony and Cleopatra, with some even seeing Cleopatra as a possible alternative to Roman control.

4.5 The Donations of Alexandria

Texts record that as Antony returned victorious from Armenia in 34 BC, he confirmed the rule of Cleopatra and Caesarion over Egypt and Cyprus, and granted his children the following provinces: Phoenice and Cilicia Tracheia to Ptolemy Philadelphus; Cyrenaica and Libya to Cleopatra Selene II; and Armenia, Media and Parthia to Alexander Helios (Dio 49.41.1–3; Plutarch, *Mark Antony* 54.3–5). Other monarchs also received land as part of Antony's reorganisation of the region, but Cleopatra's share was 'exceedingly rich' (Syme 1939: 260). Dio further records that Antony decreed that Cleopatra be called 'Queen of Kings', a title that appears on Roman denarii (Fig. 4.6). The assignment of territory to Cleopatra and her offspring can also be identified via numismatic evidence: cities in these regions began to strike coinage featuring Cleopatra VII, reflecting the fact that, given the youth of her children, Cleopatra was the *de facto* ruler.

An interesting variation on the double portrait types (Figs. 4.6–7) is found in Cyrenaica after the region had been gifted to Cleopatra Selene. This issue, consisting of a larger and smaller denomination, bears no imagery but carries an abbreviated Greek legend naming the queen as *thea neotera* on the obverse, and Antony as consul for the third time on the reverse (Fig. 4.21; RPC 1 924–5).

Cleopatra is also described as *thea neotera* on a double portrait type struck at Chalcis (Fig. 4.22; RPC 1 4771–3). On these issues Cleopatra's

Figure 4.21. Bronze 26–27mm, Cyrenaica, Cleopatra VII, 31 BC (RPC 1 924). **Obv.** BACIΛ ΘΕΑ ΝΕ. **Rev.** ΑΝΤΩ ΥΠΑ Γ.

Figure 4.22. Bronze 20mm, Chalcis, 32/31 BC (RPC 1 4771). **Obv.** Bust of
Cleopatra, ΒΑCΙΛΙCCΗC ΚΛΕΟΠΑΤΡΑC. **Rev.** Head of Antony, ΕΤΟΥC ΚΑ
ΤΟΥ ΚΑΙ G ΘΕΑC ΝΕWΤΕΡΑC.

titles are listed on both the obverse and reverse of the coin – Antony's
portrait is shown, but he is not named or mentioned in the legend. This is
a nice counterpart to the Roman coinage of Antony that shows Octavia but
does not name her (Fig. 3.12). Chalcis was now under the control of
Cleopatra so it is she who dominates the coin.

The reverse legend on Fig. 4.22 gives two regnal dates: 6 and 21. Other
coinage struck in Syria reveals that after the donations of Alexandria, two
dating systems were in use: one counting the years of Cleopatra's reign
(Egyptian dates) and another era beginning from her assumption of power
in Phoenicia (Phoenician dates) (Baldus 1987: 125). This dual dating system
is also found on coins struck for Cleopatra at Berytus (RPC 1 4530). The city
of Dora, however, only used the Egyptian regnal system (Burnett, Amandry
and Ripolles 1992: 583). The adoption of new eras by cities was not new:
after the arrival of Pompey in Syria, several cities had adopted a 'Pompeian'
or 'Roman' era, and some later adopted a 'Caesarian' era. But the adoption
of a new era to reflect their new queen was not universal: Ptolemais, for
example, continued to use a local dating system (RPC 1 4741–2). This
suggests that the adoption of the dating systems was the decision of the
local elite rather than imposed from above.

Cleopatra's portrait appears on coins of other Syrian cities that fell under
her control. The elite of Tripolis, having previously struck a coin issue dated
to the Pompeian era (year 23) showing Antony on the obverse and a female
bust that may be Fulvia on the reverse (Fig. 4.23), changed their coin designs

Figure 4.23. Bronze 20mm, Tripolis, 42/41 BC (RPC 1 4509). **Obv.** Head of Antony. **Rev.** Female bust (of Fulvia?), ΤΡΙΠΟΛΙΤΩΝ ΛΓΚ.

Figure 4.24. Bronze 21mm, Tripolis, 36/5 BC (RPC 1 4510). **Obv.** Draped bust of Cleopatra. **Rev.** Prow with Nike holding wreath and palm, star in field. ΤΡΙΠΟΛΙΤΩΝ ΛΒ.

to show their new ruler with her Phoenician regnal years (year 2, Fig. 4.24). But can we take this one step further and say that the appearance of Cleopatra's portrait on the coinage of a particular city is an indication that the city had passed under her control? The case of Damascus suggests that the situation was not so simple. Cleopatra's portrait appears on coinage in Damascus (Fig. 4.25; RPC 1 4781–5), although the city continued to use the Seleucid era (year 276). Baldus concluded from this that Damascus struck coinage to honour Cleopatra, although the town had not been gifted to her (Baldus 1987: 142). The editors of RPC, however, suggest that the coin may indicate Damascus had been given to her by Antony; Ptolemais continued to use a local dating system, and so Damascus may have done likewise (Burnett, Amandry and Ripolles 1992: 583). The case remains open.

Figure 4.25. Bronze 25mm, Damascus, 37/6 BC (RPC 1 4781). **Obv.** Diademed bust of Cleopatra. **Rev.** Tyche seated on rock with outstretched right hand, holding cornucopia in left, river god below, ΔΑΜΑΣΚΗΝΩΝ ΓΟΣ. All within wreath.

Figure 4.26. Denarius, mint moving with Antony, Mark Antony, c. 32–31 BC (RRC 544/29). **Obv.** Ship decorated with an *aplustre* and equipped with a dolon-mast (a mast that slants over the bow of the ship), ANT AVG III VIR R P C. **Rev.** *Aquila* between two standards, LEG XIV.

4.6 The Legionary Denarii of Mark Antony

In the lead up to Actium, Antony struck a large coin series that has been labelled Antony's 'legionary denarii' (RRC 544/1–39; Woytek 2007: 503–18). The obverse design was a galley accompanied by a legend referring to Antony's position as augur and triumvir (Fig. 4.26). The triumviral agreement had officially ended the year before in 33 BC, so Antony legally no longer held the position. Octavian had abandoned the title and instead sought legitimacy by having the provinces swear an oath of allegiance to him (Richardson 2012: 69). The reverse legends named different military

Figure 4.27. Denarius, mint moving with Antony, Mark Antony, c. 32–31 BC (RRC 544/12). **Obv.** Ship decorated with an *aplustre* and equipped with a dolon-mast (a mast that slants over the bow of the ship), ANT AVG III VIR R P C. **Rev.** Three standards, CHORTIS SPECVLATORVM.

units (e.g. the fourteenth legion on Fig. 4.26), accompanied by an image of an *aquila* (a military standard with an eagle atop it) between two military standards. The issue naming the *cohors speculatorum* (an elite group of messengers and scouts) carried a different reverse image, with three naval standards on the reverse (Fig. 4.27; Keppie 2000: 79).

Why not use a portrait on this series? Perhaps it was a reaction to Octavian's public justification for war: that Antony was under the spell of Cleopatra, who had her sights set on Rome. In this context, a decidedly 'non-Hellenistic' set of images may have been thought advisable. But the size of this issue (the largest of this period) and its imagery marks it out as unique: with this 'monument in miniature' Antony was demonstrating his economic and military dominance, both on land and on sea, with the number of legions he had supporting him quite literally spelt out.

A small issue released by Antony's lieutenant Pinarius Scarpus in Cyrenaica combined the reverse legionary design (in this case naming the eighth legion) with an obverse showing the head of Jupiter Ammon (RRC 546/1; after Antony's defeat Scarpus switched his allegiance to Octavian and began striking coinage celebrating the victory at Actium, RIC 1^2 531–5). Scarpus' coinage may be a 'matching series' to the other legionary denarii (Keppie 2000: 79); at any rate the almost simultaneous production of a similar type elsewhere suggests a broader awareness of Antony's iconography. In hoards different legionary types are often found together. This suggests that if, as seems likely, these coins were used to pay soldiers fighting at Actium, they were distributed at random – it is improbable that each legion was paid only with the coinage struck in their name (Keppie 2000: 81). A hoard found at Actium, for example, contains a mix of different legionary types (Table 5). The legionary denarii are the latest coins in this hoard, suggesting it was buried soon after their release. A hoard from Delos buried around the same time is mainly composed of legionary denarii (80%, the Actium hoard is 93%) (DEL in Lockyear 2013, RRCH 465). This demonstrates the quantity in which these coins were struck and hints at the impact they must have had on coin circulation in Greece before and after Actium (Lockyear 2007: 170). Antony's legionary denarii are commonly found in hoards for years after they were struck (Lockyear 2007: 170). Indeed, they seem to have constituted about a fifth of the denarii in circulation until at least the reign of Vespasian (Woytek 2012a: 330).

It was only during the Late Republic (the 40s and 30s BC) that denarii circulated in quantity in Greece, a result of the permanent presence of Roman military forces and the arrival of military mints (Kroll 1997: 140). The arrival of the denarius in Greece may have meant that the production of other local silver currencies declined (e.g. the silver coinage of Athens ceases around this time; Kroll 1993: 15). Antony's release of an extremely large denarius series contributed to these changes in the monetary system of the region.

Table 5 Contents of the Actium hoard (ACT in Lockyear 2013, RRCH 473). Coins in hoard: 41. *Terminus post quem* 31 BC.

RRC Reference	Moneyer	Date	Brief description of obverse / reverse	No. of examples
281/1	M. Furius Philus	119 BC	Head of Janus / Roma crowning trophy	1
290/1	C. Fonteius	114–13 BC	Janiform head of Dioscuri / Ship	1
366/1a	C. Annius L. Fabius Hispaniensis	82–81 BC	Female bust / Victory in *quadriga*	1
458/1	Julius Caesar	47–46 BC	Head of Venus / Aeneas carrying Palladium and Anchises	1
463/1a	Mn. Cordius Rufus	46 BC	Jugate heads of Dioscuri / Venus holding scales and sceptre	1
542/1	Mark Antony M. Junius Silanus	33 BC	Head of Antony / Inscription	1

Table 5 (cont.)

RRC Reference	Moneyer	Date	Brief description of obverse / reverse	No. of examples
542/2	Mark Antony	33 BC	Head of Antony / Inscription	2
543/1	Mark Antony	32 BC	Head of Antony / Bust of Cleopatra	1
544/12	Mark Antony	32–31 BC	Galley / Three standards (CHORTIS SPECVLATORVM)	1
544/14	Mark Antony	32–31 BC	Galley / *Aquila* between two standards (LEG II)	1
544/15	Mark Antony	32–31 BC	Galley / *Aquila* between two standards (LEG III)	4
544/18	Mark Antony	32–31 BC	Galley / *Aquila* between two standards (LEG V)	2
544/19	Mark Antony	32–31 BC	Galley / *Aquila* between two standards (LEG VI)	1
544/20	Mark Antony	32–31 BC	Galley / *Aquila* between two standards (LEG VII)	1
544/21	Mark Antony	32–31 BC	Galley / *Aquila* between two standards (LEG VIII)	2
544/22	Mark Antony	32–31 BC	Galley / *Aquila* between two standards (LEG VIIII)	1
544/23	Mark Antony	32–31 BC	Galley / *Aquila* between two standards (LEG IX)	2
544/24	Mark Antony	32–31 BC	Galley / *Aquila* between two standards (LEG X)	2
544/25	Mark Antony	32–31 BC	Galley / *Aquila* between two standards (LEG XI)	3
544/26	Mark Antony	32–31 BC	Galley / *Aquila* between two standards (LEG XII)	2
544/30	Mark Antony	32–31 BC	Galley / *Aquila* between two standards (LEG XV)	3
544/33	Mark Antony	32–31 BC	Galley / *Aquila* between two standards (LEG XVIII)	1
544/34	Mark Antony	32–31 BC	Galley / *Aquila* between two standards (LEG XVIIII)	1
544/36	Mark Antony	32–31 BC	Galley / *Aquila* between two standards (LEG XX)	2
544/37	Mark Antony	32–31 BC	Galley / *Aquila* between two standards (LEG XXI)	1
544/38	Mark Antony	32–31 BC	Galley / *Aquila* between two standards (LEG XXII)	1
544/39	Mark Antony	32–31 BC	Galley / *Aquila* between two standards (LEG XXIII)	1

Coin Hoards

A coin hoard is traditionally defined as two or more coins that have been intentionally brought together, although a single coin (particularly of gold) may also have constituted a valuable store of savings for its owner. Hoards can also contain jewellery or other valuable objects in addition to coinage. We find hoards of widely varying sizes throughout antiquity.

Hoards provide us with a general idea of what coinage was in circulation at a particular time and place. Consequently they can be used for a variety of purposes: to trace how quickly a particular coin issue entered circulation; to trace where particular coins circulated; and to gain an idea of the relative size of different coin issues (if a particular issue turns up more frequently in hoards than other contemporary coinages, it was probably larger). They can also help us deduce the relative chronology of particular coins, as discussed in the introduction. Hoards can also reveal information about cultic practice, landscape, the economy, trade and other activity.

A find from Ateste (Este) in Italy demonstrates what might be learnt from the study of hoards (RRCH 519; ES2 in Lockyear 2013). Ateste was a colony founded by Octavian after Actium for his veterans. The Ateste hoard contained 307 coins (304 denarii, 2 quinarii and 1 as), all within a pot. The last dateable coin was a denarius of 4 BC, which provides us with the earliest possible date the hoard might have been buried, a *terminus post quem* (note that the hoard may have been deposited many years after this date). The earliest coin in the hoard is a denarius struck in c. 150 BC (RRC 206/1); in total 64 coins in the hoard were minted in the second century BC, demonstrating the continued circulation of much earlier coinage in this region at the beginning of the principate. 50 examples of Antony's legionary denarii were found in the hoard, as well as 3 contemporary issues struck by Antony's supporters (2× RRC 546/2a, 1× RRC 545/1). This makes 53 in total struck by or for Antony in c. 32–31 BC. By comparison, there are only two issues of Octavian from the same period (RIC 1^2 256 (Fig. 5.4) and RIC 1^2 257).

This and similar hoard compositions suggest that Antony had far more coinage than Octavian at his disposal in the lead up to Actium; in fact, his coinage may have been as much as ten times larger than that of the future Augustus (Dillon 2007: 39). While die studies are the best way to gauge the relative size of different coinages, for very large issues this is very difficult, and a comparison of how many times a particular coin occurs in hoards (in comparison to other contemporary coins) can provide a rough idea of relative sizes (Metcalf 2006: 41). Another hoard found in Ateste, with a *terminus post quem* of 27 BC, contains only one legionary denarius; this suggests that it may have taken some time for the legionary denarii to move west (RRCH 466; ES1 in Lockyear 2013). A full description of both hoards can be found at http://numismatics .org/chrr/id/ES2 and http://numismatics.org/chrr/id/ES1.

Antony's silver denarii were slightly debased, meaning that their silver content was not as high as denarii struck at Rome. Octavian's issues from this period are of 96.84% fineness, while Antony's are 92.2%, a silver content closer to that found in the local cistophoric currency (Dillon 2007: 45). Conforming to local practice is the most probable explanation for the lower silver content of Antony's denarii, but the slight debasement of these issues had a stark effect on their circulation, as discussed below.

The third-century historian Cassius Dio notes that Antony was better funded than Octavian before Actium (Dio 50.18.2) and the numismatic evidence supports this claim. In coin hoards, Antony's legionary denarii occur much more frequently than Octavian's issues of the same time period, suggesting that Antony's coinage was more numerous. That the coins of Octavian and Antony are found together in hoards, in regions where Octavian settled soldiers after Actium (e.g. in Ateste; see 'Coin Hoards' inset), suggests that Octavian may have used Antony's denarii to pay soldiers after his victory (Dillon 2007: 43). As victor Octavian would have obtained Antony's treasury, which he could have used alongside his own funds to pay the discharged legionaries. Oddly then, the victor at Actium may have used coinage bearing the imagery of his defeated opponent to pay his soldiers. In this context it is worth remembering that the war was officially being waged against Cleopatra, not Antony; Octavian was reluc-tant to wage a campaign against Antony's memory after his defeat (Lange 2013: 83). This may help to explain the use of Antony's currency, which, as we have discussed, bore military imagery rather than Antony's portrait, again perhaps making it more palatable for use by the opposition. Octavian may also have been trying to avoid the cost and time required to melt Antony's coinage and re-strike it: the fact that Antony's issues were debased meant if Octavian had chosen to restrike the coinage and improve the fineness, he would have ended up with fewer denarii than he started with (Dillon 2007: 45). The time and effort it would have taken to recall and reissue Antony's coinage was probably the decisive factor in Octavian's decision to simply make use of it.

Antony's legionary coinage, like his cistophori (see p. 85) remained in circulation long after they were struck. The lower silver content of the legionary denarii meant, ironically, that they continued to circulate well after the coinage of Octavian and early emperors had disappeared. During the imperial period older or obsolete currency could be recalled to the mint and re-struck; as the fineness of denarii decreased over time, worn coinage with higher silver content was occasionally recalled (Dio 68.15.3; Butcher and Ponting 2014: 35–8). Numismatists believe that the lower silver content of Antony's denarii meant that it was not recalled alongside other coinages, and it was less likely to be hoarded than coins with higher silver content (instead you would probably choose to save a coin with a higher silver content and try and pass Antony's coin onto the next person). Consequently, Republican and early imperial denarii disappear from coin hoards over time suggesting they were no longer in circulation, but Antony's legionary denarii continue to appear. Antony's denarii continue to be found in reasonable quantity in hoards dating from up to the third-century AD, often worn to almost blank discs (e.g. the third-century Shapwick villa hoard in Britain had 260 legionary denarii; Abdy and Minnitt 2002). Ironically, then, Antony's 'monuments in miniature' well outlasted those of Octavian.

Restitution Coinage

Figure 4.28. Denarius, Rome, Marcus Aurelius and Lucius Verus (AD 161–9) (RIC III *Marcus Aurelius* 443). **Obv.** Ship with sceptre tied with fillet on prow, ANTONIVS AVGVR III VIR R P C. **Rev.** *Aquila* between two standards, LEG VI, ANTONINVS ET VERVS AVG REST.

Under the emperor Marcus Aurelius a coin issue was struck that carries almost the same iconography and legend as Antony's legionary denarii, accompanied by an additional legend on the reverse: *Antoninus and Verus Augusti restored (it)*. Just as an emperor may restore an earlier building, so too he could restore coins as 'monuments in miniature', even using the same language to communicate his actions (REST, an abbreviation found in many restored building inscriptions). Slight changes were made to the obverse legend to make it more legible for the imperial viewer: Antony's name is not abbreviated as on his Republican denarii, but is spelt out in full, as is his position as augur. This was particularly necessary since the abbreviation AVG in the second century AD meant Augustus.

Other emperors also 'restored' old coin types, with the best-known example being the restoration of Republican types under Trajan (Komnick 2001). Several explanations of this phenomenon have been proposed: that these coins were struck at moments when the mint was recalling and re-striking older currency; that they were issued for a particular group who had antiquarian or numismatic interests; that the types commemorated significant events or individuals of the past; or that the issues were designed to enhance the legitimacy and reputation of the current emperor (Komnick 2001: 164). The addition of the imperial titles to restoration types suggests that these issues may have been intended to communicate the virtues of the reigning emperor, much as the restoration of old buildings might. But even if we cannot be sure of the precise motivation behind this particular issue, the continued circulation of Antony's coinage may have played some role in the selection of this type to 'restore'. Antony's coinage continued to shape Roman perceptions of him well after Actium.

A detailed examination of the different types of coinage struck in this period reveals that Antony and his supporters actively engaged with provincial populations and won support from cities in the east. In many ways Antony's presence in the east was a period of innovation: the introduction of a 'universal' Roman denominational system in the form of fleet coinage, the joint issues with Cleopatra, and then the enormous, non-portrait legionary denarii. It was Antony's innovations, as well as those of others in the late Republic, which would shape the principate of Augustus. And it is to his rule that we now turn.

5

Representing the Augustan Principate (31 BC–AD 14)

Octavian's victory at Actium, his subsequent invasion of Egypt, and the deaths of Antony and Cleopatra left the young Caesar the most powerful man in the Roman world. However, his transition from triumvir to *princeps* was complex, and was accompanied by the development of an ideology of one-man rule. An important source for understanding how Augustus' extraordinary position was publicly represented is the *Res Gestae Divi Augusti* (*RGDA*), his own presentation of his achievements. When we compare the text of the *RGDA* with the messages communicated by coinage over the course of his rule, we find striking similarities. Both display a tension between the reality of a *princeps* and the ideology of the restored Republic (*res publica*), and both emphasise the return of peace to the Roman world, Augustus' building programme, his achievements in religious life and foreign diplomacy, as well as the honours he received from the Senate and People of Rome (SPQR). The parallels between these two types of evidence should not surprise us: both were official representations of the emperor seen in Rome and the provinces. Coinage here, as elsewhere, is one monument among many, and acts in conjunction with other media.

Unlike the *RGDA*, which is the final version of a text produced towards the end of Augustus' lifetime (Richardson 2012: 198), coinage allows us to trace the development of Augustan ideology over time. Like the texts produced in this period, coinage produced in Rome and the provinces displays some extraordinary innovations as people sought to represent the new political landscape. Similar to the authors of this period, coin designs were probably produced not on Augustus' orders, but within a framework inspired by Augustan ideology and the new political and cultural landscape (Richardson 2012: 211–19). Both Roman and provincial coinage reveal Augustus' careful negotiation of his own divinity, as well as the complex process of establishing an heir. Surveying the coin evidence in its context, we can see that multiple strategies of representation, arising from multiple authors, all contributed to creating the image of Augustus.

Figure 5.1. Denarius, uncertain Italian mint, c. 34–29 BC (RIC 1^2 250a). **Obv.** Bare head of Octavian. **Rev.** Venus leaning against column, half-draped, holding helmet and transverse sceptre; shield bearing eight-rayed star leans against the column, CAESAR DIVI F.

Figure 5.2. Denarius, uncertain Italian mint, c. 34–29 BC (RIC 1^2 251). **Obv.** Head of Venus wearing crown (*stephane*) and necklace. **Rev.** Octavian in military dress advancing to the right, holding transverse spear, CAESAR DIVI F.

5.1 Octavian the Divine: Coinage before and after Actium

Before and after Actium a series of gold and silver coins were struck for Octavian in Italy bearing the legend CAESAR DIVI F or IMP CAESAR (RIC 1^2 250a-277; Dillon 2007: 37; Sutherland 1976b). These coins are extraordinary because they assimilate Octavian to a series of deities (Pollini 1990). The coins were clearly conceived as pairs: on one issue the portrait of a deity would grace the obverse and Octavian would be shown on the reverse (Fig. 5.2), while on the other Octavian would be shown on the obverse and the deity on the reverse (Fig. 5.1). The overall impression is that Octavian is interchangeable with the gods. On the series carrying the legend CAESAR DIVI F (words that further communicate Octavian's connection to the divine as the son of a god) pair types exist for Octavian and Venus, Octavian and Pax (Peace), and Octavian and Victory (Figs. 5.3–4).

Figure 5.3. Denarius, uncertain Italian mint, c. 34–29 BC (RIC 1² 254B). **Obv.** Bare head of Octavian. **Rev.** Victory standing on globe holding wreath and palm, CAESAR DIVI F.

Figure 5.4. Denarius, uncertain Italian mint, c. 34–29 BC (RIC 1² 256). **Obv.** Bust of Victory with wings. **Rev.** Octavian as Neptune (?) standing with foot on globe, holding *aplustre* and vertical sceptre, CAESAR DIVI F.

The assimilation of Octavian to the divine is made even more explicit on Fig. 5.4, where Octavian is shown in a similar manner to Neptune. It has been suggested that this image may represent a statue erected for Octavian after his defeat of Sextus Pompey at the battle of Naulochus (Zanker 1988: 39–40), but in the absence of any other evidence that such a statue existed, we should be cautious in using coinage to draw this conclusion. The Octavian/Neptune figure recalls the earlier denarius type that showed Pompey the Great as Neptune (Fig. 3.23), so it might be a direct response to Sextus Pompey's coinage, communicating that Sextus' mastery of the seas and the support of Neptune had now fallen to Octavian. The image may have even been referencing the iconography of the Hellenistic king Demetrius Poliorcetes, who is shown as Neptune in a very similar manner on Hellenistic coinage in the early third century BC (Pollini 1990: 347). There are similarities to the representation of Demetrius but also differences: an *aplustre* and globe are added, and

Figure 5.5. Denarius, uncertain Italian mint, c. 29–27 BC (RIC 1² 269a). **Obv.** Bare head of Octavian. **Rev.** Laureate herm figure on winged thunderbolt, IMP CAESAR.

Figure 5.6. Denarius, uncertain Italian mint, c. 29–27 BC (RIC 1² 270). **Obv.** A herm of Octavian as Jupiter, laureate, with a thunderbolt behind. **Rev.** Octavian, togate, seated on curule chair holding victoriola, IMP CAESAR.

a sceptre is used instead of a trident, suggesting that an established statue type was adapted to show Octavian as a naval victor. Significantly, while Antony's coinage assimilating him to Dionysus was struck in the east (see p. 84) where such representations had precedent, Octavian's coins were struck in Italy where such imagery was more unusual. Octavian may have been inspired by the ideologies of his contemporaries in portraying himself not only as the son of a god, but a divinity in his own right. The picture of Octavian we see here is very different to his later policy of restricting a ruler cult to select provincial locations.

Direct and indirect assimilation of Octavian to the divine can also be seen on the later IMP CAESAR series. Again, representations of Octavian and deities are interchanged, and again one 'pair' aligns Octavian directly with the divine (Burnett 1983: 563): on Figs. 5.5–6 Octavian is shown as Jupiter on a herm statue (a statue type that had a plain, square base decorated with a portrait). Octavian's assimilation to the divine on this pair is underscored

Figure 5.7. Denarius, uncertain Italian mint, c. 29–27 BC (RIC 1² 271). **Obv.** Laureate male head with features of Octavian. **Rev.** Rostral column surmounted by cloaked figure of Octavian (?) holding spear and *parazonium*, IMP CAESAR.

by the reverse design on Fig. 5.6: here Octavian is seated holding a victoriola (a small statue of Victory), a reference to the famous statue of Zeus holding Nike created by Phidias (Koortbojian 2006). Although the image of Zeus carrying Nike had been used on the coinage of Alexander the Great, no Hellenistic king had been shown holding a victoriola in this manner; here Octavian went beyond the imagery of Hellenistic monarchs.

The coinage of the late Republic saw competing claims to the divine; the IMP CAESAR and CAESAR DIVI F series are the culmination of this discourse. The IMP CAESAR types, struck after Octavian's victory at Actium, communicate the divine support that ensured his success: along with the Octavian/Jupiter herm portrait, the portraits of Apollo, Diana, and Mars appear. The reverse types celebrate victory, with imagery of a military trophy, arches, and temples. Fig. 5.7 carries the image of a rostral column, erected to celebrate naval victories, accompanied by an obverse showing Octavian wearing a laurel wreath. Dio mentions that Octavian had been granted the right to wear the laurel wreath at all times (49.15.1), and later emperors would be shown wearing the wreath almost ubiquitously. The wreath on Fig. 5.7 differs from these later imperial portraits though, and is remarkably similar to the wreath worn by Apollo on another issue in the series (Fig. 5.8). We might thus see Fig. 5.7 as a representation of Octavian *as* Apollo, similar to the representation of Octavian as Jupiter discussed above. Again this extraordinary assimilation is paired with an extraordinary reverse: the rostral column is surmounted by what is probably a nude heroic statue of Octavian (Burnett 1983: 563–4). The reverse of Fig. 5.8 shows Octavian as a founder of a city, perhaps suggesting his role as the (re)founder of Rome and the Republic.

Table 6 Number of dies for the CAESAR DIVI F and IMP CAESAR series.
Data taken from Sutherland and Carson 1984: 30.

Series	Metal	Obv. dies	Rev. dies	No. of specimens examined
CAESAR DIVI F				
	Gold	20	18	36
	Silver	124	152	286
IMP CAESAR				
	Gold	13	16	32
	Silver	216	227	402

Figure 5.8. Denarius, uncertain Italian mint, c. 29–27 BC (RIC 1^2 272). **Obv.** Laureate head of Apollo. **Rev.** Octavian veiled and laureate ploughing with yoke of oxen and holding whip, IMP CAESAR.

A die study of both series demonstrates that the later IMP CAESAR issue had a much higher production in silver, while the earlier CAESAR DIVI F series had slightly more gold dies (Table 6). This shift is probably connected to the acquisition of Egypt in 30 BC and its associated booty (meaning more metal was available to make more coinage), which, as discussed on p. 7, appears to have had an effect on the Roman economy as a whole (Sutherland and Carson 1984: 30). If you look closely at Table 6 you will notice it also includes the number of coins in the study sample. This is because mathematical formulae exist which allow numismatists to predict how many dies an issue *should* have, based on the number of dies in their sample, and the size of their sample. These are called Esty or Carter estimates (Esty 1986; Esty 2006).

As discussed on pages 32–3, while using die numbers to calculate the *absolute* size of an issue is controversial since we don't know how many coins each die produced, we can compare the relative number of dies amongst different series to gauge *relative* sizes. Since different metals have different hardnesses (e.g. pure gold is softer than silver, and both are softer than bronze), different metals impact upon the die differently, so comparison should only be made between coins of the same metal. With this in mind, let us try some comparisons with examples already encountered in this book. The gold coinage in Table 6, for example, has a much lower number of dies than the very large aureus issue of Caesar and Hirtius (Fig. 2.10), but has more dies than the aureus series of Sextus Pompey (Fig. 3.29), and is similar in size to the triumviral gold types (p. 81). The silver issues in Table 6 are much larger than the EID MAR coin of Brutus (Fig. 3.20), for example, which had only 7 obverse dies (Woytek 2003: 525), and also much larger than the denarii struck by Sextus Pompey in Sicily (RRC 511, p. 74), which had 57 obverse and 71 reverse dies (DeRose Evans 1987). In this way we can work out the relative size of different coin issues, which in turn can reveal the purpose of the issue (small and commemorative or large for payments) and the relative wealth available to different parties.

5.2 The Restorer of the Republic

The imagery on Octavian's coinage discussed above stands in stark contrast to his later public image. Antony's defeat was presented as a victory over a foreign enemy and Octavian was voted a triumph over Egypt. Antony's name remained unmentioned (as it does in the *RGDA*), as did the names of other Romans killed (Dio 51.19.4–5; Lange 2013). Coinage celebrated the capture of Egypt (Fig. 5.9), as well as the return of Asia (RIC 1^2 276), both of

Figure 5.9. Denarius, uncertain Italian mint, c. 29–27 BC (RIC 1^2 275). **Obv.** Bare head of Octavian, *lituus* behind, CAESAR COS VI. **Rev.** Crocodile, AEGVPTO CAPTA.

Figure 5.10. Cistophorus, Ephesus, c. 28 BC (RIC 1^2 476 = RPC 1 2203). **Obv.** Laureate head of Octavian, IMP CAESAR DIVI F COS VI LIBERTATIS P(opuli) R(omani) V(index). **Rev.** Pax standing on *parazonium (?)* holding caduceus; snake emerging from *cista mystica* on right, PAX, all in laurel wreath.

which were disguised references to the end of Antony's dominance in the east.

The end of the conflict was also celebrated on a cistophorus issue struck at the mint of Ephesus in c. 28 BC (Fig. 5.10). The coin carries Octavian's portrait and names him as the champion of liberty of the Roman people, responsible for the Pax (Peace) shown on the reverse (see also *RGDA* 1.1; Cooley 2009: 108–11). Pax stands next to a *cista mystica*, the traditional symbol of the cistophorus denomination. Like the earlier cistophori of Antony, it is difficult to know whether this coin was issued by the Roman government in the region or by the provincial elite. Was the coin's message directed by Rome, or should it be seen as a provincial reaction to events? (See Rich and Williams 1999: 186 and Sutherland 1970: 112 for two opposing viewpoints). Some cistophori struck in the province of Asia utilise Augustan ideology, suggesting Roman control (e.g. a sphinx, the image on Augustus' signet ring, RIC 1^2 487), but other types have a distinctly local flavour indicative of involvement by the local elite (e.g. an Ephesian altar, RIC 1^2 479; Sutherland 1970: 100). It is difficult, then, to know who was responsible for deciding the types. This difficulty is unlikely to be resolved any time soon, but this series and others highlight the fact that the division between 'imperial' and 'provincial' issues was not clear-cut. In fact, the mints of Pergamum and Ephesus also struck denarii and aurei under Augustus, as did mints in Spain.

Fig. 5.10 demonstrates a movement away from the divine iconography of the 'pair' series towards the more sober presentation of Octavian's power that developed during 28–27 BC (Rich and Williams 1999: 172). While Octavian's earlier coins are suggestive of what the principate *might* have looked like (a Hellenistic-style monarchy with one man ruling absolutely), there was a shift towards a more complex ideology with Octavian ruling as 'the first man' of the Senate. We also see a conscious movement away from a Hellenistic-style monarchy in Octavian's decision to melt down silver statues of himself, and the decision to share his consulate with Agrippa in 28 and 27 BC (*RGDA* 8.2, 24.2; Suetonius, *Augustus* 52). In these years Augustus theoretically shared his power with Agrippa, creating a rule of two consuls that echoed traditional Republican government. Agrippa also shared the power of the censorship with Augustus (not the office itself, merely the 'power of a censor') that revised the list of senators. The importance of Augustus sharing his power can be seen in the *RGDA* 34 (quoted below), where Augustus emphasises that he had no more power (*potestas*) than his colleagues.

In addition to the Pax cistophori, the mint at Ephesus was probably responsible for an extraordinary aureus type, Fig. 5.11, currently known from only two specimens (Abdy and Harling 2005; Rich and Williams 1999). The reverse shows Octavian seated on a curule chair holding a scroll accompanied by the sentence *He has restored to the people of Rome their laws and rights*. The coin refers to the political settlement that began in 28 BC (according to this coin and the *RGDA*, which records that he

Figure 5.11. Aureus, Ephesus (?), c. 28 BC. **Obv.** Laureate head of Octavian, IMP CAESAR DIVI F COS VI. **Rev.** Togate Octavian seated on curule chair, holding scroll, scroll case (*scrinium*) before, LEGES ET IVRA P(opulo) R(omano) RESTITVIT.

transferred the *res publica* from his power back to the Senate and People of Rome at this time). The process continued the following year with Octavian's renouncement of his command of the army, provinces, and finances (Galinsky 2012: 66). The language used on Figs. 5.10–11 probably derives from a decree issued in Octavian's honour (Rich and Williams 1999: 187); both are thus perhaps (provincial) responses to events that occurred in Rome.

5.3 Senatorial Honours and Augustus' Titles

The *RGDA* records that in 28–27 BC, in response to Octavian surrendering his powers, the senate voted him a series of honours:

> I was named Augustus by senatorial decree, and the doorposts of my house were publicly clothed with laurels, and a civic crown was fastened above my doorway, and a golden shield was set up in the Julian senate house; through an inscription on this shield the fact was declared that the Roman senate and people were giving it to me because of my valour, clemency, justice, and piety. After this time I excelled everyone in influence, but I had no more power than the others who were my colleagues in each magistracy (*RGDA* 34; trans. Cooley 2009: 98–9).

These honours featured on coins from c. 27 BC. Coinage often refers to the fact that the honours were given to Augustus by the senate through the legend S P Q R, or S C (for the meaning of S C on bronze though see p. 16). The honour of the *corona civica* and the title of Augustus were also commemorated on obverses that displayed Augustus wearing an oak-wreath crown and/or carried the legend AVGVSTVS.

A survey of Augustus' coins reveals that issues celebrating these senatorial honours were largely struck in Spanish mints in the period c. 20–18 BC, well after they had been awarded. Only Fig. 5.12, a rare aureus struck in c. 27 BC, makes a contemporary reference. The decision to place these honours on coinage may thus have been made after the return of the standards lost by Crassus at Carrhae in 53 BC, which was achieved by diplomatic negotiation (*RGDA* 29; Cooley 2009: 243). A close connection between the return of the standards in 20 BC and the person of Augustus can be found in other media. The cuirass of Augustus on the Prima Porta statue, for example, is decorated with a barbarian handing over a standard to a Roman soldier. The juxtaposition of Augustus' honours with the return

Figure 5.12. Aureus, uncertain Italian mint, c. 27 BC (RIC 1² 277). **Obv.** Bare head of Augustus right, CAESAR COS VII CIVIBVS SERVATEIS. **Rev.** Eagle with wings spread standing on oak wreath flanked by S C; two laurel branches behind, AVGVSTVS.

Figure 5.13. Denarius, uncertain Spanish mint 2 (Colonia Patricia?), c. 19 BC (RIC 1² 86a). **Obv.** Bare head of Augustus right, CAESAR AVGVSTVS. **Rev.** *Aquila* on left and standard on right, flanking S P Q R arranged around shield inscribed CL V, SIGNIS RECEPTIS.

of the standards can be clearly seen on Fig. 5.13. The shield or *clipeus virtutis* (identified by the abbreviation CL V) awarded to Augustus by the Senate and People of Rome (communicated through the legend S P Q R) is flanked by an *aquila* and a military standard, accompanied by the legend SIGNIS RECEPTIS, 'standards having been recovered' (RIC 1² 85a–87b). This coin, and others like it, demonstrate that the senatorial honours awarded to Augustus transformed over time into symbols of power used in contemporary contexts (Zanker 1988: 94–7). Here the honours are used to align the recovery of the standards with the virtues of the *princeps*.

Augustus became *pontifex maximus* after the death of the existing office holder Lepidus in 12 BC (*RGDA* 10.2; Cooley 2009: 149). The title is added to Augustus' titles on bronze coinage struck at Lugdunum from 12 BC and

Figure 5.14. Denarius, Rome, L. Lentulus, 12 BC (RIC 1² 415). **Obv.** Bare head of Augustus, AVGVSTVS. **Rev.** Augustus, laureate and togate, resting on shield inscribed C V placing star on half-clad figure of Julius Caesar, who holds a victoriola and spear, L LENTVLVS FLAMEN MARTIALIS.

at Rome from 7 BC (RIC 1² 229–30, 426–36), but it only appears on precious metal coinage in AD 13–14 (Fig. 5.16). But Augustus' role as *pontifex maximus* may have been referenced in other ways at the Roman mint. An aureus issue of the moneyer Caninus Gallus in 12 BC shows on its reverse a closed door flanked by laurel branches, with a laurel wreath above (RIC 1² 419). This must be a representation of Augustus' house, and it might commemorate the fact that Augustus did not move into the public house of the *pontifex maximus* but instead remained on the Palatine, giving the other property to the Vestal Virgins and making part of his own house public property (Fullerton 1985: 479).

A further, oblique reference may have been made to Augustus' position on the extraordinary denarius issue of Lentulus (Fig. 5.14). Augustus is shown on the reverse of this coin placing a star over a statue of Julius Caesar holding a victoriola, but what is surprising is that Lentulus names his position as a priest of Mars or *flamen Martialis*. This priesthood was normally awarded by the residing *pontifex maximus*, and so perhaps here Lentulus is using coinage to reference his own appointment to the priesthood by Augustus while simultaneously honouring the *princeps* (Küter 2011: 767–9). The naming of a *flamen Martialis* on coinage in this manner is without precedent.

When Augustus was proclaimed *pater patriae* in 2 BC, the title appeared on coinage that same year (e.g. RIC 1² 204–12; i *RGDA* 35.1; Cooley 2009: 273–5). The title of *parens* had precedent in the Republic: Julius Caesar was named as *parens patriae* in 44 BC. Agrippa had been hailed as *parens municipi* (father of the *municipium*) on coinage of Gades in Spain (RPC 1

Figure 5.15. Denarius, uncertain Spanish mint 2 (Colonia Patricia?), c. 18 BC (RIC 1² 96). **Obv.** Triumphal dress (*toga picta* over *tunica palmata*) between *aquila* and wreath, S P Q R PARE CONS SVO. **Rev.** *Quadriga* with ornamental panels surmounted by four miniature galloping horses, CAESARI AVGVSTO in exergue.

77–84; he was also named as patron), and Augustus had been named as *parens* on coinage of 19/18 BC. Fig. 5.15 is one example of this, which also references Augustus as a *triumphator* (see also RIC 1² 96–101). *Pater patriae* is a development from earlier usage.

Livia

Figure 5.16. Aureus, Lugdunum (RIC 1² 219), AD 13–14. **Obv.** Laureate head of Augustus right, CAESAR AVGVSTVS DIVI F PATER PATRIAE. **Rev.** Seated female figure holding sceptre and branch, PONTIF MAXIM.

This aureus is the only precious metal issue to name Augustus as *pontifex maximus*. The title occurs on the reverse accompanied by a seated female figure holding a sceptre and branch. The attributes are those of Pax,

Figure 5.17. Dupondius, Rome, Tiberius, AD 21–22 (RIC 1² *Tiberius* 47). **Obv.** Portrait of Livia, SALVS AVGVSTA. **Rev.** TI CAESAR DIVI AVG F AVG P M TR POT XXIIII around S C.

though some have seen here the representation of 'Livia as Pax'. If true this would be the only representation of Livia on coinage under Augustus; she is noticeably absent from Augustan money, particularly when one considers the representation of women on late Republican coinage. Imperial women do not feature in quantity on Roman coinage until the reign of Hadrian (Duncan-Jones 2006). But the figure on Fig. 5.16 is unlikely to be Livia since there is no legend naming her. The identification of the image as Livia is based on a later issue of Claudius, where she is shown seated in a similar manner, but this issue was struck in conjunction with her deification and she is named as DIVA AVGVSTA (RIC 1² *Claudius* 101; Wood 2001: 88). Livia first appears on imperial coinage under Tiberius in c. AD 22–3, accompanied by legends that directly reference her: SALVS AVGVSTA (*the welfare of the empress*) and IVLIAE AVGVST(AE) (Fig. 5.17; Wood 2001: 88–9).

5.4 Innovation and Tradition in Rome

The tension between the influence held by Augustus and his public insistence on the restoration of the *res publica* manifested itself in several ways. In the *RGDA*, for example, we discover that Augustus frequently held the *power* of a certain position (censor, tribune) without actually holding the office, and that he returned the *res publica* and provinces to the Senate only to have certain honours and provinces returned back to him. The coinage struck in the city of Rome in this period also, quite literally, reflects this incongruity: often one side of a coin refers to Augustus while the other references Republican traditions. Coinage thus embodied the political tension of the period.

Coinage continued to be shaped by the political situation throughout Augustus' reign. The movement towards one-man rule was not complete until after Augustus' death, but coins reveal how a single individual gradually came to dominate the public currency. Over time references to the moneyers responsible for the coinage decrease, and from 11 BC they are no longer named on precious metal coinage struck in Rome. At around the same time the erection of public buildings in Rome by the Roman elite also ceases, which cannot be a coincidence (Wallace-Hadrill 1986: 79). The cessation of public building activity by the Roman elite is likely because Augustus gradually monopolised military triumphs and the money associated with them, which had traditionally been spent by Roman generals on monuments in the capital.

After the disruption of the civil wars, production of coinage resumed in Rome from 23 BC, the same year we know Augustus fell seriously ill. He renounced his consulship and received several honours in return including permanent tribunician and proconsular power, meaning he could continue to hold *imperium* within the city walls for the rest of his life (Dio 53.32.5–6; Richardson 2012: 99). Why is this significant? Because without *imperium* in Rome, Augustus could not control coinage in the city (Burnett 1977: 61). The granting of permanent *imperium* to Augustus perhaps meant that coinage could once again be produced in the city after a period of production in the provinces. The precious metal coins struck in Rome bore the names of the moneyers in accordance with Republican practice and carried a mixture of types, with some referring to Augustus and others traditionally Republican in theme (Küter 2014). But even the more traditional imagery on these issues may have been read in the light of Augustus' achievements. These were coins carrying the names of elite Roman families who acted as moneyers, circulating with imagery of Augustus and the new regime, and so the overall result might be characterised as miniature monuments of elite consensus (Küter 2014: 28).

The juxtaposition of tradition and innovation that characterises this series is seen on the coinage of L. Aquillius Florus. The reverses of his issues refer to Augustus' honours and achievements: the laurel branches and oak wreath are shown, the return of the military standards from Parthia, and, on

Figure 5.18. Denarius, Rome, L. Aquillius Florus, c. 19–18 BC (RIC 1² 306). **Obv.** Bust of Virtus, draped and wearing a feathered helmet, L AQVILLIVS FLORVS III VIR. **Rev.** Armenian wearing tiara and long robe, kneeling with both arms extended, CAESAR DIVI F ARME CAPT.

Figure 5.19. Denarius, Rome, L. Aquillius Florus, c. 19–18 BC (RIC 1² 301). **Obv.** Bust of Virtus, draped and wearing a feathered helmet, L AQVILLIVS FLORVS III VIR. **Rev.** Augustus standing in elephant *biga* holding laurel branch and sceptre, AVGVSTVS CAESAR.

Fig. 5.18, the success with Armenia. Fig. 5.19 displays Augustus in an elephant *biga* (RIC 1² 301–7). But the obverses connected to this reverse type name Florus as moneyer and bear images of Sol, Virtus, and a triskeles. There is no reference to Augustus on this side. Instead we find a continuation of Republican numismatic tradition: the bust of Virtus on Figs. 5.18–19, for example, is a familial type that had been used by one of Florus' ancestors in 71 BC (Fig. 5.20; Küter 2014: 113). Other coins of Florus display the portrait of Augustus on the obverse and carry familial references on the reverse. Fig. 5.21, for example, combines Augustus' portrait with a flower, a visual pun on Florus' name (such coin types are calling 'canting types'). Fig. 5.22 shows a warrior and the personification of Sicily, the same image used by his ancestor in 71 BC (Figure 5.20) and a probable reference to the suppression of the slave war in Sicily by Mn. Aquillius in 101 BC (Galinsky 1996: 31).

Figure 5.20. Denarius serratus, Rome, Mn. Aquillius, 71 BC (RRC 401/1). **Obv.** Bust of Virtus right, VIRTVS III VIR. **Rev.** Warrior holding shield and a half-prostrate female (Sicilia), SICIL in exergue, MN AQVIL MN F MN N.

Figure 5.21. Denarius, Rome, L. Aquillius Florus, c. 19–18 BC (RIC 1² 309). **Obv.** Bare head of Augustus right, CAESAR AVGVSTVS. **Rev.** Flower, L AQVILLIVS FLORVS III VIR.

Figure 5.22. Denarius, Rome, L. Aquillius Florus, c. 19 BC (RIC 1² 310). **Obv.** Bare head of Augustus right, CAESAR AVGVSTVS. **Rev.** Warrior holding shield and a half-prostrate female (Sicilia), L AQVILLIVS FLORVS III VIR, SICIL in exergue.

In fact, if you look closely, the obverse and reverse of the earlier coin type from 71 BC are split, with each now paired with an Augustan image. Florus' whole series, then, combines 'Republican tradition' with 'Augustan innovation' in a way that recalls the 'divine pairings' of the series discussed above.

Figure 5.23. Denarius, Rome, Q. Rustius, c. 19 BC (RIC 1² 322). **Obv.** Jugate busts of the Fortunae Antiatinae, Q RVSTIVS FORTVNAE ANTIAT. **Rev.** Altar inscribed FOR(tuna) RE(dux), CAESARI AVGVSTO Ex S C.

Of course, once in circulation, many viewers may have seen the image of a soldier holding Sicilia as a reference to Augustus' own achievements in regenerating Sicily (indeed, perhaps only select members of the Roman elite may have been able to interpret the type as a reference to the earlier slave war, and perhaps only family members of Florus would have known it was an earlier coin type). Multiple meanings are also evident on other coins. An issue struck by Quintus Rustius showed the altar of Fortuna Redux near the Porta Capena, erected in honour of Augustus' return from the east (Fig. 5.23; *RGDA* 11). The day he returned to Rome became the date of the Augustalia, celebrated by the pontiffs and vestals at the new altar (Dio 54.10.3–4). The two goddesses of Fortuna shown on the other side of this coin appear at first glance to be connected to the altar, but the legend reveals that the Fortunae shown are those from the city of Antium (ANTIAT), the region of Rustius' family (Küter 2014: 52–5). Again there is a juxtaposition of traditional Republican imagery with honours given to Augustus. But we cannot rule out the suggestion this particular familial type was selected because it fitted well with the altar of Fortuna on the reverse: the two goddesses may simultaneously refer to Rustius while honouring Augustus. As with Florus' coinage, the associations may have been dependent on the particular viewer (Küter 2014: 122).

The bronze coinage struck at Rome after the mint reopened was very different to the money struck in gold and silver. Bronze coins now carried a new-but-unchanging reverse type, with each issue carrying the moneyer's name around the letters S C (Fig. 5.24). One exception to this rule is the unusual issue of bronze coinage struck by Cn. Piso and his colleagues at

Figure 5.24. As, Rome, Cn. Piso, c. 22–19 BC (RIC 1^2 382). **Obv.** Bare head of Augustus right, CAESAR AVGVSTVS TRIBVNIC POTEST. **Rev.** CN PISO CN F III VIR AAA FF around S C.

Figure 5.25. Bronze 24mm, Rome, Cn. Piso, c. 22–19 BC (RIC 1^2 394). **Obv.** Bare head of Augustus right, CAESAR AVGVSTVS TRIBVNIC POTEST. **Rev.** Diademed, bearded head of Numa Pompilius, CN PISO CN F III VIR AAA FF.

some point after 22 BC (Fig. 5.25; RIC 1^2 390–6). The reverse of these issues displays a portrait of Numa, the legendary king of Rome. Numa was connected to the family of Piso: Calpus, the son of Numa, was the legendary founder of the Calpurnia family (Numa had also previously appeared on a coin issue of Cn. Calpurnius Piso in 49 BC; see RRC 446/1; Sutherland 1978: 174). Thus, again, we may have a mixing of traditional familial types with more Augustan themes. But given that contemporary parallels were being drawn between Augustus and Numa, the reverse may also have had a simultaneous reference to the *princeps* (Galinsky 1996: 35–6).

Unusually, these Numa bronzes do not carry the S C legend normally associated with bronze at Rome from this period, and the weights of the surviving specimens vary significantly (from 6.06g to 14.92g). These coins are extremely rare, and some have suggested they are forgeries (indeed the authenticity of Fig. 5.25 is uncertain), although most accept that at least some must be genuine (Burnett 1977: 51). Some specimens show evidence of tooling (incisions made into the coin itself after it was struck). Given their rarity, and their unusual character, the purpose of these issues remains open. Sutherland suggested it was an attempt by these moneyers, who produced no gold or silver issues, to give bronze coinage a 'new look'; if this was the case the innovation was quickly abandoned (Sutherland 1978: 174). Wallace-Hadrill suggested that these pieces formed a medallic series (Wallace-Hadrill 1986: 81). If Küter's suggested date of 22 BC is correct for these pieces, then this is the first time the emperor is shown with a laurel wreath, strengthening the identification of the piece as a medal (Küter 2014: 45).

Medallions and Presentation Pieces

Figure 5.26. Gold multiple (Au4, 30mm, 31.97 g), uncertain mint, 27 BC (RIC 1² 546). **Obv.** Bare head of Augustus right, small Capricorn below neck, IMP CAESAR DIVI F AVGVST COS VII. **Rev.** Hippopotamus right, AEGYPTO CAPTA above and below.

Presentation pieces, or 'medallions', were struck under Augustus, although whether we include the Numa bronzes in this category remains uncertain. Medallions differed from normal coinage in both size and weight and were probably intended as gifts to high-ranking civilian and military officials. In the later imperial period medallions were struck onto large bronze flans from specifically designed dies, but under Augustus presentation pieces were struck in gold. Heavy gold coins are known from this period, each equivalent in weight to four aurei (RIC 1^2 204–5). Two issues carry imagery known from other coinage: on one is the goddess Diana, accompanied by a reference to Sicily, and on the other is a representation of Gaius and Lucius Caesar as leaders of the youth (*principes iuventutis*). The multiple showing Diana was found in 1759 in Pompeii alongside 11 other gold coins from the emperors Augustus, Tiberius, Caligula and Claudius – the piece was obviously a store of wealth and hoarded alongside gold coins. Fig. 5.26 is a gold multiple that was found in Madrid in 1919 that refers to the conquest of Egypt, but its authenticity remains uncertain (Gorini 1968).

There are no known presentation pieces like these for the Republic. Aurei may have been given as gifts, but the pieces themselves did not differ from normal currency in size or weight. The development of the medallion as a genre in the Roman world is thus connected with the beginning of the principate. Suetonius records that Augustus gave coins (sometimes foreign or old coins) as gifts during the Saturnalia (Suetonius, *Augustus* 75.1; see also Dio 54.35.3). Bronze medallions from the later imperial period often carry Happy New Year messages, suggesting they formed a gift during New Year's celebrations (Rowan 2014b: 111). As presentation pieces, their use differed to normal coinage (many may have never entered circulation). One must keep in mind that these are rare pieces whose imagery was designed for a specific (and presumably receptive) group. The piece from Pompeii for example, weighing 30.88g, is known from a single example, stolen from the Museo Nazionale in Naples in 1977.

5.5 The Saecular Games

The movement towards coinage focused only on Augustus can be seen on the series struck in connection with the saecular games (*ludi saeculares*) in

Figure 5.27. Denarius, uncertain Spanish mint 1 (Colonia Caesaraugusta?), 19–18 BC (RIC 1² 37a). **Obv.** Head of Augustus with oak wreath right, CAESAR AVGVSTVS. **Rev.** DIVVS IVLIVS on either side of a comet.

Figure 5.28. Denarius, Rome, M. Sanquinius, 17 BC (RIC 1² 340). **Obv.** Saecular herald holding caduceus and shield with six-pointed star, AVGVST DIVI F LVDOS SAE. **Rev.** Youthful head of Julius Caesar, comet above, M SANQVINIVS III VIR.

17 BC: these coins carry the name of a moneyer, but the imagery on both sides is Augustan. The saecular games were held every *saeculum* (about 100 years) to ensure the continuity of Roman power. Their celebration under Augustus was connected with Julius Caesar. More specifically, the games were connected to the comet that appeared at a festival (the *ludi Victoriae Caesaris*) held by Octavian a few months after Caesar's death (Weinstock 1971: 379). The comet was seen as a sign of Caesar's acceptance among the gods, and Octavian made the most of the occurrence by erecting a statue of Caesar with a star above his head (Fig. 5.14; Dio 45.7.1). The star or *sidus Iulium* appeared with Caesar on coinage from c. 38 BC (RRC 534/1), on issues marking the construction of the temple to the deified Caesar in 36 BC (Fig. 5.29), and formed a reverse design for denarii struck in Spain in 19–18 BC (Fig. 5.27). Saecular games coinage show the star on the shield of the herald who was sent out to announce the celebration, as well as over Caesar's portrait (Fig. 5.28). Double portrait types were also struck

showing Augustus on the obverse, styled as DIVI F, and the deified Julius Caesar on the reverse (RIC 1^2 338). Thus while Horace's *Carmen Saeculare* and the surviving epigraphy attest to the connection of the celebrations with Apollo, Diana, and Augustus' reforms (e.g. his marriage legislation), coinage communicated their connection to Julius Caesar, the divine father of the emperor.

An aureus issue showing Augustus distributing purification materials (*suffimenta*) for the saecular games was struck in Rome in 16 BC, the year after the festival was held (RIC 1^2 350). Coinage could refer to festivals after they occurred, or could anticipate an event. Augustus' saecular coin types would become a model for later emperors: Domitian, for example, released coins that consciously recalled those of Augustus during his saecular celebration. Septimius Severus would also later reference Domitianic coinage, and the reappearance of the same imagery after intervals of more than 100 years suggests that the die engravers had access to a record of earlier coin types (the original coins would have ceased to circulate). Thus coin designs recorded the proper performance of the games for contemporary audiences as well as for posterity, functioning in much the same way as the inscriptions (*acta*) that recorded the celebration (Rowan 2013c: 50–65). Augustus adopted a traditional Roman festival to highlight his own position and his policies, and this, in turn, became the tradition that was adopted. The way coinage is used here suggests that the release of coinage may have become part of the ritual itself.

5.6 The Augustan Building Programme

The political and cultural changes Augustus brought to the Roman world also impacted its physical landscape. The concentration of powers in the hands of one man meant that the city of Rome could be redesigned in a centralised way not possible under the Republic, when building programmes were sporadic and funded by individuals. The messages of the principate contained in inscriptions, coins and festivals were also communicated via the marble, bricks and concrete erected in the city (Favro 2005; Wallace-Hadrill 1993). Rome was transformed into an imperial capital of an Empire (Wallace-Hadrill 2008: 259–312).

Much of the building programme carried dense messages aimed at the Roman elite (Hölscher 2009: 331); the audience of these monuments was restricted to those who lived in or visited the city. Coinage, however, provided a medium by which these buildings might reach a wider audience, both geographically and socio-politically. Unlike Roman buildings, which stood firm in their urban context, coins moved from region to region and person to person. The *RGDA* performs a similar function: a significant portion of the text details the building activities of Augustus in the capital and the provincial copies of the inscription spread the message to a broader audience (*RGDA* 19–21). Many of the buildings Augustus vowed took decades to complete. The temple of Mars Ultor, for example, was vowed in 42 BC, but was still incomplete upon the dedication of the Augustan forum in 2 BC. But the image of a finished building could be placed on coinage very quickly. In this sense, coinage could communicate the idea of a renovated Rome before the renovations were completed.

Though it is tempting to use the representation of buildings on coinage to uncover what lost monuments might have looked like, these representations are not photographs (Burnett 1999). Coins celebrated the idea of a monument; they were not architectural plans or images reproduced to scale. Numismatic representations are *interpretations* of buildings, something that allows the historian to deduce what the contemporary perceptions of these monuments were, and what aspects of them were thought important (Burnett 1999: 152). Coinage, then, provides an insight into how buildings were *viewed*, not necessarily what they actually looked like.

Sometimes structures that were never finished were represented on coinage (Prayon 1982). A well-known example is the temple of Caesar's Clemency, portrayed on a coin of P. Sepullius Macer in 44 BC (Fig. 3.1). The temple was shown on coins before construction began, and in all probability the temple was never built (Fishwick 1984: 265). The portrayal of a building that did not (yet) exist may have meant that it was difficult for the viewer to know what they were looking at; in this context the legend plays an important role in identifying the image, and it is no surprise that the legend is prominent on this coin (CLEMENTIAE CAESARIS; Prayon 1982: 321). Those living in the provinces were unlikely to know whether a building existed or not (they probably saw little of the monuments Roman coinage portrayed); here too, the legend would help in clarifying the image.

Similarly Octavian's temple to the deified Julius Caesar is shown on coinage in 36 BC, seven years before its dedication (Fig. 5.29). Like the building, the cult statue of the deified Julius Caesar shown in the temple is also imagined at this stage – after all, how does one represent the cult of someone who had so recently been living (Koortbojian 2013: 45–9)? The solution was to show Caesar as he was in life: veiled and holding a *lituus* in his role as a priest. Whether this was envisaged as the final statue

Figure 5.29. Denarius, mint moving with Octavian, Octavian, 36 BC (RRC 540/2).
Obv. Bearded head of Octavian, IMP CAESAR DIVI F III VIR ITER R P C. **Rev.**
Tetrastyle temple with veiled statue of Julius Caesar within, holding *lituus*. DIVO IVL
on architrave, star within pediment, lighted altar on left, COS ITER ET TER DESIG.

is unknown. The temple is given an abbreviated inscription labelling the structure as consecrated to the deified Caesar (DIVO IVL), and the *sidus Iulium* that became associated with Caesar's divinity is shown in the architrave above. Next to the temple is an altar. This was perhaps a representation of the altar that was erected on the spot where Caesar was cremated; given these coins were struck before the construction of the temple, it need not refer to an altar planned as part of the new complex (Koortbojian 2013: 42). This series has traditionally been thought to mark the beginning of the construction of the temple, but there is little evidence apart from the coin design to suggest this (Burnett 1999: 142). What is key is that the decision to build a monument, or even the idea of a monument, was thought worthy of commemoration on coinage.

The differing representations of the temple of Mars Ultor highlight the dangers of using coins to reconstruct ancient structures. Four mints struck coins celebrating the temple of Mars Ultor in 19–18 BC: two Spanish mints (RIC 1^2 28, 39a–b, 68–74, 103–6, 114–120A), Pergamum (RIC 1^2 507), and Alexandria (RPC 1 5003). The date suggests the coins were all struck in connection with the recovery of the Parthian standards. While each mint portrayed a domed structure, there are also differences between the mints and even within the same mint, demonstrating that the portrayal of Roman architecture could vary according to what the die engraver or monetary official considered important. While both Spanish mints show a four-columned (tetrastyle) temple with a statue of Mars inside (Fig. 5.30), they also showed a temple with six columns (hexastyle) containing the recovered standards (Fig. 5.31), and a tetrastyle temple enclosing a triumphal chariot

Figure 5.30. Denarius, uncertain Spanish mint 1 (Colonia Caesaraugusta?), 19–18 BC (RIC 1^2 39b). **Obv.** Bare head of Augustus, CAESAR AVGVSTVS. **Rev.** Circular domed temple with four columns showing Mars, who is helmeted and holding an *aquila* and standard, MARTIS VLTORIS.

Figure 5.31. Denarius, uncertain Spanish mint 2 (Colonia Patricia?), c.18 BC (RIC 1^2 105a). **Obv.** Laureate head of Augustus, CAESARI AVGVSTO. **Rev.** Domed temple with six columns and *aquila* and two standards within, MAR VLT on either side.

(Fig. 5.32). The cistophori of Pergamum carry a tetrastyle temple with a single *vexillum* inside (Fig. 5.33), similar to the portrayal of the structure at Alexandria (Fig. 5.34). All these coins purportedly show the same structure (and the similarities between them suggest they were all working from a central design), but each representation is different. The portrayal of structures on coinage could even change from die to die, meaning we should look at as many examples as possible when studying the representation of buildings (Kleiner 1985; Krmnicek and Elkins 2014).

Remarkably, all these representations differ completely from the remains of the temple of Mars Ultor in the Augustan Forum, which is a rectangular structure. This has led to the theory that there were two structures dedicated to Mars Ultor: one on the Capitoline mentioned by Dio (54.8.3), which is our circular building, and another in the Augustan forum. The theory

Figure 5.32. Denarius, uncertain Spanish mint 2 (Colonia Patricia?), c.18 BC (RIC 1^2 115). **Obv.** Laureate head of Augustus, CAESARI AVGVSTO. **Rev.** Domed temple with four columns and triumphal wagon containing *aquila*, S P Q R below.

Figure 5.33. Cistophorus, Pergamum, 19–18 BC, (RPC 1 2220 = RIC 1^2 507). **Obv.** Bare head of Augustus, IMP IX TR PO V. **Rev.** Circular temple with four columns containing a military standard, MART VLTO.

Figure 5.34. Bronze 25mm, 13.76 g, Alexandria, after 19 BC, (RPC 1 5003). **Obv.** Bare head of Augustus, CEBACTOC. **Rev.** Temple with four columns containing a military standard, KAICAP.

concludes that the recovered standards were initially housed on the Capitoline until the completion of the Augustan forum in 2 BC (Burnett 1999: 148; Hannah 1998: 423–4; Zanker 1988: 186–7). But coinage may merely have commemorated the decision to build the temple: by this argument there was only ever one structure, that in the Forum of Augustus (Fishwick 1984: 266). It is also possible that the temple may have originally been suggested for the Capitoline by the Senate, but that it was later built in the forum (leading to Dio's confusion, Rich 1998: 84–5). According to this theory the coin types used by the various mints in 19–18 BC may reflect the original Capitoline plan before the change of location. This may be the case, but the coins could equally reflect the projected temple for the Forum of Augustus, which may have changed as it was built. Of interest is the fact that the coins also displayed the different items that would be located within the temple. Coinage allowed the recovered Parthian standards to be shown in the temple well before they could ever be physically placed there.

Augustus' road repairs are also shown on coinage (*RGDA* 20.5; RIC 1^2 140–4, 360–2; Cooley 2009: 195–6). Not as spectacular as large temples, road repairs may have been a challenge to communicate visually, and different mints responded in different ways. In the Roman mint the repairs are celebrated through the representation of an inscription reading *The Senate and People of Rome to Imperator Caesar because the roads have been paved out of the money which he gave to the treasury* (trans. Cooley 2009: 80–1; Fig. 5.35). Like the temples, the representation of the inscription, on a small pillar (*cippus*), may not reflect what the physical inscription looked

Figure 5.35. Denarius, Rome, L. Vicinius, c. 16 BC (RIC 1^2 362). **Obv.** Equestrian statue of Augustus with pedestal inscribed S P Q R IMP CAES, before city-walls and gate. **Rev.** *Cippus* inscribed S P Q R IMP CAE QVOD V(iae) M(unitae) S(unt) EX EA P(ecunia) Q(u)IS AD A(erarium) DE(dit); L VICINIVS L F III VIR around.

Figure 5.36. Denarius, Rome, L. Mescinius Rufus, c. 16 BC (RIC 1² 356). **Obv.** *Imago clipeata* of Augustus, bare-headed and facing three-quarters right within laurel wreath, S(enatus) C(onsulto) OB R(em) P(ublicam) CVM SALVT(e) IMP(eratoris) CAESAR(is) AVGVS(ti) CONS(ervatam). **Rev.** Mars holding spear and *parazonium* on pedestal inscribed S P Q R V(ota) PR(o) RE(ditu) CAES(aris). L MESCINIVS RVFVS III VIR around.

like (if one existed), and the Latin is probably an abbreviated form of any original text. The unusual decision to represent an inscription on a coin is paired here with an unusual obverse showing an equestrian statue of Augustus before the walls of a city, perhaps a representation of the beginning of the Flaminian Way, a major road from Rome to Ariminum (Rimini).

We should view this representation as part of a broader innovation by the moneyers of 16 BC. Fig. 5.36 shows a portrait of Augustus on a round shield (an *imago clipeata*), and another contains nothing but a Latin legend within an oak wreath (Fig. 5.37). The latter is combined with a reverse showing another inscribed *cippus*, meaning that there is little other than writing on the coin. The example shown in Fig. 5.36 demonstrates what might have happened to these types as they circulated and became worn: the legend would disappear and a significant portion of the message would be lost.

The college of moneyers in 16 BC was one of the first to strike coinage that only referred to Augustus with no familial types (Sutherland 1943: 43). The coin types focus on honours voted to Augustus by the Senate (Wallace-Hadrill 1986: 78): the dedication of an honorary arch (RIC 1² 359); an equestrian statue (Fig. 5.35); prayers for the return of Augustus (*S P Q R vota pro reditu Caesaris*, Figs. 5.36–7); an *imago clipeata*; a dedication 'to the general saviour Imperator Caesar Augustus' (*Imperator Caesar Augustus communi conservatori*, Fig. 5.37; Küter 2014: 196–7); and the thanksgiving of the Senate to Jupiter Optimus Maximus for Augustus' recovery from illness, since through him the *res publica* had been preserved (Fig. 5.36). Although epigraphic forms like the *cippus* were used on later

Figure 5.37. Denarius, Rome, L. Mescinius Rufus, c. 16 BC (RIC 1^2 358). **Obv.** I(ovi) O(ptimo) M(aximo) S P Q R V(ota) S(uscepta) PR(o) S(alute) IMP(eratoris) CAE(saris) QVOD PER EV(m) R(es) P(ublica) IN AMP(liore) AT Q(ue) TRAN(quilliore) S(tatu) E(st) within oak wreath (*Vows offered to Jupiter Optimus Maximus by the Senate and People of Rome on behalf of the safety of Imperator Caesar because through him the Republic is in a more ample and tranquil state*). **Rev.** *Cippus* inscribed IMP(erator) CAES(ar) AVGV(stus) COMM(uni) CONS(ervatori), flanked by S(enatus) C(onsulto); L MESCINIVS RVFVS III VIR around.

Figure 5.38. Aureus, uncertain Spanish mint 2 (Colonia Patricia?), c. 18–17/16 BC, (RIC 1^2 140). **Obv.** Bare head of Augustus, S P Q R IMP CAESARI. **Rev.** Augustus crowned by Victory in an elephant biga on a double arch on a viaduct, QVOD VIAE MVN SVNT.

coinage, a series of coins with such extensive use of Latin does not appear again. This was an experiment that was not repeated.

Coins from Spanish mints referring to road improvements, by contrast, have less epigraphic and more visual emphasis. They portray a bridge (viaduct) decorated with honorific arches; these must have been one of the more impressive features of the road system (Figs. 5.38–40). These issues carry the same Latin legend as the Roman mint (Fig. 5.35), suggesting a central ideology from which all the imperial mints worked, but on the Spanish issues the Latin runs over both the obverse and reverse. As with the

Figure 5.39. Denarius, uncertain mint 2 (Colonia Patricia?), c. 18–17/16 BC, (RIC 1² 142). **Obv.** Bare head of Augustus, S P Q R IMP CAESARI. **Rev.** QVOD VIAE MVN SVNT in four lines between two arches on a viaduct, each bearing an equestrian statue and a trophy.

Figure 5.40. Denarius, uncertain mint 2 (Colonia Patricia?), c. 18–17/16 BC, (RIC 1² 145). **Obv.** Bare head of Augustus, S P Q R CAESARI AVGVSTO. **Rev.** Augustus crowned by Victory in a *quadriga* on a double arch adorned with *rostra*, on a viaduct, QVOD VIAE MVN SVNT.

temple of Mars Ultor, the bridges vary in their depiction: it is uncertain whether we are being shown different perspectives of one bridge, or differ- ent bridges (Cooley 2009: 197). Dio mentions that statues of Augustus were erected on arches on the bridges of the Flaminian Way at Ariminum and over the Tiber (Dio 53.22.1), but we should be hesitant in concluding that it is these statues that are shown here. The statues on these coins are repre- sented on a scale that must have been much larger than their original size (they are almost the same size as the arch that carries them, and sometimes larger). This may reflect how the bridges were mentally visualised (even if only by the die engravers): the statues may have been the aspect that came most quickly to mind, the feature that best communicated the connection of the road works with Augustus.

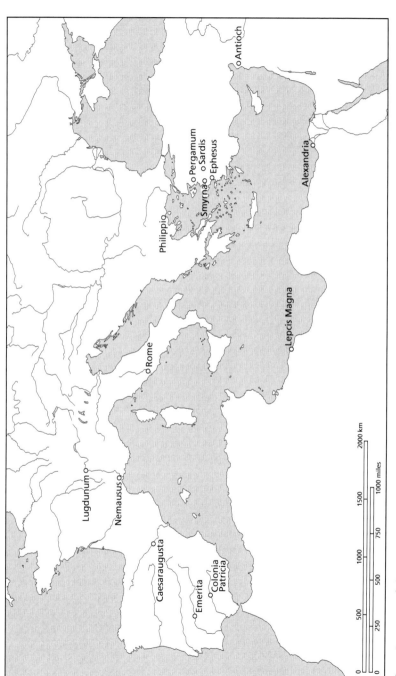

Figure 5.41. Map of places mentioned in Chapter 5.

5.7 Imperial or Provincial? Augustan Coinage in the Provinces

The building programme in Rome is one example of how the experience of the Augustan principate in the capital differed from that of the provinces. But what other differences might have existed? How did the geographically and culturally diverse provinces incorporate changes at Rome within local culture? The coinages of local cities are an important source in answering this question, since they carry both 'provincial' and 'imperial' references in their designs. The representation of the imperial family in the provinces by provincials contributed to the overall image of the emperor in a particular region; cities could adapt or extend the imperial image on their coinage (and other monuments), contributing to new conceptualisations of imperial rule. For example, Livia and other members of the imperial family are more commonly represented on provincial coins than on the official coinage of Rome, and often the emperor is shown in association with local deities, a connection not found in the capital. Different regions would have had different images of Augustus. In this sense, the public image of the emperor should be seen as a collaborative process involving multiple authors.

The 'Augustan Revolution' sparked a slow but significant change in local currencies, a process that lasted into the Julio-Claudian period. Portraiture became more common and increasingly focused on the imperial family. Reverse types increase in diversity, probably a result of the adoption of the Roman approach to money as a 'monument in miniature'. This same change in mindset also resulted in a higher number of depictions of buildings and other structures – this emphasis on representing civic space is more Roman in character than Greek (Burnett 2011; Howgego 2005a: 4). The spread of Roman culture was likely assisted by the overseas colonies that began to be founded in number in this period: colonies favoured the depiction of civic structures (though the practice is by no means confined to them). The denominations used by local mints also changed, probably in response to the spread of Roman precious metal coinage.

But the division between 'Roman' and 'provincial' coinage in this period is a difficult one. As mentioned above, official Roman gold and silver coinage continued to be struck outside Rome at the beginning of Augustus' rule. This may simply have been a continuation of the decentralised minting of the civil war period, but Burnett points out that once Augustus had officially resigned the consulship he would no longer

Figure 5.42. Denarius, Emerita Augusta, P. Carisius, c. 25–23 BC (RIC 1² 7a). **Obv.** Bare head of Augustus, IMP CAESAR AVGVST. **Rev.** Helmet between dagger and *bipennis*, P CARISIVS LEG PRO PR.

have possessed the constitutional power to control coinage at Rome. By having precious metal mints in the provinces, Augustus could maintain direct control of the process through his proconsular power (Burnett 1977). This may explain why the minting of precious metals was largely conducted in Gaul and on the Iberian Peninsula in this period, although location of these mints may also have been more convenient for troop payments.

The coinage struck in Spain for Augustus demonstrates a mixture of 'Roman' and 'local' in its designs. Denarii and quinarii of c. 25–23 BC carry the portrait and titles of Augustus on the obverse, while the reverses depict local armour such as the Iberian curved sword (RIC 1² 8), a helmet with stag's horns, and a *bipennis* (a double-bladed axe) (Fig. 5.42). Bronze coinage struck in Spain also carries representations of local armour (RPC 1 1–4). These were objects of local significance, used by Augustus to represent his victories in the Cantabrian wars. The imagery was both 'local' and 'imperial'.

Other coins carry a representation of the city-walls of Emerita Augusta (Fig. 5.43), emphasising that, having achieved victory, the emperor is now focused on peace and city-building (Trillmich 2009: 428–31). Emerita Augusta was founded for demobilised soldiers (*emeriti*) after an Augustan campaign in Lusitania in 26–25 BC. Publius Carisius oversaw the foundation of the colony as Augustus' legate, and the coins carry his name on the reverse. For veterans who settled in Emerita Augusta, the image of the city walls on Fig. 5.43 may have suggested what their home might look like in the future (much of the city was still under construction for decades after the foundation), providing a focal point for the creation of a new civic

Figure 5.43. Denarius, Emerita Augusta, P. Carisius, c. 25–23 BC (RIC 1² 9). **Obv.** Bare head of Augustus, IMP CAESAR AVGVST. **Rev.** Circular city-wall with EMERITA inscribed above the gate, P CARISIVS LEG PRO PR.

identity. In the Roman world coinage was often struck at the moment of a city's foundation (sometimes this was the *only* time coinage was issued in the name of the city), and this was likely because money, and its imagery, could generate a collective sense of identity for a newly formed community. But for those who did not live in Emerita Augusta, Fig. 5.43 communicated Augustus' role as a builder of cities and colonies, and his efforts to demobilise and support his soldiers (communicated by the legend EMERITA; Trillmich 2009: 431), an activity also recorded in the *RGDA* (16, 28). Depending on who used the coin, the associations of the image will have changed.

Bronze coinage struck at the colony of Nemausus also has both 'imperial' and 'provincial' characteristics. These coins began to be produced around 27 BC, with production lasting for more than a decade. As demonstrated on Fig. 5.44, the bronzes carried the heads of Augustus and Agrippa on the obverse, and a crocodile chained to a palm tree on the reverse, accompanied by the name of the town, COL(onia) NEM(ausus) (RIC 1² 154–61, RPC 1 522–4). The chained crocodile references the capture of Egypt, and given that other artefacts with Egyptian motifs have been found in the colony, it is likely that Nemausus was founded for veterans who had served in Egypt (Sauer 2005: 22). The obverse iconography is simultaneously a reference to the ruling authority and a statement of local loyalty to the emperor (Suspène 2012: 27). The palm had previously decorated local currencies in the area, but the addition of the crocodile changed the image from one that was strictly local to one recalling Augustus' achievements and (perhaps) the achievements of the veterans settled in the colony. Both obverse and reverse designs, then, simultaneously hold imperial and local significance.

Figure 5.44. Bronze 27mm, Nemausus, c. 16/15(?)–10 BC (RPC 1 523). **Obv.** Head of Agrippa (wearing rostral crown) and Augustus (bare-headed) back-to-back, IMP DIVI F. **Rev.** Crocodile chained to a palm tree; wreath with long ties above, COL NEM.

Though the imagery and legend are provincial in character, the quantity in which this type was struck (particularly between c. 16/15 and 10 BC) demonstrates that the issue was made for imperial use (Sutherland 1976a: 29). In fact, these coins have been found throughout the region of the three Gauls and along the Rhine frontier in Roman military camps, indicating that they had a relatively wide regional circulation and were probably given to soldiers (Suspène 2012: 30).

Finds also reveal that after 10 BC the production of the Nemausus mint declined in volume, with the coinage of Lugdunum instead becoming the important regional bronze currency in the west (Fig. 5.45; RIC 1² 229–48). Augustus established an imperial mint in Lugdunum in 15 BC. The coins display the altar to Rome and Augustus that had been placed in the sanctuary of the Three Gauls in the city, one of the earliest places to be granted an imperial cult (Fishwick 1999: 96–8). Ruler cult was another area in which the inhabitants of Rome had a different experience to the provinces: no structure was erected to Augustus as a god in the capital, but Pergamum (Asia) and Nicomedia (Bithynia) were granted permission to build temples. The altar at Lugdunum was established by Drusus, and functioned as both a monument of Roman victory as well as a reference to the divinity of Augustus and his family (Richardson 2012: 210).

Figure 5.45. Sestertius, Lugdunum, AD 9–14 (RIC 1² 231a). **Obv.** Laureate head of Augustus, CAESAR AVGVSTVS DIVI F PATER PATRIAE. **Rev.** The altar of Lugdunum decorated with the *corona civica* between laurels, flanked by stylized nude male figures, Victories left and right on columns, ROM ET AVG.

Like the issues of Nemausus, the Lugdunum coins are simultaneously 'imperial' and 'local'. They did not carry the city's name, but bore an image of regional significance, an apt choice for a regional currency. Similar regional 'imperial' currencies were also struck in the east: one large series is characterised by a reverse with the legend C A within a wreath (Fig. 5.46). The attribution of this coinage to Asia is based on the idea that C A stands for *Commune Asiae* (RPC 1 2227–35), but finds suggest that some variants may have been struck in Syria (RPC 1 4101–7). The abbreviation C A may, then, refer to the fact that the coinage was struck with the permission of Augustus (*Caesar Augustus* or *Caesari auctoritate*, Küter 2014: 14). Coins with the legend S C within a wreath were struck at Antioch in Syria, with the obverse legend in either Latin or Greek (Fig. 5.47; RPC 1 4246–9, 4260–1, 4264; Howgego 1982). Both the C A and S C series are found throughout the region and were used by the military, as indicated by legionary countermarks (on countermarks see inset on "Countermarking" on p. 177).

5.8 Provincial Responses to Augustan Ideology

Although it can be difficult at times to distinguish between imperial and provincial coinage, many coins from this period are clearly the products of local mints, struck for use within a city and its hinterland. It is to these that

Figure 5.46. Brass 35mm, mint in Asia (?), c. 25 BC (RPC 1 2234). **Obv.** Bare head of Augustus; AVGVSTVS. **Rev.** C A within rostral wreath.

Figure 5.47. Bronze 27mm, Antioch, c. 5/4 BC (RPC 1 4246). **Obv.** Laureate head of Augustus, ΚΑΙΣΑΡΟΣ ΣΕΒΑΣΤΟΥ. **Rev.** S C within laurel wreath.

we now turn. These coins have a wide variety of designs referring to cults, festivals, myths, and historical events (Howgego, Heuchert and Burnett 2005). Provincial coin types can also respond to imperial ideology and articulate the relationship of a particular city to the emperor.

A good example is Fig. 5.48, a coin of Philippi. The reverse shows a statue of Augustus being crowned by a statue of the deified Julius Caesar. The design was probably inspired by actual statues erected in the colony, which served as a declaration of support for Augustus as well as a local focal

Figure 5.48. Leaded bronze 26mm, Philippi, reign of Augustus (RPC 1 1650). **Obv.** Laureate head of Augustus, COL AVG IVL PHIL IVSSV AVG. **Rev.** Three bases. On the central base is a statue of Augustus in military dress crowned by a statue of Divus Julius wearing a toga, AVG DIVI F DIVO IVL.

point that connected the inhabitants with their ruler. The representation of monuments, buildings and other structures on coins is typically Roman, and so the use of this particular design can be connected to a broader cultural shift in how civic identity was represented (Burnett 2011: 24–5). The legend specifically mentions the fact that the colony had been (re) founded by Augustus (IVSSV AVG), which, along with the full name of the colony (*Colonia Augusta Iulia Philippensis*), underscored the close connection between the city and the emperor.

Pergamum provides another local representation of Augustus and his position (Fig. 5.49). The obverse portrays the *demos* (a personification of the citizens) of Pergamum and of Sardis with a legend referring to both citizen bodies, celebrating an alliance or *homonoia* between the two (the alliance is also shown on coinage of Sardis; RPC 1 2988). The reverse shows the temple of Rome and Augustus with the cult statue of Augustus inside, accompanied by a legend that places the name of Augustus directly above the temple (CEBACTON), and then names the local official (*grammateus*) Kephalion. Dio observes that Pergamum's temple to Augustus (granted to the *koinon* or association of the Hellenes in Asia), along with that in Nicomedia (granted to the *koinon* of Bithynia), marked the beginning of ruler cult in the Roman Empire (Dio 51.20.6–9). Being one of the first to receive the honour would have been a source of local pride, and it is little wonder that the privilege is advertised on coinage. These provincial

Figure 5.49. Brass 20mm, Pergamum, c. AD 1 (?) (RPC 1 2362). **Obv.** The *demos* of Pergamum crowning the *demos* of Sardis with a wreath, ΠΕΡΓΑΜΗΝΩΝ ΚΑΙ ΣΑΡΔΙΑΝΩΝ. **Rev.** Temple with two columns enclosing a statue of Augustus, ϹΕΒΑϹΤΟΝ, ΚΕΦΑΛΙΩΝ ΓΡΑΜΜΑΤΕΥΩΝ.

imperial cults were known as *neokoria* and formed a point of rivalry between different cities, often featuring on provincial coin types (Burrell 2004).

Suetonius records that Augustus agreed to cults in the provinces only if they were shared with the goddess Roma (Suetonius, *Augustus* 52). On cistophori issued in the name of the commune of Asia (COM ASIAE) the temple was shown without any cult statues (Fig. 5.50). Later under the emperor Claudius the temple was shown with the statues of both Roma and Augustus (RPC 1 2221). But on Fig. 5.49 the figure of Roma is absent: only Augustus is portrayed. The different representations of the temple may be a reflection of the different audiences of the different coins – on the local brass coins of Pergamum the cult statue of Augustus could be shown alone, but this was not the case on the silver regional coinages (Burrell 2004: 20).

Cities could also connect themselves with the *princeps* by adopting imperial imagery directly. One of the best examples of this practice is the use of the Capricorn, Augustus' star sign (Fig. 5.51). Suetonius' comment that Augustus 'made his horoscope public and issued a silver coin stamped with the sign of the constellation Capricornus' reveals that, whatever the reality, the Romans believed the emperor had a role in the design of his coinage (Suetonius, *Augustus* 94.12). The Capricorn appears on denarii, cistophori, and aurei (RIC 1^2 125–30, 477–82, 547–8; the sign was also

Figure 5.50. Cistophorus, Pergamum, 19–18 BC (RPC 1 2219). **Obv.** Bare head of Augustus, IMP IX TR PO V. **Rev.** Temple with six columns inscribed ROM ET AVGVST on entablature, in field COM ASIAE.

Figure 5.51. Denarius, uncertain Spanish mint 2 (Colonia Patricia?), 18–17/16 BC (RIC 1² 128). **Obv.** Bare head of Augustus. **Rev.** Capricorn holding globe attached to rudder, cornucopia above its back; AVGVSTVS.

adopted in many other contexts, e.g. on signet rings and intaglios; see LaRocca et al. 2013: 251). The Capricorn is then adopted on the currency of local cities; Fig. 5.52 is an example from the North African city of Lepcis Magna. Fig. 5.53 is a coin of the client king of Mauretania, Ptolemaeus, son of Juba II. Ptolemaeus (AD 23–40), similar to other client kings, struck coinage using Roman and local motifs, including the Capricorn, reflecting his position as a ruler whose power was dependent on Rome (Salzmann 1974: 180). Examples such as these provide evidence for the reception of Augustan imagery. The die engravers of these local issues may have taken their designs from Augustan coinage, or from other Augustan visual media. But the adoption of imperial imagery was neither universal across

Figure 5.52. Bronze 20–22mm, Lepcis Magna, reign of Augustus (RPC 1 845). **Obv.** Bare head of Augustus. **Rev.** Capricorn with globe and cornucopia, LPQY in neo-punic below.

Figure 5.53. Denarius, Mauretania, King Ptolemaeus, AD 38/9. **Obv.** Diademed head of King Ptolemy of Mauretania, REX PTOLEMAEVS. **Rev.** Capricorn right, R A XV below.

the provinces nor uniform, demonstrating that the design of local coinage was not centrally regulated (Burnett 2011: 28). The decision to imitate or utilise a design associated with the emperor was thus probably the decision of the local provincial elite.

Provincial cities could also extend or adapt the emperor's image, particularly by connecting the imperial family with local cults. The empress in particular was frequently aligned with local goddesses, and was shown more frequently on provincial issues than on imperial coinage, at least before the reign of Hadrian. A good example of this phenomenon is provided by the coinage of Smyrna in Asia. As well as issuing a coin decorated with a Capricorn (Fig. 5.54), the city also released coins showing Augustus and Livia jugate (Fig. 5.55; Klose 1987), even though Livia did not appear on imperial coinage under Augustus. In this way the city of Smyrna, like other

Figure 5.54. Bronze 13mm, Smyrna, c. AD 4–14 (RPC 1 2468). **Obv.** Bare head of Augustus, ΣΕΒΑΣΤΟΝ. **Rev.** Capricorn, ΚΟΡΩΝΟΣ ΖΜΥΡΝΑΙΩΝ.

Figure 5.55. Leaded bronze 19mm, Smyrna, c. 10 BC (?) (RPC 1 2464). **Obv.** Laureate head of Augustus and draped bust of Livia, ΣΕΒΑΣΤΩΙ ΖΜΥΡΝΑΙΟΙ. **Rev.** Aphrodite Stratonikis leaning on column holding sceptre and Nike, dove on right, ΔΙΟΝΥΣΙΟΣ ΚΟΛΛΥΒΑΣ.

provincial cities, developed their own representations of the emperor and his family within a local context.

Fig. 5.56 is a later issue of Smyrna, struck some time between AD 4 and 14. The obverse carries the busts of Augustus and Tiberius, while the reverse aligns Livia to the local goddess Aphrodite Stratonikis. The goddess is shown leaning on a column holding a sceptre and Nike, as on earlier coins (Fig. 5.55), but the legend names the figure as Livia: ΛΙΒΙΑΝ. The alignment of imperial women to local cults can also be seen in other cities and on other media (Matheson 1996; Bartman 2012: 416). Under Tiberius, the bust of Livia is placed alongside that of the local Senate on an issue of Smyrna (RPC 1 2469). Caligula's sister Drusilla is later aligned with Persephone (RPC 1 2472), and Nero's wife Poppaea is shown as Nike (RPC 1 2486). This seeming freedom in the interpretation of the imperial image (with cities often going further than 'official' imperial imagery) is most frequently seen for imperial women, who appear to have formed a point of contact between the emperor and his subjects (on this same phenomenon in portraiture see Fejfer 2008).

Figure 5.56. Leaded bronze 19mm, Smyrna, c. AD 4–14 (RPC 1 2467). **Obv.** Bare heads of Augustus and Tiberius facing each other, CEBACTON TIBEPION KAICAPA. **Rev.** Livia as Aphrodite Stratonikis leaning on column holding sceptre and Nike; dove to right, monogram to left, ΛΙΒΙΑΝ ΖΜΥΡΝΑΙΩΝ ΚΟΡΩΝΟC.

5.9 Establishing the Succession: Gaius, Lucius and Tiberius

Augustus' position was a collection of powers, not an established hereditary monarchy. What would happen to the Roman world after the *princeps'* death was consequently something that had to be negotiated. Augustus wanted a successor but how exactly this might take place was tricky. Succession became an issue as Augustus fell ill in 23 BC: the *princeps* gave his ring to Agrippa and state documents to his fellow consul Calpurnius Piso. He did not name, and probably did not have, an heir at this stage (Dio 53.30.1–2). After all, naming a successor would immediately reveal the real power of Augustus' position, diminishing the Republican façade (Gruen 2005: 39).

An heir could not be appointed or named in a will, since Augustus' position was dependent on a series of magistracies and powers that were not transferable. But after 23 BC, Augustus sought to grant some of these powers to others, enabling them to succeed him upon his death. Agrippa married Augustus' daughter Julia in 21 BC and was granted tribunician power in 18 BC. The marriage also bore grandchildren for Augustus: Gaius and Lucius, whom Augustus adopted as his own sons (Dio 54.18.1; Suetonius, *Augustus* 64.1; Velleius Paterculus 2.96.1).

While the sharing of powers and magistracies may have been the political mechanism for a succession, coinage reveals a different, altogether more

Figure 5.57. Leaded bronze 18mm, Aegae (Asia), 10–1 BC (RPC 1 2428). **Obv.** Bare head of Lucius Caesar, ΑΙΓΑΕΩΝ ΛΕΥΚΙΟΝ. **Rev.** Bare head of Gaius Caesar, ΓΑΙΟΝ ΔΙΦΙΛΟC ΦΑΙΤΑ ΑΓΩΝΟΘΕΤΑC.

overt statement. Agrippa is shown alongside Augustus on Roman coinage, but Gaius and Lucius come to dominate Rome's currency. It must have been clear to anyone who used Roman coinage in the later years of Augustus' life that Gaius and Lucius were the appointed successors. Indeed, if we look at provincial coinage, we find that the message was received loud and clear.

Over 40 provincial cities struck coinage showing Gaius and Lucius (Wolters 2002: 315). Portraits of the brothers were shown (e.g. Fig. 5.57), as well as full figure portrayals of both wearing togas (e.g. in Tarracco in Spain; RPC 1 212). In Caesaraugusta a statue group of Augustus, Gaius and Lucius was chosen as an obverse type (RPC 1 319). The appearance of the two adopted sons of Augustus on provincial coinage is not surprising: they had a prominent public role, particularly after 2 BC when both brothers became leaders of the youth (*principes iuventutis*) (*RGDA* 14; Cooley 2009: 162–7; Pollini 1987: 2).

Gaius and Lucius Caesar appear on imperial coinage with Julia in 13 BC as part of a series marking the renewal of tribunician power for both Augustus and Agrippa (Fig. 5.58). On the coins, as in the *RGDA*, Agrippa is presented as Augustus' colleague, shown seated next to Augustus (Fig. 5.59; *RGDA* 8.2; Cooley 2009: 140). Types with the portrait of Augustus on one side and Agrippa on the other were also struck (RIC 1^2 408–9): on denarii both Augustus and Agrippa are shown bare-headed, while on the aureus issue Augustus wears an oak wreath and Agrippa a combined mural and rostral crown (Figure 5.60). The honour of this crown

Figure 5.58.
Denarius, Rome,
C. Marius c.f. Tro,
13 BC (RIC 1² 405).
Obv. Bare head
of Augustus within
oak wreath,
AVGVSTVS DIVI
F. **Rev.** Head of Julia
with wreath above,
between the heads
of Gaius and Lucius,
C MARIVS TRO III
VIR.

Figure 5.59. Denarius, Rome, C. Sulpicius Platorinus, 13 BC (RIC 1² 407). **Obv.** Bare head of Augustus, CAESAR AVGVSTVS. **Rev.** Augustus and Agrippa both bare-headed and togate seated on *bisellium* (two-person seat) on platform decorated with *rostra*, upright staff or spear to the left, C SVLPICIVS PLATORIN.

Figure 5.60. Aureus, Rome, C. Sulpicius Platorinus, 13 BC (RIC 1² 409). **Obv.** Head of Augustus with oak wreath, CAESAR AVGVSTVS. **Rev.** Head of Agrippa wearing combined mural and rostral crown, M AGRIPPA PLATORINVS III VIR.

Figure **5.61.** Denarius, Lugdunum, 9–8 BC (RIC 1² 199). **Obv.** Laureate head of Augustus, AVGVSTVS DIVI F. **Rev.** Gaius Caesar galloping on horse holding sword and shield in his left hand, *aquila* between two standards on ground, C CAES AVGVS F.

Figure **5.62.** Denarius, Lugdunum, 9–8 BC (RIC 1² 201a). **Obv.** Laureate head of Augustus, AVGVSTVS DIVI F. **Rev.** Augustus, togate, seated on stool on platform, extending right hand to infant held out by cloaked barbarian, IMP XIIII in exergue.

was given to Agrippa by Augustus, and is described by Dio as a 'golden crown adorned with ship's beaks' (49.14.4).

Gaius Caesar appears in a military context riding a horse on the reverse of coins struck at Lugdunum in c. 8 BC named as the son of Augustus (AVGVS F.) (Fig. 5.61). The type probably refers to Gaius' participation in military exercises with the legions (Dio 55.6.4); this issue may have been used by Augustus to pay the soldiers the donative mentioned by Dio in connection with this event (Pollini 1985). This issue is die linked with another that has a reverse showing Augustus receiving a child from a barbarian (Fig. 5.62), perhaps a reference to the peace and subsequent exchange of child hostages that followed Tiberius' successful German campaigns.

The *RGDA* records that the Roman equestrians hailed 'each of them [Gaius and Lucius Caesar] as leader of the youth, and honoured them with silver shields and spears' (*RGDA* 14.1; Cooley 2009: 166–7). This honour

Figure 5.63. Denarius, Lugdunum, c. 2 BC–c. AD 5 or later (RIC 1^2 207). **Obv.** Laureate head of Augustus, CAESAR AVGVSTVS DIVI F PATER PATRIAE. **Rev.** Gaius Caesar on left and Lucius Caesar on right, each standing togate resting hand on shield; behind each shield is a spear, above on left a *simpulum*, and above on right a *lituus*, C L CAESARES AVGVSTI F COS DESIG PRINC IVVENT.

was commemorated on coinage struck at Lugdunum showing Gaius and Lucius with the shields and spears, along with a *simpulum* (symbolising Gaius' position as *pontifex*) and *lituus* (representing Lucius' position as augur), with a legend naming them as *principes iuventutis*, consuls designate, and as the sons of Augustus (Fig. 5.63, RIC 1^2 205–12). The accumulation of honours shown on this series is significant, since the two brothers could only 'succeed' Augustus by acquiring powers similar to his. RIC dates the production of these coins to the period c. 2 BC–AD 4 'or beyond', and archaeological finds suggest production continued until at least AD 5 (Wolters 2002: 310). In fact, the *only* aurei and denarii produced between 8 BC and AD 13 were of this type, which was struck in extremely large quantities. Coins of this series are found not only within the borders of the Roman Empire, but in regions of Germany and as far north as Scandinavia; they are also one of the most common Roman coins found in India (Wolters 2002: 298). The concentrated production of a single type over several years, focused on the young Caesars, indicates a concentrated effort by Augustus to place his heirs in the spotlight.

Some of these coins carry an additional X on the reverse (Fig. 5.64). This 'X' has variously been thought to stand for 'ten' or *denarius*, or been identified as a mint or control mark. Most recently Wolters has suggested the X refers to the posthumous honours granted to Gaius and Lucius after their deaths. The *Tabula Hebana* and *Tabula Siarensis* (two bronze inscriptions from the reign of Tiberius) record that their names were to be added to the hymn of the *Salii* (priests of Mars) and that ten *centuriae* were to be

Figure 5.64. Denarius, Lugdunum (?), c. 2 BC–c. AD 5 or later (RIC 1² 212). **Obv.** Laureate head of Augustus, CAESAR AVGVSTVS DIVI F PATER PATRIAE. **Rev.** Gaius Caesar on left and Lucius Caesar on right, each standing togate resting hand on shield; behind each shield is a spear, above on right a *lituus*, and above on left a *simpulum*. X above shields, C L CAESARES AVGVSTI F COS DESIG PRINC IVVENT.

named after them (Wolters 2002: 305–6). The suggestion that the X refers to these ten centuries is strengthened by the fact that these 'X' coins appear to be found mostly in Rome and Italy (although it may be that not all publications list whether the coin is of the 'X' variety; Wolters 2002: 317–21). Given that the other types of this series are found throughout the Empire, Wolters argues that the localised finds of the 'X' series suggest either that this series was produced in Rome, or that it was shipped to Rome and Italy from Lugdunum. It may thus have been produced with a particular audience in mind who would have understood the significance of the small addition.

Imitations

Figure 5.65. Perfunctory imitation of the RIC 1² 207.

Figure 5.66.
Anonymous
imitation of
RIC 1² 207.

Given the quantities in which the type was struck, it is no surprise that the Gaius and Lucius issue was a popular design for imitation. Different types of coin imitation existed in the ancient world, a fact recognised by the Athenian law of Nikophon in 375/4 BC (*SEG* 26.72), which listed five categories of imitations, not all of which were considered invalid currency. In his study of imitations van Alfen identified seven types of coins: the prototype (original coin); artistic imitation (where the original coin type was adapted); anonymous imitation (very close to the prototype); marked imitation (which imitates the prototype but with intentional differences); perfunctory imitation (the coin refers to a known prototype but we cannot be sure it is a direct imitation of the original – it may be an 'imitation of an imitation'); plated or debased imitation (not of good silver); and the counterfeit coin (privately manufactured coins aimed at winning profit through fraud) (van Alfen 2005). Two types of imitations of the Gaius and Lucius type are shown above. Fig. 5.65, with its rough rendering of the portrait of Augustus and nonsense lettering, might be classified as a perfunctory imitation, while Fig. 5.66 is perhaps best labelled an anonymous imitation. Both, however, are probably of good silver and thus cannot be labelled 'counterfeit'.

Like other posthumous monuments erected for Gaius and Lucius, coinage was produced in their name after their deaths in AD 4 and AD 2 respectively. Augustus was forced to alter his plans for succession, but it was some time before this was communicated on coinage. It was only in AD 10–12 that asses were produced in Rome bearing Tiberius' name and titles

Figure 5.67. Denarius, Lugdunum, AD 13–14 (RIC 1² 222). **Obv.** Laureate head of Augustus, CAESAR AVGVSTVS DIVI F PATER PATRIAE. **Rev.** Tiberius laureate in triumphal *quadriga* holding laurel branch and eagle-tipped sceptre, TI CAESAR AVG F TR POT XV.

Figure 5.68. Denarius, Lugdunum, AD 13–14 (RIC 1² 226). **Obv.** Laureate head of Augustus, CAESAR AVGVSTVS DIVI F PATER PATRIAE. **Rev.** Bare head of Tiberius, TI CAESAR AVG F TR POT XV.

(RIC 1² 469–71), and that bronze coinage produced at Lugdunum began to carry his portrait. When the design of aurei and denarii finally changed from the Gaius and Lucius type in AD 13–14, it is to highlight Tiberius as successor (RIC 1² 219–26). Tiberius is shown as triumphator (Fig. 5.67), and a double portrait issue was struck (Fig. 5.68). Thus from 8 BC until the end of Augustus' rule, precious metal coinage focused on succession, a reflection no doubt of the genuine concern as to what would happen after the *princeps'* death. Coinage provides a powerful contemporary insight into what must have been a very real source of anxiety in Rome. It also suggests that Augustus and his advisors recognised that any successor not only had to possess magistracies and official powers, but also needed to be well known amongst the population of the Roman Empire. Coinage offered a medium to help achieve this goal.

5.10 After Augustus

The image of Tiberius as *triumphator* continued to be produced at Lugdunum after Augustus' death in AD 14 (RIC 1² *Tiberius* 1–2; see Strabo, *Geography* 4.3.2 on Lugdunum as a mint under Tiberius). Overall, in fact, Tiberius' precious metal coinage was largely unchanging in its design. This is less surprising when we consider that precious metal currency was also largely static in design in the final years of Augustus' rule, with the Gaius and Lucius type being produced year after year. Tiberius' bronze coins, however, were more varied in their imagery. Coinage of all metals commemorated the deification of Augustus and his status as a *divus*. Like *Divus Iulius* before him, Augustus' portrait was now accompanied by a star, and bronze types were struck in Rome showing Augustus with a radiate crown, another symbol of his divinity (Fig. 5.69; from Nero the meaning of the radiate crown would change as it came to be used as a denominational indicator). At times Augustus' portrait is accompanied by Jupiter's thunderbolt. The radiate Augustus is also shown in a *quadriga* of elephants (Fig. 5.70).

These references to the divine Augustus are not only found at the beginning of Tiberius' reign, but continue to be struck throughout his rule, underscoring Tiberius' role as Augustus' (pious) successor. An example of this is Fig. 5.71, struck in c. AD 34–7 and decorated with Augustus' divine portrait on the obverse and an eagle on a globe on the reverse. The eagle would later

Figure 5.69. As, Rome, AD 14–37 (RIC 1² *Tiberius* 72). **Obv.** Radiate head of Augustus with star above and thunderbolt in front, DIVVS AVGVSTVS PATER. **Rev.** Draped female figure seated on stool holding patera and sceptre, S C on either side.

Figure 5.70. Sestertius, Rome, AD 35–36 (RIC 1² *Tiberius* 62). **Obv.** *Quadriga* of elephants with riders with radiate figure of Augustus seated in car holding laurel branch and long sceptre, DIVO AVGVSTO S P Q R. **Rev.** TI CAESAR DIVI AVG F AVGVST PM TR POT XXXVII around S C.

Figure 5.71. As, Rome, AD 34–37 (RIC 1² *Tiberius* 82). **Obv.** Radiate head of Augustus, DIVVS AVGVSTVS PATER. **Rev.** Eagle standing on globe with wings spread and head turned right, S C.

come to be a standard image used to communicate imperial deification ceremonies (*consecratio*). This issue and others like it demonstrate the continued presence of Augustus on Roman coinage after AD 14. The coins struck for him during his lifetime would also not have immediately disappeared, but would continue to circulate for decades. Augustus continued to have a presence in daily life well after his death.

6

Coins and Daily Life

This volume has largely focused on the significance of particular coins and their imagery. The examples discussed have revealed how the elite used coinage to express specific ideas at specific moments in time, revealing that in the Roman world at this time coin design was taken seriously as a medium of communication. But this money, once created, was used by different segments of society in different contexts. Ancient coinage did not exist in a modern-day museum collection to be studied one type at a time; rather, coinage joined the mass of currency already in circulation, and was used in economic, social, and cultic contexts. Understanding the different contexts of coin use in the Roman world, and how experiences of Roman money differed according to class, occupation and where one lived is vital. These considerations not only allow us to better analyse coinage and its imagery, but add to our understanding of daily life in antiquity.

6.1 Supplying the Army

Keeping the army paid and well supplied was obviously important in the Roman world, and this was one reason for striking coinage (Howgego 1995: 36). Military expenditure must have formed a significant part of the Roman economy: the wages for a single legion in the first century BC cost 713,550 denarii (although expenses were deducted from their pay), and Cicero notes that the cost of an army was around 2,235,417 sestertii (Cicero, *Verrine Orations* 2.1.36; Rosenstein 2011: 140). But we cannot simply equate the number of coins struck to the cost of a particular war: coinage already in circulation, returned to the government through taxes, rents, or other means could also be used to make state payments (Burnett 1987b: 86–99). Rather than only striking brand new coinage to pay for a particular war, some or many of the costs may have been met from existing money or resources (e.g. grain).

Indeed, keeping the army supplied was more complicated than simply shipping some gold to the frontier. If soldiers were to buy products they had

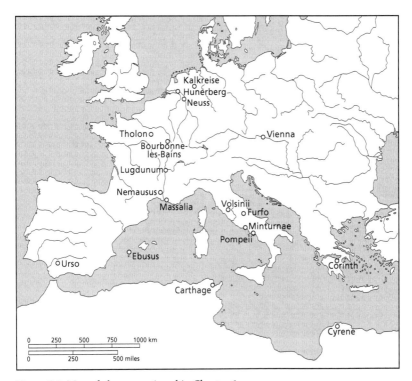

Figure 6.1. Map of places mentioned in Chapter 6.

to have access to a variety of denominations. The annual pay of a legionary
was 300 denarii, but a loaf of bread cost around a semis in the Republic, and
a half litre of ordinary wine cost around an as, though prices might vary
from region to region and according to season (Burnett 1987b: 96). Just as
today we would rarely go to buy milk with a $100 note or £100 note (and if
we did we would probably be chastised by the shopkeeper), or would not
think to buy a new car using only penny or cent coins, so too the Roman
world needed a variety of denominations in order to facilitate different
types of transaction. The Roman government had to ensure there was a mix
of denominations in the military camps which would have enabled the
soldiers to make purchases.

The gap in the production of bronze coinage during the Republic (see
p. 11) suggests that coin production for everyday transactions was not
a primary concern of the Republican government. But we do find small
change in imperial Roman army camps. Soldiers from this period were

likely paid in a mix of denominations; for the army at least, the Roman government was concerned about liquidity (that is, that there was enough money to meet demand). In German military camps in particular, asses from Lugdunum and Nemausus are common, and other bronzes from Spain are found; these coins were probably brought by Roman soldiers as they moved from Spain to the northern frontier (García-Bellido 2008). Silver denarii had been the common method of paying soldiers in the Republic, and it was assumed that the practice continued into the imperial period, but scholars are now increasingly entertaining the idea that under Augustus gold and bronze coins may also have been included in military pay, although we don't know in what quantities (Wolters 2001). One imagines that the supply of small change would have been particularly important to soldiers in regions where there was no locally available currency.

What happened if there was not enough money? We find some evidence of liquidity problems in an Augustan camp on the Hunerberg (Nijmegen, The Netherlands). The camp was occupied between c. 19 and 16/12 BC and is probably connected with the campaigns of Drusus. Excavations revealed silver coins in the Augustan contexts, among which were three plated denarii (coins with a bronze or lead core just coated in silver rather than being wholly made of silver). In fact, plated coins are found quite frequently on archaeological sites (Kemmers 2006: 34; at the site of Neuss in Germany plated coins make up around 50% of the silver finds). Plated coins have traditionally been interpreted as counterfeit issues, but their frequency in archaeological contexts suggests that the Roman government may have been responsible for them, or at the very least tolerated their presence as long as they were not used in official governmental transactions (Kemmers 2006: 35–6). The high volume of plated denarii here and elsewhere might suggest they came into existence to solve a liquidity problem, ensuring enough silver coinage to allow the economy to function smoothly at moments when there was a shortage. On the other hand, their presence in archaeological strata may simply be because their users realised the coins were plated and threw them away, or didn't bother to look for them once lost (whereas the loss of a high value gold coin would likely have sparked an intensive search by the user, meaning that these types of coins are less frequently found in excavations). Whatever the reason, soldiers on the frontiers used a variety of coins, not all of which may have been 'official' or of pure silver.

Looking closely at the types of coins found on military sites reveals that, for some locations at least, the government chose specific imagery to send to the army. In the Flavian period Victory types were common amongst the coins found on the northern frontier, while in Italy building types were more common. This phenomenon, choosing particular imagery to decorate particular coins for particular audiences, is called audience targeting (Kemmers 2006). Some coin types may have specifically been designed for military pay, and the messages on these coins may have been different to the coins struck to pay for public buildings, for example. This is an emerging area of research, and future work will determine whether audience targeting also existed in other periods. The series of temporary legionary camps in northern Europe connected with the campaigns of Drusus, Tiberius, and others form an excellent body of evidence for this type of exploration. Each camp was only occupied for a short amount of time (several years at most) before being abandoned, meaning that the coins found in the excavations of these camps can be associated with military activity in a specific time period. Examining the coin finds from these camps reveals the types of coinage used by soldiers under Augustus.

6.2 Kalkriese and the Battle of Teutoburg Forest

A good case study for studying the coins used by soldiers on the frontier is the site of Kalkriese in Germany, the suggested location for the battle of Teutoburg Forest in AD 9. The battle resulted in a significant Roman defeat: several legions and cohorts were lost under the leadership of Publius Quinctilius Varus (Dio 56.18–24; Suetonius, *Augustus* 23; Tacitus, *Annals* 1.55–71; Velleius Paterculus 117–20; Berger 1996; Berger 2000). The connection of Kalkriese with the battle of Teutoburg forest is not universally accepted (some connect it with a later campaign of Germanicus, see Kemmers 2006: 57), but the site clearly saw a battle between Roman and Germanic forces. Thus, finds from the site reveal what coinage soldiers used along the frontier. Although the corpses of Roman soldiers may have been robbed after the German victory, the coin finds that survive provide us with some idea of what was carried onto the battlefield (Berger 2000: 16). A large portion of the aurei and denarii found at Kalkriese were of the Gaius and Lucius as *principes iuventutis* type (Fig. 5.63): 7 out of 19 Augustan aurei and 26 of the 115 denarii carried this design (Berger 1996). As mentioned in the previous chapter, this coin type was struck in quantity, but now we possess evidence that some of these coins were shipped to the troops on the northern frontier, communicating Augustus' succession plans to a vital power base.

Coins that are found close together at Kalkriese, and a reasonable distance from other coins, may represent the 'purses' of individual soldiers who died on the battlefield. Some of these are detailed in Table 7. Though some of these 'purses' contained only asses or denarii, others contained a mix of metals; those containing higher value coins may have belonged to officers, those with lower value coins perhaps the property of lower ranking troops. What these coin groups demonstrate is that these soldiers had access to a mix

Table 7 Selection of 'purses' from Kalkriese.

Purse	Find spot	Berger catalogue nos.	Coins and associated finds	Publication
1	50	17072–3	5 Lugdunum asses (*4 of them stuck together in a roll, one with slash marks on the obverse*)	Berger 1996, 124
			4 denarii (*RRC 458/1, 318/1, RIC 1² 207, one illegible type*)	Berger 2000, 17
			1 silver rivet	
2	50	18124a–e	5 denarii (*RRC 320/1, 463/1, 468/1, RIC 1² 187a, RIC 1² 210*)	Berger 1996, 128–30 Berger 2000, 17
3	83	55–63, 67–8	10 Lugdunum asses (*all countermarked. Countermarks include 1 x IMPL, 3x rectangles, 1 x AVC, 1 x VAR. One coin with cuts on the obverse*)	Berger 1996, 136
			1 halved Vienna as (*RPC 1 517*)	Berger 2000, 17
4	100	H1-19	15 denarii (*RRC 299/1a, 316/1, 342/5, 360/1, 372/2, 455/1, 463/1, 463/2, 494/23, 544/14, 544/24, RIC 1² 207 (3 examples), RIC 1² 208*)	Berger 1996, 148–50
			3 quinarii (*RRC 332/1, 333/1, RIC 1² 376*)	Berger 2000, 17
			1 aureus (*RIC 1² 206*)	
5	121	5–7	3 Lugdunum asses (*all countermarked. Countermarks are: 1x circle, 1 x rectangle, 1x unknown*)	Berger 1996, 154 Berger 2000, 17

of denominations, and that the currency was of mixed age: recent Augustan coins were used alongside older coinage from the Republic, with some coins more than 100 years old at the time of their loss (e.g. Purses 1 and 2, which contained denarii originally struck in 104 BC and 103 BC respectively). You can look up the images of the coin types by typing in the RIC numbers into *Online Coins of the Roman Empire* (http://numismatics.org/ocre/) and the RRC numbers into *Coins of the Roman Republic Online* (http://numismatics .org/crro/). The impression formed by the designs of currency in circulation was thus a juxtaposition of Augustan ideology against old Republican types, an intersection one imagines that Augustus, with his emphasis on restoring the *res publica*, would not have minded at all.

The purses also reveal that coins could be cut in half to create smaller denominations, like the halved as from the Vienna mint in purse 3 (Fig. 6.2 is a similarly halved Vienna as). This phenomenon was probably a solution to a local shortage of semisses or other smaller denominations (although the cutting of older, heavier coins could be performed to create pieces that matched a new metrological standard). If one did not have the correct change, one could simply cut a coin in half to create the desired denomination. That this practice was common is also suggested by the Augustan finds from the Hunerberg: 81 of the 90 Republican bronze coins found here were halved (Kemmers 2006: 81). But although this practice suggests a functional approach to coinage, the coin's design may have still have played a role. The double-headed Janus on the obverse of Republican issues and the double portraits on the issues from Vienna and Lugdunum would have

Figure 6.2. Halved as, Vienna, 36 BC (?) (RPC 1 517). The original coin would have been decorated with bare heads of Caesar on the left and Octavian on right with the legend IMP CAESAR DIVI F DIVI IVLI; only Caesar survives on this halved specimen. On the reverse is the remains of a prow with superstructure, C(olonia) I(ulia) V(iennensis).

provided a rough guideline for cutting the coin down the middle (with each half then carrying one portrait), although the reverse design of the coin would be destroyed in the process. This is an important reminder that coinage was first and foremost an economic instrument intended to serve the economy.

Many of the coins found at Kalkriese (including those in 'purses') have countermarks, which are commonly found on coins from the early imperial period along the Rhine and Danube rivers (Berger 1996: 47). Indeed, 195 of the 205 Lugdunum bronze coins found at Kalkriese published by Berger had countermarks. A countermark could be applied to a coin for a variety of reasons, but those found along the Roman northern frontier in this period stem from a very particular context: military donatives. When generals gave money to their troops, they would stamp the coins with a countermark carrying their name or a symbol (Berger 1996: 47–8). This money was given to soldiers in addition to their normal pay to ensure loyalty and support. Amongst the countermarks found from Kalkriese are some referencing Varus (VAR, and perhaps also C.VAL which may stand for C. Numonius Vala, Varus' cavalry commander). By deciding to countermark a coin in this way, the original design of the issue is transformed to meet a new context. On Fig. 6.3, for example, the countermark has been stamped over Augustus' portrait, demonstrating the primacy of the countermark over the original message of the coin. A soldier receiving this coin as a bonus to his normal pay would perhaps associate the design and the object with his commander, not necessarily the emperor.

Figure 6.3. Lugdunum as with countermark VAR on the obverse.

Countermarking

The countermarking of coinage by Roman generals is a phenomenon concentrated in the early imperial period. More generally, the practice was probably confined to local civic authorities and the Roman government. Local cities may have countermarked their coinage on the occasion of an imperial visit or an imperial victory, to mark a change in imperial titulature, upon the death or as part of the posthumous condemnation (*damnatio memoriae*) of an emperor, or to reflect changes to a city's titles. Countermarks could also change or confirm the value of a (worn) coin, or clarify how a coin related to others in circulation. Countermarks carrying the name of particular legions on worn coins may have been placed there to ensure the coin was accepted as valid currency by the troops. In sum, the practice was used for a variety of purposes, some of which may be impossible for the historian to reconstruct.

Purses 1 and 3 contained coins with slash marks, a phenomenon found in high concentration on the Lugdunum altar asses at Kalkriese: about half of the first series of these issues found at the site were intentionally defaced through stabbing, cuts and slashes (Fig. 6.4). Berger, observing that for the most part the defacement was performed on the side of the coin carrying the portrait of Augustus, suggested that the mutilation was performed by soldiers dissatisfied with the emperor (Berger 1996: 55). Kemmers and Myberg suggested instead that the mutilation of Roman coins at Kalkriese may have been performed by the Germans – after defeating the Romans, the victors may have decided to deface this symbol of Roman power (Kemmers and Myrberg 2011: 98). The differing opinions here demonstrate the difficulties associated with interpreting coinage within the archaeological record. If Berger is correct then the finds suggest that the money continued to be used after its defacement (otherwise there would be little point carrying it in a purse), whereas the theory of Kemmers and Myberg suggests that after the coins were mutilated they were abandoned. Other known examples of the ritual mutilation of coins, discussed below, suggest that Kemmers and Myberg may be correct: it is unlikely a coin remained acceptable currency once subjected to this treatment. In this case, the coins from Kalkriese reveal the barbarian opposition to Augustus and the Roman Empire he represented.

Similar concentrations of defaced coinage have been found elsewhere in Germany and throughout the Roman Empire. It is not always clear why the

Figure 6.4. Lugdunum as from Kalkriese with cut marks and piercings.

coins were treated in this way. 48 aurei were recently uncovered in the excavations of a building in Tholon (France). The coins, all struck between 46 and 27 BC, contained many specimens that had been folded or warped. Issues of Antony, Octavian and Caesar were all treated in this fashion, so it cannot have been politically motivated and the find spot did not have any known cultic associations. In sum, it is a mystery, particularly given the high value of the deposit, although the mutilation of coinage is a known phenomenon in Gaul until the reign of Claudius (Suspène, Chausserie-Laprée and Rétif 2016).

6.3 Coins in Ritual Practice

Coins could also play a role in religious activity, and were often given as an offering to deities. Giving a coin as part of a ritual act could, at times, involve the mutilation of the coin involved. Destroying the coin in this way ensured that, once offered to a deity, the coin stayed in the deity's possession and could no longer be used to buy things in the everyday (profane) sphere. The spread of coinage across the Mediterranean thus brought with it an interesting shift in ritual practice: instead of offering a cow, or a libation, one might offer its value, represented by a particular denomination. By cutting, piercing, or folding the coin, it could be 'ritually killed' before being offered, although this was not a prerequisite (Piette and Depeyrot 2008: 52). The defacement of coinage within a ritual context is most frequent in eastern Gaul and in Germany, suggesting that it was a regional practice (Piette and Depeyrot 2008: 52; see Kiernan 2001 for Britain).

At the site of Bourbonne-les-Bains in France a mixture of mutilated and non-mutilated coins were found in what is probably a religious context. More than 4,500 Roman coins were discovered at the Roman catchment installation of a hot spring at this site, with a high number of Augustan issues (Sauer 2005: xiii). Cuts were rare on the coins dated to before AD 9–11, which may indicate that it was Roman soldiers who initially offered coins at the spring (the practice of offering coins at bodies of water is more common in Italy than in Gaul). The coins that were cut may then have been offered later in time by the local Gallic population, who ritually mutilated their offerings in accordance with local practice (Sauer 2005: 97, 147). That the coins from the spring are mostly Roman suggests that the initial dedicators were Roman soldiers; civilians in Gaul in this period would be unlikely to have had access to such a large supply of imperial coinage (Sauer 2005: 147). Although many of the cut marks on the coins from Bourbonne-les-Bains are random, some appear to have been intentionally placed: three quadrantes decorated with a bull have cuts running across the body of the animal, suggesting that perhaps in this instance the person offering the coin wanted to symbolically kill or sacrifice the animal shown. These coins, and others, demonstrate the ritual use of money (Aarts 2005). If we adopt anthropological models, offering money to the gods is classified as a 'long-term sphere of exchange' (offerings to the gods to ensure the cosmic order), as opposed to 'short-term' exchanges (daily exchanges between individuals to obtain goods) (Aarts 2005; Parry and Bloch 1989).

Many of the coin offerings found in ritual contexts are not of particularly high value. Small coins that are probably quadrantes with an eagle on the reverse compose 41.94% of the entire assemblage from Bourbonne-les-Bains (Fig. 6.5). As mentioned above, bull quadrantes are also found (Fig. 6.6), and both issues were likely struck at auxiliary mints in the region. Quadrantes were the smallest denomination available within the Roman currency system in this period. This was probably what made them attractive as votive offerings; the act was symbolic rather than a 'real' exchange of value (Sauer 2005: 37). Although not quite the same thing, think about what coin you might choose to throw into the Trevi fountain in Rome – people normally choose small coin denominations rather than large euro notes. Both quadrantes carry the portrait of Augustus on the obverse, an indication of how, even unconsciously and unintentionally, the emperor's image may have formed a backdrop to daily life.

Figure 6.5. Brass 18–19mm, quadrans (?), auxiliary mint of Lugdunum, c. 10 BC (RPC 1 508 = RIC 1² 227). **Obv.** Laureate head of Augustus, IMP CAESAR. **Rev.** Eagle with wings spread and head turned left, AVGVSTVS.

Figure 6.6. Brass 18–19mm, quadrans (?), auxiliary mint of Lugdunum c. 10 BC (RPC 1 509 = RIC 1² 228). **Obv.** Bare head of Augustus, IMP CAESAR. **Rev.** Butting bull, AVGVSTVS DIVI F.

Offerings may have been intentionally selected for their low value, but imagery might also be influential at times. The spring at Nemausus, for example, contained many halved asses of the Nemausus mint given as votive offerings. These coins had a double portrait on the obverse, with Augustus on one side and Agrippa on the other (Fig. 5.44). But the deposit contained far more halves with the portrait of Augustus on them than Agrippa. This may indicate a preference for the imperial portrait when choosing a coin half to sacrifice, perhaps because some of these offerings were for the emperor (Sauer 2005: 20). Suetonius provides evidence of this practice, observing that people would annually throw a coin into the Lacus Curtius in the Roman Forum for Augustus' welfare (Suetonius, *Augustus* 57).

Coins offered at temples might be placed in specially designed money boxes or *thesauri* (Crawford 2003). An example of this practice can be found in Volsinii (Orvieto, Italy). Here a stone *thesaurus* was found in front of a tufa altar within a large Etruscan sanctuary that was renovated in the Late Republican or early Augustan period (Fig. 6.7; Ranucci 2011). The *thesaurus* was designed so that coin offerings might be placed through a hole in the lid, falling into the container below. The excavations uncovered ash, coals and the remains of sacrifices covering the lid, including the hole. This surface layer is dated to the early imperial period, the point at which the *thesaurus* appears to have fallen out of use. 221 coins were found in the *thesaurus*, including 185 Republican asses, 1 Republican quinarius (RRC 342/2a), 2 Republican denarii (RRC 422/1a, 528/3), 18 coins with the legend DIVOS IVLIVS (Fig. 3.9 for the type), and 13 asses of Augustus. The coins were placed vertically in the *thesaurus*, sometimes in groups of four and five, and the dates of the coins do not correspond with their placement in the container (i.e. the oldest coins are not at the bottom). These features suggest that, in this particular case, the coins were intentionally deposited in the *thesaurus* at one moment in time (Ranucci 2011: 956). Whether the coins were all removed from circulation at the time of the deposit, or whether the coins had been kept elsewhere in the sanctuary as offerings and only placed together later, is impossible to know.

Coin offerings at temples were, in theory, reusable. If not cut or mutilated, they could be spent for the upkeep of the sanctuary, a practice evident in surviving epigraphic evidence (Crawford 2003). For example, the charter of the Caesarian colony at Urso in Spain (*colonia Iulia Genetiva*) states that any money brought to the temples as a sacred offering could only be used for the benefit of that temple or cult; similarly laws at the Italian city of Furfo dating to 58 BC note that 'whatever money is received, that money may be used to buy, lend, put out at interest or give, so that the temple may be improved and more handsome' (Adamik 2003). The regulations at Furfo specifically state that money used in this manner is to be considered 'profane' (*profanum*). This stipulation indicates the need to declare that the money was able to shift between the divine and profane spheres of exchange.

These regulations indicate that, once offered at a temple, coinage was earmarked for use by (or on behalf of) a deity. Although official definitions of money characterise it as a neutral medium of all-purpose exchange, we often 'classify' or 'earmark' our money, meaning it is put

1

2

Figure 6.7. *Thesaurus* from Orvieto *in situ*. The top image shows the *thesaurus* lid before the altar, and the bottom image shows the vessel that lay beneath to catch the coins offered.

aside for a particular purpose or purchase (e.g. setting aside money for college; Zelizer 1997). This has been characterised as the 'social life' of money, and was also present in the Roman world, where particular sums of money could only be spent on particular things (Rowan 2013b). Another example from this period is the *sanctius aerarium*, the Roman treasury where money was kept specifically for use against the Gauls. Caesar was criticised for removing the money from this treasury; Appian writes there was a curse on anyone who removed the money for any purpose other than to fight the Gauls. Caesar reportedly retorted that he had subjugated the Gauls completely and so had freed Rome from the curse (App. 2.6.41).

Coins are also found in foundation deposits, placed beneath the foundation of a temple or other structure as an offering to the gods, probably for the protection of the structure (Crawford 2003). Although often overlooked in excavations, coinage could also be placed below the floors of other structures like baths, between the joinery of Roman buildings, and even beneath the masts of ships – again, one imagines, for the protection of the structure or as a good omen (Rowan 2011: 7–8). The practice was not confined to architectural structures: a coin of Commodus was found inside the colossal bronze statue of Hercules now in the Vatican, perhaps placed there by the statue's maker, and in 1660 a coin of Domitian was reportedly discovered inside the bronze doors of the Curia (Donderer 1984: 181; Pietrangeli 1949–51: 46). Thus coins, as everyday objects that carried images of the emperor and the gods, were used, much like today, as small 'good luck' offerings in a variety of contexts throughout the Roman world.

Votive offerings of coinage may be connected to a belief that coinage, a medium of commensuration, could transcend worlds or world-orders. Just as money could mediate between Roman and barbarian worlds, or between different individuals and cities, it could also mediate between the divine and profane. This idea can be seen in the practice of burying the dead with coinage. According to mythology one needed an obol to pay the ferryman Charon in the underworld (Stevens 1991), and this belief can be demonstrated in the frequent occurrence of coinage in Roman tombs. There are also literary references to this practice: Juvenal, for example, humorously writes in his *Satires* of a wealthy man killed by a cartload of Ligurian marble, and, not having an appropriate coin (*triens*) to hand, he is forced to sit at the side of the river since he is unable to pay his fare (Juvenal, *Satires* 3.249–67). The deposition of coins within liminal spaces (e.g. under boundary markers) may have been a product of this same association of money and (the crossing of) boundaries (Rowan 2011: 8). Suffice to say, coins were used in numerous contexts and for numerous purposes, and people sometimes treated money in a variety of ways.

6.4 Small Change in the City

Our focus thus far has been on official coins (struck by a governmental authority), but archaeological evidence demonstrates that official money circulated alongside old coins, imitations, and other types of money. This meant that the everyday experience of currency was different from city to city, and very different from the impression given by RRC and RIC. Diversity is most apparent at the level of small change. Although military camps may have been supplied with smaller denominations, it appears that cities were often not and so had to develop their own local solutions. These local innovations are not well studied, but they formed part of the experience of daily life.

One of the best-known examples of this phenomenon is Pompeii. One of the more surprising things to emerge from excavations in the city is that Pompeii was awash in coinage similar to that found in Ebusus, decorated with images of the Egyptian god Bes. Coinage similar to that struck by the Greek city Massalia is also found in quantity, carrying the image of Apollo on one side and a butting bull on the other. In the recent excavations of Insula 1 in Regio VI, coins of Ebusus and Massalia types accounted for 45% of the coin assemblage (Hobbs 2013: 32). Detailed analysis of these coinages reveals that they differ from the 'official' issues of Ebusus and Massalia, and must have been the product of a single mint, likely located in Pompeii itself (Stannard 2005). This 'pseudo-mint', as it has been labelled, probably arose because the city did not possess enough small change for daily transactions. And although Bes was originally an Egyptian god, its presence on a local coinage used daily may have meant that, over time, Bes came to be seen as a 'Pompeian' image, linked to local Pompeian identity. These non-governmental high volume currencies are more common in Italy than we might think, and need to be examined when discussing local economies or identities. Another pseudo-mint, for example, was probably located at Minturnae towards the end of the first century BC and produced coinage with types similar to the 'official' issues of Panormos (Sicily) and Paestum (Italy) (Fig. 6.8; Stannard and Frey-Kupper 2008).

Why pseudo-mints chose particular designs over others was probably due to a combination of factors, not least the existence of the original currency in the region. The motivations behind these pseudo-mints and whether they were tacitly tolerated by the authorities is still open to discussion, but the sheer number of imitative coinages in this period suggests they were accepted by the Roman authorities to some

Figure 6.8. Bronze 16mm, first century BC, pseudo-mint (Minturnae?) (Stannard and Frey-Kupper 2008 no. 13). **Obv.** Beardless helmeted head. **Rev.** Helmeted warrior holding patera and spear, ΛVH.

extent (Bransbourg 2011: 134). These mints filled a demand for small change before the rule of Augustus, a need driven by an increasingly monetised economy in Italy (Stannard and Frey-Kupper 2008: 376–8). As more people began to use money, more transactions took place with money, leading to a greater need for small denominations, but Rome before the late Republic had ceased to produce bronze coins. Local pseudo-currencies were one solution to this problem. Imitations were another. Crawford has identified some 117 groups of Roman Republican coin imitations, demonstrating the scale on which local variations of 'official' currency may have existed (Crawford 1982). The role of these coinages in the Roman economy, and in Roman society, still needs further study.

In addition to locally produced coinages, old currency continued to circulate even after the Roman conquest of particular regions. The majority of examples of this practice are of bronze coins – precious metal (gold and silver) was likely to be absorbed by the Roman treasury. The bronze coins of Carthage, for example, remained in circulation in Africa until the imperial period (Burnett 1987a: 179). Contemplate what the effect might be of using coinage carrying Carthaginian imagery well after their historic defeat! Bronze Ptolemaic coinage also continued to circulate after the Roman acquisition of Egypt, Crete and Cyrenaica (Picard et al. 2012: 127–8). Many of these Ptolemaic coins in Alexandria are very worn, suggesting that they were frequently being passed from person to person.

About two thirds of the coin finds from the sanctuary of Demeter in Cyrene were small denominations of the Ptolemaic dynasty, a proportion

Figure 6.9. Bronze coin of Cyrene, 260–96 BC, 13mm, 1.85 g (BMC 30). **Obv.** Head of a Ptolemaic king. **Rev.** Head of Libya, ΠΤΟΛΕΜΑΙΟΥ ΒΑΣΙΛΕΩΣ.

Figure 6.10. Bronze coin of Corinth, 400–200 BC, 11 mm, 1.58 g. **Obv.** Pegasus, koppa below. **Rev.** Trident.

similar to other sites in the region. This suggests that Ptolemaic bronzes remained the circulating medium of small change in this area as well (Buttrey 1997: 6–7). Ptolemaic issues showing Libya on the reverse similar to Fig. 6.9, naming King Ptolemy in the legend, have been found in strata as late as the third century AD (Buttrey 1987: 165). Again, this provided small denominations for daily transactions, but the effect is something we need to think more about. Imagine an inhabitant of Cyrene in the first century AD, using a coin showing the emperor for one transaction, and a coin showing an old Ptolemaic king for the next! Then again, perhaps the use of old and new coinage together should be seen along the lines of other monuments from antiquity: Augustus' buildings in Rome, for example, sat alongside much older structures, as did Roman monuments in Egypt.

Similarly, excavations at Corinth demonstrate that the local bronze coinage of the city, struck before its destruction by the Roman general Mummius in 146 BC, formed part of the circulating currency of the city after its re-foundation by Julius Caesar in 44 BC. These Pegasus/trident bronzes (Fig. 6.10) are one of the most common coins of the Republican and imperial period strata from the city (Mac Isaac 1987: 98). Where precisely all these local Corinthian bronzes came from is another question; they may have been circulating in the region ever since Corinth's destruction.

The continuing presence of older, obsolete, imitative and alternative currencies in cities throughout the Empire (of which only a few examples have been detailed here) demonstrates that, for small change at least, the value and acceptability of a coin must have been locally constructed (Butcher 2001–2: 21–2). In addition to coinage issued by the state, there were other forms of currency that people employed within their social and economic relationships. In the Roman world, particular forms of money were accepted in particular places and not in others, but this practice seems restricted to small change. The Romans appear to have exerted far more control over precious metal currencies. Nonetheless, when we explore what images and messages currency might have brought to its users, local currencies like these need to be included in the discussion. Just as the Bes that graced the coinage of Ebusus may have transformed into a symbol of local identity in Pompeii, the persistence of the original coinage of Corinth must also have contributed to shaping the identity of the new colony.

Coins, and coin imagery, were also used in a variety of other ways. As portable, decorative pieces of metal, coinage was easily converted into jewellery, a practice that became increasingly common in the imperial period. The reasons for using coins in jewellery were varied: coinage might act as a statement of connection to Rome, a public display of a close connection to the emperor, or a display of status and wealth. Unless found in a controlled excavation, it is difficult to know when a coin was converted. The Anglo-Saxons, for example, often pierced Roman coins and reused them, as did populations in medieval Serbia (Ciric 2014; Eckardt and Williams 2003). We cannot know, then, when Fig. 6.11 or Fig. 3.38 were pierced. Coinage might also be converted into other objects, or used as stamps to decorate other materials (Rowan 2011: 6). One such instance can be seen on an Arretine vase that used a coin carrying the portrait of Octavian as a stamp repeatedly in the design (Stenico 1955). In this way the designs of coinage could appear on other media, and in other contexts.

Coinage also became part of festivals. For example, they were commonly given as gifts on New Year's Day. Wall paintings from Pompeii show coinage alongside other traditional New Year's gifts like dates and figs; these objects also appear on New Year's Day lamps (Fig. 6.12) (Thüry 2012). The Augustan poet Ovid connects dates, figs and coins (*stipis*) to the New Year in his *Fasti* (1.185–240; Green 2004: 67–113). Here and in other contexts coinage was used to establish and maintain social relationships as well as economic ones.

Figure 6.11. Pierced denarius, Rome, L. Livineius Regulus, 42 BC (RRC 494/29). **Obv.** Head of L. Regulus Pr., REGVLVS PR. **Rev.** Modius with a corn-ear on either side, L LIVINEIVS REGVLVS.

Figure 6.12. Terracotta lamp of the first century AD, decorated with Victory holding a shield inscribed with a New Year's wish for happiness, surrounded by three coins and dried fruit.

Coinage was struck by a mint for a particular purpose, carrying a particular message, at times targeted at a particular audience. But once it entered circulation, the meanings and values of the coin and its imagery were continually (re)constructed by different individuals. Both these perspectives allow us to fully appreciate how coinage, as well as its messages, functioned in the period 49 BC–AD 14.

Guide to Further Reading

General Overviews of Money, Minting and the Development of Coinage in the Roman World

For **general introductions** to ancient coinage see Howgego 1990, Howgego 1995 and von Reden 2010. Good overviews of **Roman coinage** are Burnett 1987b, Crawford 1970, Metcalf 2006, and relevant chapters in Metcalf 2012. For the **historical development** of Roman coinage in the Republic see Burnett 2012 and Woytek 2012a. On the types and functions of money in the Roman world see Harris 2006, Harris 2008, Hollander 2007, Kay 2014, Verboven 2002, Verboven 2003, and Verboven 2009. Discussions of the **mints**, moneyers and monetary developments for this period can be found in RRC and RIC, as well as Burnett 1977. A good list of known mint sites can be found in Serafin 2001. Further discussion of Crawford's method in creating die estimates can be found in Hollander 2008: 114–15, Kay 2014: 90–3, Lockyear 2007: 226–7, and Metcalf 1999: 7. On coin **hoards** see Lockyear 2007, and the general discussion in Casey 1986.

Images and Coin Reference Works

Searchable versions of RRC and RIC can also now be found online with excellent images: see *Coinage of the Roman Republic Online* (http://nu mismatics.org/crro/) and *Online Coins of the Roman Empire* (http://nu mismatics.org/ocre/). Many hoards from the Roman Republic (RRCH) are also now available online at *CHRR Online* (http://numismatics.org /chrr/). Good images and an introduction to the coinage of the Republic can also be found online in E. Ghey and I. Leins (eds), *Roman Republican Coins in the British Museum*: www.britishmuseum.org/rese arch/publications/online_research_catalogues/rrc/roman_republican_ coins.aspx.

Money as a Monument in Miniature and Medium of Communication

On the role of coinage as '**monuments in miniature**' see Chueng 1998, and Meadows and Williams 2001. On the **selection of coin types** see Pink 1946, Jones 1970, Levick 1999, and Rowan 2013c: 19–24. For coinage as a **medium of communication** see Noreña 2011. For **provincial coinage** see Butcher 1988, and Howgego, Heuchert and Burnett 2005.

The Late Republic

Good discussions of **Sextus Pompey** and his coinage can be found in DeRose Evans 1987, Powell and Welch 2002, Welch 2012, and Zarrow 2003. Buttrey 1960a remains important. Woytek 2003, in German, has an excellent and detailed discussion of the issues of 49–42 BC. Weinstock 1971 is a good historical discussion of **Julius Caesar**, with some reference to coin types. A good introductory website to the coinage of Julius Caesar is L. Horne and C. Rowan, *The Coinage of Julius Caesar*: www.humanities .mq.edu.au/acans/caesar/Home.htm. For the coins of the **provinces** in the Republican period see Burnett 1987b. For **Scipio Metellus** see Linderski 1996. Good discussions of the conflicting iconography of **Antony and Octavian** can be found in Newman 1990, and a detailed analysis of the **triumviral gold issues** is Buttrey 1956. For the representation of **women** in the Late Republic and Early Empire see Wood 2001.

On the monetary system of **Ptolemaic Egypt** see Lorber 2012 and von Reden 2007. A catalogue of the coinage of the Ptolemies was published in Greek by J. N. Svoronos, and an online English translation by Lorber can be found at http://www.coin.com/images/dr/svoronos_book2.html. A full in-depth treatment in English of the iconography of **Antony and Cleopatra** is lacking, but a good recent article is Haug 2008. On **legionary denarii** see Dillon 2007.

Augustus

There are numerous works on ideology and material culture under Augustus (e.g. Galinsky 1996 and Zanker 1988). Good discussions that focus specifically on coinage can be found in Burnett 2011 and Wallace-Hadrill 1986, as well as in the introduction to RIC 1 (second edition). For **imperial women** on coinage see Duncan-Jones 2006. See

Dahmen 2010 for **client kings**. On 'central' and 'local' interaction on material culture more broadly see Mattingly 2010, Terrenato 1998, Versluys 2013, and Wallace-Hadrill 2008. For the **Nemausus** coins see Kraay 1955, Sutherland 1976a and Suspène 2012. On **medallions** see Clay 1976 and Toynbee 1944; medallions from the imperial period are catalogued in Gnecchi 1912. For buildings on Roman coins see Burnett 1999.

Money and Society

On the various functions of money within Roman society see Aarts 2005 and Rowan 2011. On **coins and archaeology** see DeRose Evans 2013, Kemmers and Myrberg 2011, Luley 2008, and Sauer 2005. For **audience targeting** see Kemmers 2005 and Kemmers 2006. On **countermarks** see Howgego 2005b. For coins placed within buildings see Carlson 2007 and Donderer 1984. On **imitations and pseudo-mints** see Stannard and Frey-Kupper 2008. The *Portable Antiquities Scheme* database contains information about archaeological finds in Britain, including an enormous number of coins, with images and geographical data: http://finds.org.uk/.

APPENDICES

1 Timeline

A more detailed timeline of this period can be found in the relevant volumes of the *Cambridge Ancient History*.

Year	Historical event	Monetary developments
BC		
49	Caesar crosses the Rubicon. Battle of Ilerda.	Credit crisis at Rome. Caesar obtains the Roman treasury. Caesar's elephant denarius.
48	Battle of Pharsalus. Pompey killed in Egypt. Alexandrine war. Caesar meets Cleopatra.	Denarii reference Caesar's Gallic victories.
47	Birth of Caesarion.	Venus motifs appear on the coinage of Caesar and his supporters. Nicaea strikes coins carrying the portrait of Caesar (47/46 BC). Metellus Scipio striking coins in Africa (47/46 BC).
46	Battle of Thapsus. Series of measures introduced by Caesar between 46 and 44 including reform of the calendar. Caesar's triumph, dedication of the Julian forum.	Large aureus issue of Caesar and Hirtius. Sons of Pompey striking coinage in Spain (46–45 BC).
45	Battle of Munda.	
44	Caesar becomes dictator for life. Assassination of Caesar. Brutus and Cassius move east.	Number of moneyers in Rome increased to four by Caesar. Caesar's portrait appears on coinage at Rome.
43	Battle of Mutina; Hirtius and Pansa (consuls) killed. Death of Cicero. Formation of second triumvirate. Proscriptions. Sextus appointed prefect of the fleet. Colony founded at Lugdunum. Octavian becomes consul.	Double-portrait coinage struck by the triumvirs referencing their new positions. Issues of Brutus and Cassius (43–42 BC), including EID MAR issue.
42	Deification of Caesar. Sextus Pompey in control of Sicily. Battle of Philippi. Foundation of colony at Philippi.	Pompey the Great aligned with Neptune and Janus on the coins of Sextus. Large emission of coinage at Rome (possibly using bullion from the proscriptions). Fulvia (?) appears on coinage at Lugdunum.
41	Antony in the east, meets Cleopatra.	Octavian begins to use the title DIVI F on his coinage.

(cont.)

Year	Historical event	Monetary developments
40	Treaty of Brundisium. Parthian invasion of Syria. Antony marries Octavia. Herod granted Judea.	Octavia appears on an aureus issue of Antony in the east.
39	Pact of Misenum. Antony and Octavia winter in Athens. Antony hailed as the New Dionysius.	Octavia appears on cistophori. Sosius begins to produce coinage on Zacynthus. Athens strikes coins showing Dionysius.
38	Renewal of triumviral powers for 5 years. Marriage of Octavian and Livia.	Antony styles himself as M F M N on coinage. Fleet coinage. *Sidus Iulium* appears on coinage of Octavian.
37	Capture of Jerusalem by Sosius and beginning of reign of Herod. Marriage of Antony and Cleopatra in Antioch. Antony appoints client kings in Asia Minor.	
36	Lepidus removed from triumvirate. Sextus Pompey defeated at Naulochus.	Double portrait coinage of Antony and Cleopatra.
35	Death of Sextus Pompey.	
34	Antony victorious in Armenia. Donations of Alexandria. Triumph of Sosius over Judea.	Antyllus appears on Antony's coinage.
33	Octavian consul for the second time.	
32	Antony divorces Octavia. Release of Antony's will.	Legionary denarii of Antony begin to be produced.
31	Battle of Actium. Octavian becomes consul for the third time.	
30	Death of Antony and Cleopatra, Octavian victorious in Egypt.	
29	Octavian's triple triumph. Dedication of the temple of *Divus Iulius*. Doors on the temple of Janus closed. Octavian and Agrippa conduct the census.	Wealth from Egypt floods Rome.
28	Octavian is *princeps senatus*. Dedication of the temple of Apollo on the Palatine. Octavian consul for the sixth time, sharing the consulate with Agrippa.	Pax cistophorus and LEGES ET IVRA type.

Year	Events	Coinage
27	Senatorial honours granted to Octavian, who is given the title Augustus. Augustus goes to Gaul and Spain until 24 BC.	Beginning of Nemausus bronze production?
25	Juba II made king of Mauretania. Augustus falls ill. Marriage of Marcellus and Julia.	
24	Augustus returns to Rome from Spain and is consul for the tenth time.	
23	Augustus ill. Death of Marcellus. Augustus receives *imperium maius* and *tribunicia potestas* for life.	
22	Augustus goes to Greece and Asia and remains in the region until 19 BC. Temple of Jupiter Tonans.	
21	Marriage of Agrippa and Julia.	
20	Recovery of Parthian standards. Dedication of temple of Mars Ultor. Tigranes becomes King of Armenia.	
19	Augustus returns to Rome and is given the grant of consular *fasces* and a seat between the consuls in the Senate. Dedication of the altar of Fortuna Redux and arch of Augustus in the forum. Death of Virgil.	Mint at Rome restarts production.
18/17 (?)	Augustus' moral legislation.	
17	Augustus adopts Gaius and Lucius. Saecular games.	'Epigraphic' series of the moneyers at Rome. Beginning of the chained crocodile coinage of Nemausus (?).
16	Augustus in Gaul and Agrippa in the east until 13 BC.	Numa issue of the moneyer Piso. Imperial mint established at Lugdunum.
15	Tiberius and Drusus invade Bavaria.	
13	Inauguration of the Ara Pacis. Death of Lepidus.	Julia, Lucius and Gaius appear on coinage at Rome.

(cont.)

Year	Historical event	Monetary developments
12	Augustus becomes *pontifex maximus*. Death of Agrippa. Drusus campaigns in Germany until 9 BC. Dedication of the altar of the three Gauls.	
11	Tiberius marries Julia. Death of Octavia.	Moneyers cease to be named on coinage struck at Rome.
10		Lugdunum altar types overtake the Nemausus issues as the important regional bronze currency in the west.
9	Death of Drusus the Elder.	
8		Gaius shown on horseback on coinage at Lugdunum (9–8 BC).
7	14 *regiones* of Rome established. Triumph of Tiberius.	
6	Tiberius retires to Rhodes.	
5	Augustus is consul. Gaius assumes *toga virilis* and is *princeps iuventutis*.	
4	Death of Herod.	
2	Dedication of the forum of Augustus and temple of Mars Ultor. Augustus is consul and *pater patriae*. Lucius assumes the *toga virilis* and is *princeps iuventutis*. Exile of Julia.	Beginning of coinage showing Gaius and Lucius as *principes iuventutis*.
AD		
2	Lucius dies at Massalia. Tiberius returns from Rhodes.	
4	Death of Gaius. Augustus adopts Agrippa Postumous and Tiberius, who in turn adopts Germanicus. Tiberius campaigns in Germany.	
6	Judea becomes a province.	
7–8	Agrippa Postumous and Ovid banished.	
9	Battle of Teutoberg forest.	
10		Tiberius appears on imperial coinage.
12	Illyrian triumph of Tiberius. Germanicus in Gaul and Germany.	
14	Death of Augustus. Tiberius becomes *princeps*.	

2 Latin Numismatic Abbreviations

Coins use many of the abbreviations that are found in Latin inscriptions. The more complicated legends on the coins illustrated within this volume have been discussed in the relevant sections of text. A list of common Latin abbreviations used on coinage of this period is found below. Coins often carried the name of the magistrate, and magistracies are often followed by Roman numerals to indicate the number of times the position has been held (e.g. COS III means *consul for the third time*).

III VIR	*tresvir* (moneyer)
III VIR R P C	*III vir rei publicae constituendae consulari potestate* (triumvir for confirming the Republic with consular power)
III VIR AAA FF	*tresviri auro argento aere flando feriundo* (the three men for the casting and striking of gold, silver and bronze)
AVG	*augur* (Republican period), *Augustus* (imperial period)
COS	*consul*
COS DES	*consul designatus* (consul designate)
DEVICTA	having been conquered
DICT	dictator
DIVI F	*divi filius* (son of the god)
EID MAR	Ides of March
F	*filius* (son of)
HS	*sestertii*
IMP	*imperator*
ITER	a second time
LEG	*legatus* or legion
LEG F C	*legatus fisci castrensis* (a financial official in the provinces)
MAG, or MGN	*magnus* (the Great)
N	*nepos* (grandson of)
(IN) PERPETVO	in perpetuity
P M	*pontifex maximus* (chief priest)

PONT	*pontifex*
PONT MAX	*pontifex maximus* (chief priest)
P P	*pater patriae* (father of the country)
PR	*praetor* (likely prefect in the case of Hirtius)
PRO COS	*proconsul*
PRO PR	*propraetor*
Q	*quaestor*
QVART	a fourth time
QVINC	a fifth time
REX	king
S C, or EX S C	*ex senatus consultum* (by decree of the Senate)
S P Q R	*Senatus populusque Romanus* (the Senate and People of Rome)
TER	a third time
TR POT	tribunician power

3 Glossary (by Andrew Meadows, updated and revised by the author)

Readers are also encouraged to consult *The Dictionary of Roman Coins* (William Stevenson 1964), also available online at *NumisWiki* (http://www.forumancientcoins.com/numiswiki/view.asp) for any unfamiliar terms.

AE: numismatic abbreviation for the Latin word *aes*, an alloy of copper.

apex: a round or conical hat with a wooden pointed piece of wood on top, worn by Roman priests.

aplustre: the curved stern of a ship and its ornaments.

aquila: a Roman legionary standard surmounted by an eagle.

AR: numismatic abbreviation for silver (from Latin *argentum*).

as: Roman bronze or copper coin denomination, weighing c. 9–11g under Augustus with a diameter of c. 27mm.

aspergillum: an instrument used to sprinkle holy water, associated with Roman priests.

attribute: something held by or worn by a figure portrayed on a coin.

aureus: Roman gold coin denomination worth 400 asses or 25 denarii, weighing c. 7.7–7.9g under Augustus with a diameter of c. 19–21mm.

authority: the formal guarantor of the value of a coin. For civic coinages, the authority is generally presumed to be the government of the city itself. Within kingdoms and empires, the authority may be the supreme ruler (e.g. king or emperor), or an appointee (e.g. satrap or provincial governor).

AV: numismatic abbreviation for gold (from Latin *aurum*).

axis: see 'die-axis'.

BI: numismatic abbreviation for billon, a heavily debased silver.

biga: a chariot of two horses (or elephants).

bipennis: a double-bladed axe.

bisellium: a seat with room for two people to sit on it, often richly decorated.

brockage: a mint error that occurs when a previously-struck coin sticks to the die and is then impressed onto the next blank.

bucrania: ornaments containing ox-heads (singular is *bucranium*).

caduceus: a herald's staff, also carried by Mercury.

candelabrum: a candlestick.

carnyx: a type of trumpet associated with Iron Age populations in Gaul and Britain.

cippus: a pillar, often used to describe gravestones, tombstones and boundary stones.

circulation: the movement of coinage once it has been issued. The circulation of ancient coinage can be studied through the evidence of hoards and single finds, as well as from documentary sources.

circulation wear: the wear, or deterioration, in condition visible on a coin due to the time it has spent in circulation.

cista: a wooden box or basket.

cista mystica: a basket used for housing sacred snakes, connected with initiation rites into the cult of Dionysius.

cistophorus: a silver denomination originally struck by the Attalids. The coins weighed c. 12g, were c. 27–29mm in diameter and received their name ('basket-bearer') due to their *cista* type.

control-mark: a mark engraved, generally into the reverse die, apparently to indicate some aspect of the administration of the production of the coin.

cornucopia: a symbol of abundance: a horn-shaped vessel overflowing with fruits or other produce.

corona civica: oak wreath crown awarded to someone who had saved the life of a Roman in battle.

countermark: mark in the form of letter(s), a symbol, a monogram, or a combination of these punched into a coin. The reason for the application of such marks is not always certain, and probably varied from case to case. Some served to reauthorise a coin for circulation in new areas. Others perhaps assigned new denominations to old coins.

Cu: abbreviation for copper.

cuIullus: a vessel associated with the Vestal Virgins and Roman priests.

damnatio memoriae: memory sanctions that could be imposed upon a 'bad' emperor after his death.

demos: on coinage, often a personification of a citizen body.

denarius: silver Roman denomination worth 16 asses in this period, weighing c. 3.65–3.85g with a diameter of c. 18mm.

denarius serratus: a denarius with a toothed or etched edge.

denomination: the value of an ancient coin. These values are generally expressed in a standard set of units, subdivisions and multiples thereof. See further Appendix 4: Denominational Systems.

desultor: a rider who jumped from horse to horse during circus games.

die: a piece of metal engraved with a design and then used to strike coins. Two dies were required to strike the two faces of a coin: the obverse die and the reverse die.

die-axis: the relative orientation of obverse and reverse images on a coin.

die-engraver: the artist responsible for the engraving of the design onto dies. They are generally anonymous on ancient coinage, although a few signatures are recorded, particularly in late fifth-century Sicily.

die study: a technical numismatic study of a coinage that involves the identification of the dies used to strike a coinage. Such studies allow for the establishment of the relative chronology of a coinage. They also permit quantification of a coinage by identifying the number of dies used to produce a given coinage.

die-wear: the wear, or damage, experienced by a die in the course of its use to strike coins. This may take the form of gradual deterioration or sudden breaks. It can be used by numismatists as part of a die-study to determine the relative chronology of production.

double-strike: when a coin is struck by the same die twice, often leaving a 'ghost' or shadow on the coin.

drachma: Greek coin denomination, worth 6 obols, or ¼ of a tetradrachm.

dupondius: a Roman denomination introduced by Augustus, made of brass or orichalcum. It was worth 2 asses and weighed c. 11.5–13.5g under Augustus, rising to 13.5–15.5g under Tiberius.

emergency hoard: a hoard of coins, and perhaps other precious objects, secreted together in antiquity at a time of emergency. Such deposits tend to consist of a cross-section of coins in circulation at the time of deposit. They may thus serve as evidence for the nature of the coin supply at a given time.

equestrian statue: a statue of a rider on a horse.

ethnic: a legend indicating the identity of the people (e.g. the citizens of a city) acting as the authority behind a coinage.

exergue: the area on a coin below the ground-line of a design.

fabric: a term used to refer to the general appearance of a coin as a piece of metal, including its shape, weight, diameter and thickness.

fasces: a bundle of rods, often with an axe. A symbol of the authority of Roman magistrates or other officials.

fasti: yearly chronological or calendar based records.

fiduciary: coinage that takes its value not from the content of the metal that it contains, but from the *fiat* of the authority behind it.

field: an empty area of a coin design wherein subsidiary symbols such as mint-marks, control-marks, or legends may be placed.

fineness: the amount of pure metal (gold or silver) that a coin contained.

flan: the metal blank from which a coin is struck.

hasta pura: a spear staff without the iron head.

herm: a type of statue with a head or bust above a plain squared lower section.

hoard: a group of coins deposited together in antiquity, thus forming a single archaeological context for multiple objects. The reasons for deposit are likely to have varied, and are rarely recoverable with certainty from the archaeological deposits. Categories of hoard include but are perhaps not limited to savings hoards, emergency hoards and ritual deposits.

imago clipeata: shield portrait.

imitation: a coin that, more or less slavishly, copies the types of a model coinage, but is not a product of the same authority as its model.

intrinsic: coinage that takes its value from the quantity (weight) of metal that it contains.

issue: either the process of officially placing a coin into circulation; or a specific subsection of a period of coin production, identifiable by specific control-marks or mint-magistrate's signatures.

issuer: the person administratively responsible for the production of a coin. The identity and indeed status of the issuer of an ancient coin is often unclear. The terms moneyer and mint-magistrate are often used to refer to officials known or assumed to have been responsible for the production of coin within a state.

janiform: two heads or busts back-to-back like the double-headed god Janus.

jugate: two heads or busts facing in the same direction, with one placed atop the other in the design so as to appear closer to the viewer.

laureate: wearing a laurel wreath.

legend: the inscription(s) that appear on a coin. These most often occur on the reverse in the Greek world, but appear on Roman coins on the obverse too, whence the habit passed to the Greek and modern worlds.

lituus: the curved staff of an augur.

metrology: the study of coin weights and coin metal composition.

mint: a place where coins are produced. In the vast majority of ancient cases, no evidence exists for the nature of physical locations of mints, and many may not have consisted of permanent facilities. The term is therefore rather loosely used for the ancient world to indicate place and facility of production.

mint-magistrate: the official, whether elected or appointed, responsible for oversight of the production of coins within the mint. The names of many private individuals that appear on ancient coins are assumed to be those of mint-magistrates.

modius: a unit of measurement for grain.

monogram: an identifying mark made up of a number of letters overlaid and/or ligatured. These are often found on coins as mint-marks or control marks, or in countermarks.

multiple: a coin weighing the equivalent of several precious metal pieces (e.g. 4 aurei).

mural crown: a crown in the form of a city wall with towers. Given to a general who was first to scale the ramparts of an enemy's town. Also worn by personifications of cities (Tyche), or other tutelary deities associated with a city.

obverse: the 'heads' side of a coin, produced by the obverse die. It is most of the time the side of the coin on which a portrait or other form of head is depicted, and sometimes provides an indication thereby of who was the authority behind the coin. See also 'reverse'.

obverse die: the die used to strike the obverse side of a coin.

oppidum: a town.

Or: numismatic abbreviation for orichalcum or brass, an alloy of copper and zinc.

overstrike: a coin produced by striking an existing coin with a new pair of dies. Overstrikes tend to be imperfect, and thus allow identification of the designs of both the original coin and those struck over it.

parazonium: a weapon similar to a dagger, but longer.

patera: a bowl used for libations.

pelta: a small shield.

phalerae: a metal disc won as military decoration.

plated: when a coin has a base metal core and is only coated in silver.

posthumous coinage: a coinage produced in the name of an individual after his or her death.

praefericulum: a metal vase used by the Roman augurs and priests.

quadrans: Roman denomination worth ¼ of an as, struck in bronze during the Republic and in copper under Augustus.

quadriga: a chariot of four horses (or elephants).

quaestor: a Roman magistracy charged with financial affairs.

quinarius: a silver Roman denomination worth 8 asses, weighing c. 1.6–1.8g and with a diameter of 12–14mm.

radiate: wearing a radiate crown, a reference to divinity. From the reign of Nero, however, the radiate crown was used on coinage to signal a 'double denomination' (a dupondius or antoninianus).

restrike: the process of collecting existing coins, melting them down, and beginning the minting process again.

reverse: the 'tails' side of the coin, produced by the reverse die. It is often the side of the coin bearing the legend, and thus providing clear indication of where the coin was produced. See also obverse.

reverse die: the die used to strike the reverse side of a coin.

ritual deposit: a group of coins deposited together, not for purposes of saving, but for religious purposes such as offerings to gods. Unlike many hoards, such deposits were arguably not intended to be recovered.

rostral crown: a crown adorned with ship's prows or 'beaks', awarded to a maritime prefect or naval commander-in-chief who had won a great naval victory.

rostrum: the curved end of a ship's prow (its 'beak'), often found on war ships. Plural: *rostra.*

saltire: a diagonal cross or X.

savings hoard: a group of coins gathered together in a single deposit over a period of time by means of, or for the purposes of, saving.

sella curulis: or curule chair: the magistrate's seat given to dictators, consuls, praetors, censors, aediles, and the prefect of the city. Pontiffs and vestals also had the right to the curule chair.

semis: a denomination that was worth half an as.

sestertius: Roman denomination worth four asses, struck in silver in the Republican period, and in orichalcum after the monetary reforms of Augustus.

simpulum: a vessel with a long handle used to make libations.

single find: a coin found in isolation either by accident or by deliberate means such as metal-detecting. This may occur within a controlled archaeological survey or excavation environment, or not.

strike: the process by which the majority of ancient coins were produced. This consisted of placing a blank of metal (flan) on the obverse die, positioning the reverse die on top of the blank, and then applying force in the form of hammer blows (striking) to imprint the designs of the two dies onto the piece of metal.

style: a word used to refer to the appearance of the types of a coin.

terminus ante quem: the latest date an event could have occurred. The event must have occurred at this time, or beforehand.

terminus post quem: the earliest time an event could have occurred. The event must have occurred at this time or afterwards.

test-cut: a cut made into an intrinsic value coin to make sure that it is made of solid metal, and not plated.

tetradrachm: a Greek silver coin worth 4 drachms or 24 obols. On the Attic weight standard it was c. 17.2g.

toga picta: part of the costume worn by *triumphators* (and consuls during their annual procession). It was embroidered with figures of various colours.

togate: wearing a toga.

tooled: used to describe a coin that has been altered after it has been struck by incising or other methods.

triskeles: a symbol consisting of three bent human legs.

tunica palmata: the dress worn by *triumphators*, and by those who presided over the circus. It was purple with gold edging.

type: the numismatic term for the design that appears on a coin; this may thus be subdivided into obverse- and reverse-types.

undertype: the original type of a coin before it has been overstruck.

unicum: a coin known from only one specimen.

vexillum: a flag-like military standard.

victoriola: a little statue of Victory.

weight standard: the official system of weights in use in an ancient state. In an intrinsic value coinage, value depended on weight. Weight standards thus became a means of unifying or dividing circulation of coinage, depending on decisions taken about adoption or rejection of specific weight standards.

4 Denominational Systems (by Andrew Meadows)

(a) Greece

The Greek world was not, at any period, unified by a single monetary system. In the archaic and classical periods, different city-states adopted different weight standards for their silver coinages. Moreover, different denominational structures were also used in different places. We are best informed about the city of Athens, thanks to the spread of Athenian influence in the 5th century BC, and the fact that the Athenian (Attic) system was adopted and spread by Alexander the Great.

The basic unit was the drachma ('handful'), which was subdivided into six obols ('spits'). All other silver denominations were named by reference to these two basic units of account. The drachma and obol were not the most common denominations, however. In many states, Athens included, the main denomination was the tetradrachm (four drachma). Decadrachms (10 drachmas), didrachms (2 drachmas), drachms (1 drachma) and hemidrachms (half drachmas) were also produced. In addition to the obol, diobols (2 obols), hemiobols (half obols), tetartemoria (quarter obols) and hemitetartemoria (eighth obols) were also produced. Such small denominations, less than a drachm in value, are often described today as 'fractions'. In this extensive array of denominations, Athens was exceptional. Most states confined themselves to one or two denominations. The principal denomination in use in a state could also be referred to as a 'stater'.

For accounting purposes, units larger than the drachma were available. A 'mna' (the denomination is known as a 'mnaieion') consisted of 100 drachmas, and a 'talent' was made up of 60 mnas or 6000 drachmas. The following table gives the equivalences in grammes of silver of the basic Athenian units of account:

1 obol = 0.72g
1 drachm = 6 obols = 4.3g
1 mna = 100 drachms = 430g
1 Talent = 60 mnas = 600 drachms = 25.8Kg.

During the Hellenistic period, bronze coinage became common in many states. At Athens the obol was divided into 8 bronze chalkoi. Half, 1, 2 and 4 chalkous coins are known.

(b) Rome

The Roman monetary system before the Second Punic War (218–201 BC) was complex and unstable. The earliest silver coinage of the late fourth/ early third century BC was essentially based on the Greek drachma system, on a variety of different standards. From the start this coinage was accompanied by bronze money in a variety of forms. The basic Roman bronze unit was the as, originally weighing one Roman pound (approx. 324g or 12 ounces). By the end of the third century BC, the weight of the as had dropped to 35g. Around 212 BC the Roman state introduced a new silver denomination known as the denarius (a 10 as piece). This would remain the basic Roman silver coin until the third century AD. In 141 BC the denarius was re-tariffed at 16 asses. The full range of denominations issued in silver and bronze under the Republic can be set out as follows:

Silver
1 denarius = 10 or 16 asses
1 quinarius = half denarius = 5 or 8 asses
1 sestertius = quarter denarius = 2 ½ or 4 asses
Bronze
1 as (= tenth or sixteenth denarius)
1 semis = half as
1 triens = third as
1 quadrans = quarter as
1 sextans = sixth as
1 uncia = twelfth as

Under Augustus the bronze coinage was reformed to produce the following denominations:

Sestertius (4 asses or quarter denarius)
Dupondius (2 asses or half sestertius)
As (quarter sestertius)

Semis (half as)

Quadrans (quarter as)

In addition, the gold aureus, which had started to be produced in serious quantities by Julius Caesar, was standardised at a value of 25 denarii.

5 The Production of Ancient Coinage
(by Andrew Meadows)

Ancient coinage was hand made, in two senses. First the actual process of striking the coins was carried out by hand. A coin was produced by placing a blank piece of metal on a die set within an anvil or similar anchoring device. This is known to numismatists as the 'obverse die', or sometimes the 'anvil die'. A second die on the end of a punch (the 'reverse die') was then placed on top of the blank and hit forcefully with a hammer, probably several times. The result was a flat, roundish piece of metal with, potentially, designs or 'types' on both sides.

The second hand-crafted element of coin production was the engraving of the designs that appeared on ancient coins. Unlike modern coin dies, which are all mechanically copied from a single master engraving, each ancient die was individually engraved and thus different from every other. These two elements of hand-production produce an interesting mixture of results. On the one hand, there is an individuality of design of dies, which allows us to trace the products of an ancient mint in a way that is impossible for modern coins. It also allows us to count the number of dies used to produce a particular coinage, and thus to quantify it. On the other, hand striking, although not nearly so fast as modern machine production, allows for the production of thousands of identical or closely similar objects within a very short space of time. Coins in this sense are one of the very rare examples from the pre-modern world of mass production.

The substance of ancient coinage was also profoundly different from that of today's coins. In origin, coinage was a monetary instrument of intrinsic value. The earliest coins, produced in Asia Minor from the mid-seventh to mid-sixth centuries BC were made of carefully controlled amounts of electrum, the alloy of gold and silver. Subsequently, most probably under the influence of the prevailing monetary tradition of the Near East, coinage was throughout the latter part of the sixth century through to the first century AD largely produced in high-quality silver, with gold being produced when circumstances of supply or demand particularly prompted it. The fact that these precious metal coins took their value from their weight often

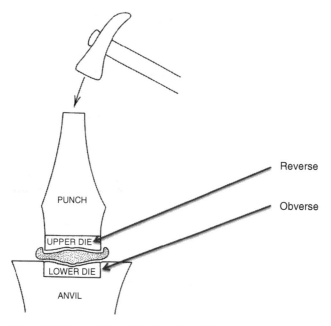

Figure 7.1. Diagram illustrating the coin striking process.

made it possible for them to circulate over wide areas, and beyond the borders of the political authorities that had produced them. Nevertheless, there were constraining factors. The novelty of coinage, in contrast to the earlier Near Eastern practice of making payments with weighed amounts of silver bullion, lay both in the carefully regulated weights (denominations) at which coins were produced, which added facility of use, and in the designs that were struck on them, which provided clear statement of origin, and thus guaranteed their metal quality (value). While both developments added convenience and functionality, they also served potentially to constrain monetary behaviour. The localised system of weight standards of the ancient world according to which ancient coins were denominated could fragment as well as unify monetary behaviour. Similarly, a mark of guarantee could only function where it was recognised. This was particularly the case when the phenomenon of bronze coinage arose in the latter part of the fifth century BC. Such coinages were, on the whole, produced as fiduciary instruments, whose value lay not so much in their metal content, which was far less tightly controlled than in precious metal coinage, but in the guaranteed system in which they circulated. Such fiduciary coinages depended for their value essentially on the confidence of the recipients of the coin in their ability to reuse it later.

Bibliography

Aarts, J. 2005. 'Coins, money and exchange in the Roman world. A cultural-economic perspective', *Archaeological Dialogues* 12: 1–28.

Abdy, R. and Harling, N. 2005. 'Two important new Roman coins', *NC* 165: 175–8.

Abdy, R. and Minnitt, S. 2002. 'Shapwick Villa', *Coin Hoards from Roman Britain* 11: 169–233.

Adamik, T. 2003. 'Temple regulations from Furfo (CIL I.2 756)', in *Latin vulgaire-latin tardif VI. Actes de vɪᵉ colloque international sur le latin vulgaire et tardif Helsinki, 29 août–2 septembre 2000*, ed. H. Solin, M. Leiwo and H. Halla-aho. Hildesheim, Georg Olms Verlag: 77–82.

Alföldi, A. 1958. 'The portrait of Caesar on the denarii of 44 BC and the sequence of the issues', in *Centennial Publication of the American Numismatic Society*, ed. H. Ingholt. New York, American Numismatic Society: 27–44.

Alföldi, A. and Giard, J.-B. 1984. 'Guerre civile et propagande politique: l'émission d'Octave au nom du Divos Julius (41–40 avant J.C.)', *Numismatica e antichità classiche* 13: 147–53.

Amandry, M. 1981. 'Le monnayage de Dymé (Colonia Dumaeorum) en Achaïe. Corpus', *Revue Numismatique* 23: 45–67.

1986. 'Le monnayage en bronze de Bibulus, Atratinus et Capito: une tentative de romanisation en Orient', *Revue Suisse de Numismatique* 65: 73–85.

1988. *Les monnayages des Duovirs Corinthiens*. Athens, École française d'Athènes.

1990. 'Le monnayage en bronze de Bibulus, Atratinus et Capito. Part III', *Revue Suisse de Numismatique* 69: 65–96.

2008. 'Le monnayage de L. Sempronius Atratinus revisité', *AJN* 20: 421–34.

Amandry, M. and Barrandon, J.-N. 2008. 'Le genèse de la réforme monétaire augustéenne', in *Del imperium de Pompeyo a la auctoritas de Augusto. Homenaje a Michael Grant*, ed. M. P. García-Bellido, A. Mostalac and A. Jiménez. Madrid, Consejo superior de investigaciones científicas: 207–33.

Bahrfeldt, M. 1905. 'Die Münzen der Flottenpräfekten des Marcus Antonius', *Numismatische Zeitschrift* 37: 9–56.

Baldus, H. R. 1973. 'Ein neues Spätporträt der Kleopatra aus Orthosia', *Jahrbuch für Numismatik und Geldgeschichte* 23: 19–43.

1987. 'Syria', in *The Coinage of the Roman World in the Late Republic*, ed. A. Burnett and M. Crawford. Oxford, British Archaeological Reports: 121–51.

Balzat, J.-S. and Millis, B. W. 2013. 'M. Antonius Aristocrates', *Hesperia* 82: 651–72.

Barbato, M. 2015. 'The coins of Clovius and Oppius (*RRC* 476/1 and 550/1-3): new evidence from find-spots', *NC* 175: 103–16.

Bartman, E. 2012. 'Early imperial female portraiture', in *A Companion to Women in the Ancient World*, ed. S. L. James and S. Dillon. Malden, MA, Wiley-Blackwell: 414–22.

Berger, F. 1996. *Kalkriese 1: Die römische Fundmünzen*. Mainz, Verlag Philipp von Zabern.

— 2000. 'Die Münzen von Kalkriese. Neufunde und Ausblick', in *Die Fundmünzen von Kalkriese und die frühkaiserzeitliche Münzprägung. Akten des wissenschaftlichen Symposions in Kalkriese, 15.–16. April 1999*, ed. R. Wiegels. Möhnesee, Bibliopolis: 11–45.

Bieber, M. 1973. 'The development of portraiture on Roman Republican coins', in *Aufstieg und Niedergang der römischen Welt 1.4*, ed. H. Temporini. Berlin, de Gruyter: 871–98.

Bland, R. 1996. 'The Roman coinage of Alexandria, 30 BC–AD 296: interplay between Roman and local designs', in *Archaeological Research in Roman Egypt: The Proceedings of the Seventeenth Classical Colloquium of the Department of Greek and Roman Antiquities, British Museum (JRA Suppl. 19)*, ed. D. M. Bailey. Ann Arbor, MI, Journal of Roman Archaeology: 113–27.

Bransbourg, G. 2011. '*Fides et pecunia numerata*. Chartalism and metallism in the Roman world. Part 1: The Republic', *AJN* 23: 87–152.

Broughton, T. R. S. 1951-2. *The Magistrates of the Roman Republic (2 vols)*. New York, American Philological Association.

Burnett, A. 1977. 'The authority to coin in the late Republic and early Empire', *NC* 137: 37–63.

— 1983. 'Review of Albeet, *Das Bild des Augustus auf den frühen Reichsprägungen*', *Gnomon* 55: 563–5.

— 1987a. 'Africa', in *The Coinage of the Roman World in the Late Republic*, ed. A. Burnett and M. Crawford. Oxford, British Archaeological Reports: 175–85.

— 1987b. *Coinage in the Roman World*. London, Spink.

— 1995. 'The unification of the monetary systems of the Roman West: accident or design?', in *Italy in Europe: Economic Relations 700 BC–AD 50*, ed. J. Swaddling, S. Walker and P. Roberts. London, British Museum: 313–20.

— 1999. 'Buildings and monuments on Roman coins', in *Roman Coins and Public Life under the Empire*, ed. G. M. Paul and M. Ierardi. Ann Arbor, MI, University of Michigan Press: 137–64.

— 2001. 'The invisibility of Roman imperial mints', in *I luoghi della Moneta. Le sedi della zecche dall'antichità all'età moderna*, ed. R. La Guardia, S. Masseroli and T. Tibiletti. Milan, Commune di Milano: 41–8.

— 2011. 'The Augustan revolution seen from the mints of the provinces', *JRS* 101: 1–30.

— 2012. 'Early Roman coinage and its Italian context', in *The Oxford Handbook of Greek and Roman Coinage*, ed. W. E. Metcalf. Oxford University Press: 297–314.

Burnett, A., Amandry, M. and Ripolles, P. P. 1992. *Roman Provincial Coinage Vol 1*. London, British Museum.

Burrell, B. 2004. *Neokoroi. Greek Cities and Roman Emperors*. Leiden, Brill.

Butcher, K. 1988. *Roman Provincial Coins: An Introduction to 'Greek Imperials'*. London, Seaby.

2001–2. *Small Change in Ancient Beirut (Berytus XLV–XLVI)*. Beirut, Faculty of Arts and Sciences, The American University of Beirut.

2004. *Coinage in Roman Syria: Northern Syria, 64 BC–AD 253*. London, Royal Numismatic Society.

2005. 'Information, legitimation, or self-legitimation? Popular and elite designs on the coin types of Syria', in *Coinage and Identity in the Roman Provinces*, ed. C. Howgego, V. Heuchert and A. Burnett. Oxford University Press: 141–56.

Butcher, K. and Ponting, M. 2014. *The Metallurgy of Roman Silver Coinage*. Cambridge University Press.

Buttrey, T.V. 1954. 'Thea Neotera on coins of Antony and Cleopatra', *American Numismatic Society Museum Notes* 6: 95–109.

1956. *The Triumviral Portrait Gold of the Quattuorviri Monetales of 42 BC*. New York, American Numismatic Society.

1960a. 'The denarii of Cn. Pompeius Jr. and M. Minatius Sabinus', *American Numismatic Society Museum Notes* 9: 75–94.

1960b. 'The 'pietas' denarii of Sextus Pompey', *NC* 20: 83–101.

1987. 'Crete and Cyrenaica', in *The Coinage of the Roman World in the Late Republic*, ed. A. Burnett and M. Crawford. Oxford, British Archaeological Reports: 165–74.

1997. 'Part I: the coins', in *The Extramural Sanctuary of Demeter and Persephone at Cyrene, Libya*, ed. D. White. Philadelphia, University of Pennsylvania: 1–66.

Camp, J. and Kroll, J. 2001. 'The Agora mint and Athenian bronze coinage', *Hesperia* 70: 127–62.

Carbone, F. 2014. *Le monete di Paestum tra I sec. a.C. e I sec. d.C. Analisi dei coni*. Milan, Società Numismatica Italiana Onlus.

Carlson, D. 2007. 'Mast-step coins among the Romans', *International Journal of Nautical Archaeology* 36: 317–24.

Carson, R. A. G. 1956. 'System and product in the Roman mint', in *Essays in Roman Coinage Presented to Harold Mattingly*, ed. R. A. G. Carson and C. H. V. Sutherland. Oxford University Press: 227–39.

Casey, J. 1986. *Understanding Ancient Coins*. London, B.T. Batsford Ltd.

Ceruti, S. 1993–4. 'Brutus, Cyprus and the coinage of 55 BC', *AJN* 5–6: 69–87.

Cheshire, W. A. 2007. 'Aphrodite Cleopatra', *Journal of the American Research Center in Egypt* 43: 151–91.

Chueng, A. 1998. 'The political significance of Roman imperial coin types', *Schweizer Münzblätter* 191: 53–61.

Ciric, G. 2014. 'The power of things? Reconsidering the value of reused Roman material culture in the Medieval period in Serbia', in *Embodying Value? The Transformation of Objects in and from the Ancient World*, ed. A. Bokern and C. Rowan. Oxford, British Archaeological Reports: 145–55.

Clay, C. L. 1976. 'Roman imperial medallions: the date and purpose of their issue', in *Actes du 8éme Congrès International de Numismatique*, ed. H. A. Cahn and G. L. Rider. Paris, International Numismatic Commission: 253–65.

Coltelloni-Trannoy, M. 1999. 'Les représentations de l'Africa dans les monnayages africains et romains à l'époque républicaine', in *Numismatique, langues, écritures et arts du livre, spécificité des arts figurés*, ed. S. Lancel. Paris, Éditions du Comité des travaux historiques et scientifiques: 67–91.

Cooley, A. 2009. *Res Gestae Divi Augusti*. Cambridge University Press.

  2013. 'Women beyond Rome: trend-setters or dedicated followers of fashion?', in *Women and the Roman City in the Latin West*, ed. E. Hemelrijk and G. Woolf. Leiden, Brill: 23–46.

Crawford, M.H. 1970. 'Money and exchange in the Roman world', *JRS* 60: 40–8.

  1973. 'Paestum and Rome. The form and function of a subsidiary coinage', in *La monetazione di bronzo di Poseidonia-Paestum (Atti del III convegno del centro internazionale di studi numismatici, Napoli 19–23 Aprile 1971)*. Rome, Istituto italiano di numismatica: 47–109.

  1974. *Roman Republican Coinage (2 vols)*. Cambridge University Press.

  1982. 'Unofficial imitations and small change under the Roman Republic', *Annali dell'Istituto Italiano di Numismatica* 29: 139–63.

  2003. 'Thesauri, hoards and votive deposits', in *Sanctuaires et sources dans l'Antiquité*, ed. O. de Cazanove and J. Scheid. Naples, Centre Jean Bérard: 69–84.

  2012. 'Review: B. Woytek, *Arma et Nummi. Forschungen zur römischen Finanzgeschichte und Münzprägung der Jahre 49 bis 42 v. Chr.*, Wien (2003)', *Gnomon* 84: 337–42.

Dahmen, K. 2010. 'With Rome in mind? Case studies in the coinage of client kings', in *Kingdoms and Principalities in the Roman Near East*, ed. T. Kaizer and M. Facella. Stuttgart, Franz Steiner Verlag: 99–112.

de Callataÿ, F. 1995. 'Calculating ancient coin production: seeking a balance', *NC* 145: 289–311.

DeRose Evans, J. 1987. 'The Sicilian coinage of Sextus Pompeius (Crawford 511)', *American Numismatic Society Museum Notes* 32: 97–157.

  1992. *The Art of Persuasion: Political Propaganda from Aeneas to Brutus*. Ann Arbor, MI, University of Michigan Press.

  2013. 'Coins and archaeology of the Roman Republic', in *A Companion to the Archaeology of the Roman Republic*, ed. J. DeRose Evans. Chichester, Wiley Blackwell: 110–22.

Dillon, J. N. 2007. 'Octavian's finances after Actium, before Egypt: The CAESAR DIVI F / IMP CAESAR coinage and Antony's legionary issue', *Chiron* 37: 35–48.

Donderer, M. 1984. 'Münzen als Bauopfer in römischen Privathäusern', *Bonner Jahrbücher* 184: 177–88.

Duncan-Jones, R. P. 2006. 'Crispina and the coinage of the empresses', *NC* 166: 223–8.

Eck, W. 1984. 'Senatorial self-representation: developments in the Augustan period', in *Caesar Augustus: Seven Aspects*, ed. F. Millar and E. Segal. Oxford, Clarendon Press: 129–67.

Eckardt, H. and Williams, H. 2003. 'Objects without a past? The use of Roman objects in early Anglo-Saxon graves', in *Archaeologies of Remembrance: Death and Memory in Past Societies*, ed. H. Williams. New York, Kuver: 141–70.

Erkelenz, D. 2002. 'Das Pörtrait des Statthalters in der Lokalprägung der römischen Provinzen', *Schweizerische Numismatische Rundschau* 81: 65–87.

Esty, W. 1986. 'Estimation of the size of a coinage: a survey and comparison of methods', *NC* 146: 185–215.

2006. 'How to estimate the original number of dies and the coverage of a sample', *NC* 166: 359–64.

Favro, D. 2005. 'Making Rome a world city', in *The Cambridge Companion to the Age of Augustus*, ed. G. K. Galinsky. Cambridge University Press: 234–63.

Fears, J. R. 1975. 'Sulla or Endymion: a reconsideration of a denarius of L. Aemilius Buca', *American Numismatic Society Museum Notes* 20: 29–37.

Fejfer, J. 2008. *Roman Portraits in Context*. Berlin, Walter de Gruyter.

Fishwick, D. 1984. 'Coins as evidence: some phantom temples', *Échos du monde classique* 27: 263–70.

1999. 'Coinage and cult: the provincial monuments at Lugdunum, Tarraco, and Emerita', in *Roman Coins and Public Life under the Empire*, ed. G. M. Paul and M. Ierardi. Ann Arbor, MI, The University of Michigan Press: 95–122.

Frederiksen, M. W. 1966. 'Caesar, Cicero and the problem of debt', *JRS* 56: 128–41.

Frey-Kupper, S. 2013. *Die antiken Fundmünzen vom Monte Iato 1971–1990. Ein Beitrag zur Geldgeschichte Westsiziliens*. Lausanne, Éditions du Zèbre.

Fullerton, M. D. 1985. 'The *domus augusti* in imperial iconography of 13–12 BC', *American Journal of Archaeology* 89: 473–83.

Galinsky, K.G. 1969. *Aeneas, Sicily, and Rome*. Princeton University Press.

1996. *Augustan Culture*. Princeton University Press.

2012. *Augustus: Introduction to the Life of an Emperor*. Cambridge University Press.

García-Bellido, M. P. 2008. 'From *imperatores* to *imperator*: the beginning of the Augustan <<military>> coinage in Hispania (27–15 BC)', in *Del imperium de Pompeyo a la auctoritas de Augusto. Homenaje a Michael Grant*, ed. M. P. García-Bellido, A. Mostalac and A. Jiménez. Madrid, Consejo superior de investigaciones científicas: 279–94.

Gitler, H. and Master, D. M. 2010. 'Cleopatra at Ascalon: recent finds from the Leon Levy expedition', *Israel Numismatic Research* 5: 67–98.

Gnecchi, F. 1912. *I Medaglioni Romani (3 vols)*. Milan, Istituto di studi romani.

Gorini, G. 1968. 'I medaglioni d'oro di Augusto', *Annali dell'Istituto Italiano di Numismatica* 15: 39–61.

Graeber, D. 1996. 'Beads and money: notes toward a theory of wealth and power', *American Ethnologist* 23: 4–24.

Green, S. J. 2004. *Ovid Fasti 1. A Commentary*. Leiden, Brill.

Gruen, E. S. 2005. 'Augustus and the making of the principate', in *The Cambridge Companion to the Age of Augustus*, ed. K.G. Galinsky. Cambridge University Press: 33–51.

Grunauer-von Hoerschelmann, S. 1978. *Die Münzprägung der Lakedaimonier*. Berlin, Walter de Gruyter & Co.

Hannah, R. 1998. 'Games for Mars and the temples of Mars Ultor', *Klio* 80: 422–33.

Harris, W. V. 2006. 'A revisionist view of Roman money', *JRS* 96: 1–24.

(ed.) 2008. *The Monetary Systems of the Greeks and Romans*. Oxford University Press.

Haug, E. 2008. 'Local politics in the late Republic: Antony and Cleopatra at Patras', *AJN* 20: 405–20.

Helly, B. 1975. 'Actes d'affranchissement thessaliens', *Bulletin de correspondance hellénique* 99: 119–44.

Hobbs, R. 2013. *Currency and Exchange in Ancient Pompeii. Coins from the AAPP Excavations at Regio VI, Insula 1*. London, Institute of Classical Studies.

Hoff, M. C. 1989. 'Civil disobedience and unrest in Augustan Athens', *Hesperia* 58: 267–76.

Hollander, D. B. 2007. *Money in the Late Roman Republic*. Leiden, Brill.

2008. 'The demand for money in the late Republic', in *The Monetary Systems of the Greeks and Romans*, ed. W. V. Harris. Oxford University Press: 112–36.

Hollstein, W. 1994. 'Apollo und Libertas in der Münzprägung des Brutus und Cassius', *Jahrbuch für Numismatik und Geldgeschichte* 44: 113–33.

Hölscher, T. 2009. 'Monuments of the battle of Actium: propaganda and response', in *Augustus*, ed. J. Edmondson. Edinburgh University Press: 310–33.

Hopkins, K. 1980. 'Taxes and trade in the Roman Empire', *JRS* 70: 101–25.

Howgego, C. 1982. 'Coinage and military finance: the imperial bronze coinage of the Augustan East', *NC* 142: 1–20.

1990. 'Why did ancient states strike coins?', *NC* 150: 1–25.

1995. *Ancient History from Coins*. London, Routledge.

2005a. 'Coinage and identity in the Roman provinces', in *Coinage and Identity in the Roman Provinces*, ed. C. Howgego, V. Heuchert and A. Burnett. Oxford University Press: 1–18.

2005b. *Greek Imperial Countermarks. Studies in the Provincial Coinage of the Roman Empire*. London, Spink.

2013. 'The monetization of temperate Europe', *JRS* 103: 1–30.

Howgego, C., Heuchert, V. and Burnett, A. (eds.) 2005. *Coinage and Identity in the Roman Provinces*. Oxford University Press.

Jones, A. H. M. 1956. 'Numismatics and history', in *Essays in Roman Coinage Presented to Harold Mattingly*, ed. R. A. G. Carson and C. H. V. Sutherland. Oxford University Press: 13–33.

Jones, J. R. 1970. 'Mint magistrates in the early Roman Empire', *Bulletin of the Institute of Classical Studies* 17: 70–8.

Justo, M. G. 1996–7. 'Las acuñaciones de Usekerte/Osicerda', *Annals de l'Institut d'Estudis Gironins* 36: 321–33.

Kay, P. 2014. *Rome's Economic Revolution*. Oxford University Press.

Kemmers, F. 2005. 'Not at random: evidence for a regionalised coin supply?', in *Proceedings of the Fourteenth Annual Theoretical Roman Archaeology Conference, University of Durham 26–27 March 2004*, ed. J. Bruhn, B. Croxford and D. Grigoropoulos. Oxford, Oxbow: 39–49.

2006. *Coins for a Legion. An Analysis of the Coin Finds from the Augustan Legionary Fortress and Flavian Canabae Legionis at Nijmegen*. Mainz, von Zabern.

Kemmers, F. and Myrberg, N. 2011. 'Rethinking numismatics. The archaeology of coins', *Archaeological Dialogues* 18: 87–108.

Keppie, L. 2000. 'Mark Antony's legions', in *Legions and Veterans. Roman Army Papers 1971–2000*. Stuttgart, Franz Steiner Verlag: 75–96.

Kiernan, P. 2001. 'The ritual mutilation of coins on Romano-British sites', *The British Numismatic Journal* 71: 18–33.

Kleiner, F. S. 1985. *The Arch of Nero in Rome*. Rome, Giorgio Bretschneider.

Klose, D. O. A. 1987. *Die Münzprägung von Smyrna in der römischen Kaiserzeit*. Berlin, Walter de Gruyter.

Knoepfler, D. 1988. 'L'intitulé oublié d'un compte des naopes béotiens', in *Comptes et inventaires dans la cité grecque*, ed. D. Knoepfler. Neuchâtel, Faculté des lettres Neuchâtel: 263–94.

Komnick, H. 2001. *Die Restitutionsmünzen der frühen Kaiserzeit*. Berlin, de Gruyter.

Koortbojian, M. 2006. 'The bringer of victory: imagery and institutions at the advent of Empire', in *Representations of War in Ancient Rome*, ed. K. Welch. Cambridge University Press: 184–217.

2013. *The Divinization of Caesar and Augustus*. Cambridge University Press.

Kraay, C. 1954. 'Caesar's *quattuorviri* of 44 BC: the arrangement of their issues', *NC* 14: 18–31.

1955. 'The chronology of the coinage of Colonia Nemausus', *NC* 15: 75–87.

Kraft, K. 1972. *Das System der kaiserzeitlichen Münzprägung in Kleinasien*. Berlin, Gebr. Mann.

Krmnicek, S. and Elkins, N. 2014. 'Dinosaurs, cocks, and coins: an introduction to "Art in the Round"', in *'Art in the Round': New Approaches to Ancient Coin Iconography*, ed. S. Krmnicek and N. Elkins. Tübingen, VML, Verlag Marie Leidorf GmbH: 7–22.

Kroll, J. 1972. 'Two hoards of first-century BC Athenian bronze coins', *APXAIOΛOΓIKON ΔEΛTION* 27: 86–120.

1993. *The Athenian Agora XXVI: The Greek Coins*. Princeton, NJ, American School of Classical Studies at Athens.

1996. 'Hemiobols to assaria: the bronze coinage of Roman Aigion', *NC* 156: 49–78.

1997. 'Coinage as an index of romanization', in *The Romanization of Athens*, ed. M. C. Hoff and S. I. Rotroff. Oxford, Oxbow: 135–50.

Küter, A. 2011. 'Die augusteischen Münzmeisterprägungen: *IIIviri monetales* im Spannungsfeld zwischen Republik und Kaiserzeit', in *Proceedings of the XIVth International Numismatic Congress Glasgow 2009*, ed. N. Holmes. Glasgow, International Numismatic Commission: 765–71.

2014. *Zwischen Republik und Kaiserzeit. Die Münzmeisterprägung unter Augustus*. Berlin, Gebr. Mann.

La Rocca, E. 1987-8. 'Pompeo Magno «novus Neptunus»', *Bullettino della commissione archeologica comunale di Roma* 92: 265–92.

Lange, C. H. 2009. *Res Publica Constituta. Actium, Apollo and the Accomplishment of the Triumviral Assignment*. Leiden, Brill.

2013. 'Triumph and civil war in the late Republic', *Papers of the British School at Rome* 81: 67–90.

LaRocca, E., Parisi Presicce, C., Lo Monaco, A., Giroire, C. and Roger, D. (eds.) 2013. *Augusto*. Rome, Electa.

Levick, B. 1999. 'Messages on the Roman coinage: types and inscriptions', in *Roman Coins and Public Life under the Empire*, ed. G. M. Paul. Ann Arbor, MI, University of Michigan Press: 41–60.

Linderski, J. 1996. 'Q. Scipio Imperator', in *Imperium sine fine: T. Robert S. Broughton and the Roman Republic*, ed. J. Linderski. Stuttgart, Franz Steiner Verlag: 145–85.

Lockyear, K. 2007. *Patterns and Process in Late Roman Republican Coin Hoards*. Oxford, Archaeopress, BAR International Series.

2013. *Coin Hoards of the Roman Republic Online, version 1*. New York, American Numismatic Society. (http://numismatics.org/chrr/)

Lorber, C. C. 2012. 'The coinage of the Ptolemies', in *The Oxford Handbook of Greek and Roman Coinage*, ed. W. E. Metcalf. Oxford University Press: 211–34.

Lowe, B. J. 2002. 'Sextus Pompeius and Spain: 46–44 BC', in *Sextus Pompeius*, ed. A. Powell and K. Welch. Swansea, Classical Press of Wales: 65–102.

Luley, B. P. 2008. 'Coinage at Lattara. Using archaeological context to understand ancient coins', *Archaeological Dialogues* 15: 174–95.

Mac Isaac, J. D. 1987. 'Corinth: coins 1925–1926. The theater district and the Roman villa', *Hesperia* 56: 97–157.

Martini, R. 1995. *Monetazione bronzea romana tardo-repubblica II. Sextus Pompeius. Le emissioni hispaniche del tipo CN. MAG, loe serie di Eppius e gli "assi" sicilani*. Milan, Ennerre.

Matheson, S. B. 1996. 'The divine Claudia: women as goddesses in Roman art', in *I Claudia. Women in Ancient Rome*, ed. D. E. E. Kleiner and S. B. Matheson. New Haven, CT, University of Texas Press: 182–94.

Mattingly, D. 2010. 'Cultural crossovers: global and local identities in the classical world', in *Material Culture and Social Identities in the Ancient World*, ed. S. Hales and T. Hodos. Cambridge University Press: 283–95.

Mattingly, H. 1948. '<<EID MAR>>', *L'antiquité classique* 17: 445–51.

Mazard, J. 1955. *Corpus Nummorum Numidiae Mauretaniaeque*. Paris, Arts et Métiers Graphiques.

Meadows, A. and Williams, J. 2001. 'Moneta and the monuments: coinage and politics in Republican Rome', *JRS* 91: 27–49.

Metcalf, W. E. 1980. *The Cistophori of Hadrian*. New York, American Numismatic Society.

1999. 'Coins as primary evidence', in *Roman Coins and Public Life under the Empire*, ed. G. M. Paul and M. Ierardi. Ann Arbor, MI, University of Michigan Press: 1–18.

2006. 'Roman imperial numismatics', in *A Companion to the Roman Empire*, ed. D. S. Potter. Malden, MA, Blackwell: 35–44.

(ed.) 2012. *The Oxford Handbook of Greek and Roman Coinage*. Oxford University Press.

Metzler, J. 1995. *Das treverische Oppidum auf dem Titelberg: zur Kontinuität zwischen der spätkeltischen und der frührömischen Zeit in Nord-Gallien. Band 1*. Luxembourg, Musée national d'histoire et d'art.

Miller, J. F. 2009. *Apollo, Augustus, and the Poets*. Cambridge University Press.

Milne, J. G. 1971. *Catalogue of Alexandrian Coins*. Oxford University Press.

Moles, J. 1983. 'Fate, Apollo, and M. Junius Brutus', *American Journal of Philology* 104: 249–56.

Molinari, M. C. 2003. 'Gli aurei a nome di Giulio Cesare e Aulo Irzo', *Rivista Italiana di Numismatica e Scienze Affini* 104: 165–253.

Morawiecki, L. 1983. *Political Propaganda in the Coinage of the Late Roman Republic (44–43 BC)*. Warsaw, Polskie towarzystwo archeologiczne i numizmatyczne.

Mwangi, W. 2002. 'The lion, the native and the coffee plant: political imagery and the ambiguous art of currency design in colonial Kenya', *Geopolitics* 7: 31–62.

Newman, R. 1990. 'A dialogue of power in the coinage of Antony and Octavian (44–30 BC)', *AJN* 2: 37–63.

Noreña, C. F. 2001. 'The communication of the emperor's virtues', *JRS* 91: 146–68.

2011. 'Coins and communication', in *The Oxford Handbook of Social Relations in the Roman World*, ed. M. Peachin. Oxford University Press: 248–68.

Nousek, D. L. 2008. 'Turning points in Roman history: the case of Caesar's elephant denarius', *Phoenix* 62: 290–307.

Papageorgiadou-Bani, H. 2004. *The Numismatic Iconography of the Roman Colonies in Greece. Local Spirit and the Expression of Imperial Policy*. Athens, Diffusion de Boccard.

Parry, J. and Bloch, M. 1989. 'Introduction: money and the morality of exchange', in *Money and the Morality of Exchange*, ed. J. Parry and M. Bloch. Cambridge University Press.

Picard, O., Bresc, C., Faucher, T., Gorre, G., Marcellesi, M.-C. and Morrisson, C. 2012. *Les monnaies des fouilles du Centre d'études alexandrines. Les monnayages de bronze à Alexandrie de la conquête d'Alexandre à l'Égypte moderne*. Alexandria, Centre d'études alexandrines.

Pietrangeli, C. 1949–51. 'Bidentalia', *Atti della Pontificia Accademia Romana di Archeologia. Rendiconti* 25–26: 37–52.

Piette, J. and Depeyrot, G. 2008. *Les monnaies et les rouelles du sanctuaire de la Villeneuve-au-Châtelot (Aube) (2ᵉ s. av. J.-C.–5ᵉ s. ap. J.-C.)* Wetteren, Moneta.

Pink, K. 1946. 'Die Triumviri monetales unter Augustus', *Numismatische Zeitschrift* 71: 113–25.

Pollini, J. 1985. 'The meaning and date of the reverse type of Gaius Caesar on horseback', *AJN* 30: 113–17.

1987. *The Portraiture of Gaius and Lucius Caesar*. New York, Fordham University Press.

1990. 'Man or God: divine assimilation and imitation in the late Republic and early principate', in *Between Republic and Empire. Interpretations of Augustus and his Principate*, ed. K. A. Raaflaub and M. Toher. Berkeley, CA, University of California Press: 334–57.

2012. *From Republic to Empire. Rhetoric, Religion, and Power in the Visual Culture of Ancient Rome*. University of Oklahoma Press.

Popovitch, L. 2013. 'Un *aureus* de Cassius frappé en 42 av. J.-C. découvert à Saint-Apollinaire (Côte-d'Or)', *Bulletin de la Société française de numismatique* 68.5: 90–7.

Powell, A. 2002. '"An island amid the flame": the strategy and imagery of Sextus Pompeius, 43–36 BC', in *Sextus Pompeius*, ed. A. Powell and K. Welch. Swansea, Classical Press of Wales: 103–34.

Powell, A. and Welch, K. (eds.) 2002. *Sextus Pompeius*. Swansea, Classical Press of Wales.

Prayon, F. 1982. 'Projektierte Bauten auf römischen Münzen', in *Praestant Interna. Festschrift für Ulrich Hausmann*, ed. B. von Freytag, D. Mannsperger and F. Prayon. Tübingen, Verlag Ernst Wasmuth: 319–30.

Raaflaub, K. A. 2003. 'Caesar the liberator? Factional politics, civil war, and ideology', in *Caesar against Liberty? Perspectives on his Autocracy*, ed. F. Cairns and E. Fantham. Cambridge, Francis Cairns: 35–67.

Ranucci, S. 2011. 'A stone *thesaurus* with a votive coin deposit found in the sanctuary of Campo della Fiera, Orvieto (*Volsinii*)', in *Proceedings of the*

XIVth International Numismatic Congress Glasgow 2009 vol 1, ed. N. Holmes. Glasgow, International Numismatic Council: 954–9.

Raubitschek, A. E. 1946. 'Octavia's deification at Athens', *Transactions and Proceedings of the American Philological Association* 77: 146–50.

1954. 'Epigraphical notes on Julius Caesar', *JRS* 44: 65–75.

Reding, L. 1972. *Les monnaies gauloises du Tetelbierg*. Luxembourg, Ministère des Arts et des Sciences.

Rich, J. W. 1998. 'Augustus's Parthian honours, the temple of Mars Ultor and the arch in the Forum Romanum', *Papers of the British School at Rome* 66: 71–128.

Rich, J. W. and Williams, J. H. C. 1999. '*Leges et ivra P.R. restitvit*. A new aureus of Octavian and the settlement of 28–27 BC.', *NC* 159: 169–213.

Richardson, J. S. 2012. *Augustan Rome: 44 BC to AD 14. The Restoration of the Republic and the Establishment of the Empire*. Edinburgh University Press.

Rizakis, A. D. 2001. 'La constitution des élites municipales dans les colonies romaines de la province d'Achaïe', in *The Greek East in the Roman Context. Proceedings of a Colloquium Organised by The Finnish Institute at Athens*, ed. O. Salomies. Helsinki, The Finnish Institute at Athens: 37–49.

Roller, D. W. 2007. 'The lost building program of Marcus Antonius', *L'antiquité classique* 76: 89–98.

Rosenstein, N. 2011. 'War, wealth and consuls', in *Consuls and Res Publica: Holding High Office in the Roman Republic*, ed. H. Beck, A. Duplà, M. Jehne and F. Pina Polo. Cambridge University Press: 133–58.

Rowan, C. 2011. 'Slipping out of circulation: the afterlife of coins in the Roman world', *Journal of the Numismatic Association of Australia* 20: 3–14.

2013a. 'Imaging the Golden Age: the coinage of Antoninus Pius', *Papers of the British School at Rome* 81: 211–46.

2013b. 'The profits of war and cultural capital: silver and society in Republican Rome', *Historia* 61: 361–86.

2013c. *Under Divine Auspices. Divine Ideology and the Visualisation of Imperial Power in the Severan Period*. Cambridge University Press.

2014a. 'Iconography in colonial contexts. The provincial coinage of the Late Republic in Corinth and Dyme', in *'Art in the Round': New Approaches to Coin Iconography*, ed. N. Elkins and S. Krimnicek. Tübingen, Verlag Leidorf GmbH: 147–58.

2014b. 'Showing Rome in the round: re-interpreting the "commemorative medallions" of Antoninus Pius', *Antichthon* 48: 109–25.

2016. 'Ambiguity, iconology and entangled objects on coinage of the Republican world', *JRS* 106: 21–57.

Salzmann, D. 1974. 'Zur Münzprägung der Mauretanischen Könige Juba II und Ptolemaios', *Madrider Mitteilungen* 15: 174–83.

Sauer, E. 2005. *Coins, Cult and Cultural Identity: Augustan Coins, Hot Springs and the Early Roman Baths at Bourbonne-les-Bains.* University of Leicester School of Archaeology and Ancient History.

Serafin, P. 2001. 'Dove erano le zecche di Roma repubblicana?', in *I luoghi della moneta*, ed. R. La Guardia. Milan, Comune di Milano: 29–40.

Shipley, F. W. 1930. 'C. Sosius: his coins, his triumph, and his temple of Apollo', in *Papers on Classical Subjects in Memory of John Max Wulfung*, ed. F. W. Shipley. St Louis, MO, Washington University Press: 73–87.

Stannard, C. 2005. 'The monetary stock at Pompeii at the turn of the second and first centuries BC: Pseudo-Ebusus and Pseudo-Massalia', in *Nuove richerche archeologiche a Pompei ed Ercolano*, ed. P. G. Guzzo and M. P. Guidobaldi. Naples, Electa Napoli: 120–43.

Stannard, C. and Frey-Kupper, S. 2008. '"Pseudomints" and small change in Italy and Sicily in the late Republic', *AJN* 20: 351–404.

Steel, C. 2013. *The End of the Roman Republic, 146–44 BC. Conquest and Crisis.* Edinburgh University Press.

Stenico, A. 1955. 'Il vaso pseudocorneliano con le monete e l'opera di C. Cispius', *Archeologia Classica* 7: 66–74.

Stevens, S. 1991. 'Charon's obol and other coins in ancient funerary practice', *Phoenix* 45: 215–19.

Suspène, A. 2012. 'Monnaies locales et identités: le cas du monnayage colonial de la Nîmes augustéene', *Revue Numismatique* 169: 23–34.

Suspène, A., Chausserie-Laprée, J. and Rétif, M. 2016. 'Un ensemble d'*aurei* (46–27 a.c.) mis au jour sur le site de Tholon lors des fouilles d'archéologie préventive du lycée Paul-Langevin à Martigues', *Bulletin de la société française de numismatique* 71: 82–90.

Sutherland, C. H. V. 1943. 'The sentorial gold and silver coinage of 16 BC: innovation and inspiration', *NC* 3: 40–9.

1970. *The Cistophori of Augustus.* London, Royal Numismatic Society.

1976a. *The Emperor and the Coinage. Julio-Claudian Studies.* London, Spink.

1976b. 'Octavian's gold and silver coinage from c. 32 to 27 BC', *Numismatica e antichità classiche* 5: 129–57.

1978. 'Some observations on the coinage of Augustus', *Numismatica e antichità classiche* 7: 163–77.

Sutherland, C. H. V. and Carson, R. A. G. 1984. *The Roman Imperial Coinage I: From 31BC to AD 69.* London, Spink.

Syme, R. 1939. *The Roman Revolution.* Oxford, Clarendon Press.

Terrenato, N. 1998. 'The Romanization of Italy: global acculturation or cultural bricolage?', in *TRAC 97. Proceedings of the Seventh Annual Theoretical Roman Archaeology Conference Nottingham 1997*, ed. C. Forcey, J. Hawthorne and R. Witcher. Oxford, Oxbow: 20–7.

Thonemann, P. 2013. 'The Attalid State, 188–133 BC', in *Attalid Asia Minor: Money, International Relations, and the State*, ed. P. Thonemann. Oxford University Press: 1–47.

2015. *The Hellenistic World. Using Coins as Sources*. Cambridge, Cambridge University Press and the American Numismatic Society.

Thüry, G. E. 2012. 'Zu Gelddarstellung auf Wandbildern der Vesuvregion', *Numismatische Zeitschrift* 119: 59–92.

Toher, M. 2003. 'Julius Caesar and Octavian in Nicolaus', in *Caesar Against Liberty? Perspective on his Autocracy*, ed. F. Cairns and E. Fantham. Cambridge, Francis Cairns: 132–56.

Toynbee, J. C. 1944. *Roman Medallions*. New York, American Numismatic Society.

Trillmich, W. 2009. 'Colonia Augusta Emerita, capital of Lusitania', in *Augustus*, ed. J. Edmondson. Edinburgh University Press: 427–67.

Tucci, P. L. 2005. '"Where high Moneta leads her steps sublime". The "Tabularium" and the temple of Juno Moneta', *Journal of Roman Archaeology* 18: 7–33.

van Alfen, P. 2005. 'Problems in ancient imitative and counterfeit coinage', in *Making, Moving and Managing. The New World of the Ancient Economies, 323–31 BC*, ed. Z. Archibald, J. Davies and V. Gabrielsen. London, Oxbow: 322–54.

Verboven, K. 2002. *The Economy of Friends: Economic Aspects of Amicitia and Patronage in the Late Republic*. Brussels, Latomus.

2003. '54–44 BCE: financial or monetary crisis?' in *Credito e moneta nel mondo romano (Incontri Capresi di storia dell'economia antica. Convegno internazionale, Capri 2000)*, ed. E. Lo Cascio. Bari, Edipuglia: 49–68.

2009. 'Currency, bullion and accounts. Monetary modes in the Roman world', *Revue Belge de Numismatique* 155: 91–121.

Versluys, M. J. 2013. 'The archaeology of Empire during the Republic', in *A Companion to the Archaeology of the Roman Republic*, ed. J. DeRose Evans. Chichester, Blackwell: 429–40.

von Reden, S. 2007. *Money in Ptolemaic Egypt: from the Macedonian Conquest to the End of the Third Century BC*. Cambridge University Press.

2010. *Money in Classical Antiquity*. Cambridge University Press.

Voutiras, E. 2011. 'Des honneurs divins pour Marc Antoine à Thessalonique?', in *More than Men, Less than Gods. Studies on Royal Cult and Imperial Worship*, ed. P. Iossif, A. S. Chankowski and C. C. Lorber. Leuven, Peeters: 457–69.

Wallace-Hadrill, A. 1986. 'Image and authority in the coinage of Augustus', *JRS* 76: 66–87.

1993. *Augustan Rome*. Bristol Classical Press.

2008. *Rome's Cultural Revolution*. Cambridge University Press.

Weinstock, S. 1971. *Divus Julius*. Oxford, Clarendon Press.

Welch, K. 1998. 'Caesar and his officers in the Gallic War commentaries', in *Julius Caesar as Artful Reporter: The War Commentaries as Political Instruments*, ed. K. Welch and A. Powell. London, Duckworth: 85–110.

2012. *Magnus Pius. Sextus Pompeius and the Transformation of the Roman Republic*. Swansea, Classical Press of Wales.

William Stevenson, S. 1964. *A Dictionary of Roman Coins, Republican and Imperial*. London, Seaby.

Wiseman, T. P. 1998. 'The publication of *de bello gallico*', in *Julius Caesar as Artful Reporter: The War Commentaries as Political Instruments*, ed. K. Welch and A. Powell. London, Duckworth: 1–10.

Wolters, R. 2001. 'Bronze, silver or gold? Coin finds and the pay of the Roman army', *Zephyrus* 53/54: 579–88.

2002. 'Gaius und Lucius Caesar als designierte Konsuln und principes iuventutis. Die lex Valeria Cornelia und RIC I² 205ff.', *Chiron* 32: 297–323.

Wood, S. E. 2001. *Imperial Women. A Study in Public Images, 40 BC–AD 68*. Leiden, Brill.

Woods, D. 2009. 'Caesar the elephant against Juba the snake', *NC* 169: 189–92.

Woytek, B. 1995. 'MAG PIVS IMP ITER. Die Datierung der sizilischen Münzprägung des Sextus Pompeius', *Jahrbuch für Numismatik und Geldgeschichte* 48/49: 79–94.

2003. *Arma et nummi. Forschungen zur römischen Finanzgeschichte und Münzprägung der Jahre 49 bis 42 v. Chr*. Vienna, Verlag der österreichischen Akademie der Wissenschaften.

2004. 'Iulius Caesar und das Nominaliensystem der römischen Reichsprägung in der Principatszeit', in *Ad fontes! Festschrift für Gerhard Dobesch zum fünfundsechzigsten Geburtstag am 15. September 2004*, ed. H. Heftner and K. Tomaschitz. Vienna, Eigenverlag der Herausgeber: 344–51.

2007. 'Die Münzen der römischen Republik und der Übergangszeit zum Prinzipat im Museum Canuntinum (mit einem Exkurs zu den Legionsprägungen des Marcus Antonius)', in *Die Fundmünzen der römischen Zeit in Österreich Abteilung III: Niederösterreich, Band 2: Die antiken Fundmünzen im Museum Carnuntinum*, ed. M. Alram and F. Schmidt-Dick. Vienna, Verlag der Österreichischen Akademie der Wissenschaften: 489–522.

2012a. 'The denarius coinage of the Roman Republic', in *The Oxford Handbook of Greek and Roman Coinage*, ed. W. E. Metcalf. Oxford University Press: 315–44.

2012b. 'System and product in Roman mints from the late Republic to the high principate: some current problems', *Revue Belge de Numismatique* 158: 85–122.

Youroukova, Y. 1976. *Coins of the Ancient Thracians*. Oxford, British Archaeological Reports.

Zanker, P. 1988. *The Power of Images in the Age of Augustus*. Ann Arbor, MI, University of Michigan Press.

Zarrow, E. M. 2003. 'Sicily and the coinage of Octavian and Sextus Pompey: Aeneas or the Catanean brothers?', *NC* 163: 123–35.

Zelizer, V. A. 1997. *The Social Meaning of Money*. Princeton University Press.

Index

47816508R00139

Made in the USA
Columbia, SC
04 January 2019